Footprints Of Famous Men

Designed As Incitements To Intellectual Industry

by

John G. Edgar

Double9 BOOKS

Footprints Of Famous Men

Designed As Incitements To Intellectual Industry

by John G. Edgar

ISBN: 978-93-60460-66-2

Published by

DOUBLE 9 BOOKS

2/13-B, Ansari Road
Daryaganj, New Delhi – 110002
info@double9books.com
www.double9books.com
Tel. 011-40042856

ABOUT THE AUTHOR

English writer John George Edgar was born in 1834 and died in 1864. A lot of his books were written for boys. Edgar was born in 1834. He was the fourth son of the Rev. John Edgar of Hutton, Berwickshire. He started working as a businessman in Liverpool and went to the West Indies to do business, but he soon gave up business and turned his attention to writing. Edgar's first book was called Boyhood of Great Men and came out in 1853. That same year, he also published a companion book called Footprints of Famous Men. Over the next ten years, he wrote up to fifteen more books for boys to read. Some of them were biographies, and the rest were works of dramatic fiction based on historical facts that showed different times in English history. Edgar knew a lot about border traditions and was especially good at learning about early English and Scottish history. He was the magazine's first editor. Edgar found time between his other work to write strongly conservative political pieces for the London press.

CONTENTS

WASHINGTON

The name, which this truly great and good man rendered for ever illustrious and venerable, is of thoroughly English origin, and was assumed, from a manor in the county of Durham, by one of the proprietors, during the dynasty of the Plantagenets. The family continued, for successive centuries, to produce men distinguished in their day and generation as knights, divines, lawyers, and agriculturists; and during the Protectorate two of its cadets, more adventurous than their predecessors, fared forth from a hereditary grange in Northamptonshire, took shipping for Virginia, sailed into the bay of Chesapeake, and settled, in the midst of silk grass and wild fruit, under the shade of the tall, bulky trees on the banks of the Potomac.

The grandson of one of these emigrants, a colonist of industry, enterprise, and repute, flourished in the earlier part of the eighteenth century. He seems to have been fully alive to the inconvenience, and steeled against the temptations of celibacy; for he was twice married, and blessed with several children, of whom George Washington—the eldest son by the second wife—was born on the 22d of February, 1732. Shortly after this joyous event, the worthy and prosperous planter removed to an estate he possessed in Stafford county; and there, on the east side of the Rappahannoc river, the childhood of the future general and statesman was passed. He soon gave indications of a natural disposition to lead and govern; and showed an innate inclination for military pursuits and athletic exercises. When at play, he took infinite delight in forming his youthful comrades into companies, which he drilled, marched, and paraded with due order and formality. Sometimes they were divided into two armies, and fought mimic battles—he acting as captain-general of one party. Then, as in maturer years, he was much given to such feats as running, leaping, wrestling, throwing bars, and others of a similar character. Moreover, he was held in great respect by his more volatile companions, who looked up to him as an extraordinary lad; and thus he was often privileged to arbitrate on and settle their casual disputes, always, it is stated, to the satisfaction of the parties concerned.

YOUNG WASHINGTON'S MILITARY ASPIRATIONS.

It has been remarked that, in general, persons attain with credit, and fill with dignity, the positions which might have been anticipated from their juvenile indications. Some, indeed, afterward display talents of which, in their first stages, they gave no sign, and others put forth a blossom not destined to bring forth the promised fruits: but most frequently the man is such as might have been predicted from the characteristics exhibited in early years. Washington can hardly be regarded as an exception to the general rule; though it is unnecessary to add, that he more than realized any hopes that could reasonably have been entertained from his puerile performances. The seminary at which he received his very scanty education was by no means of the highest class. The pupils were not even initiated into the rudiments of classical learning. Enough was taught the urchins to fit them for conducting the practical business of a planter—at that time the pursuit of nearly all gentlemen whose progenitors had left the comfort and security of merry England to encounter the toils and hardship of a colonial life. The teachers seem to have acted rigidly on the precept of a Spartan king, that the boy should be instructed in the arts likely to be useful to the man. If, on leaving school, the hopeful youths could read with decent correctness, write a tolerable hand, and keep accounts intelligibly, what more was wanting to capacitate them for growing tobacco and shipping it, to be disposed of by the commercial magnates who, arrayed in scarlet cloaks and flowing periwigs, paced, with haughty step and unvailed pride, the arched Exchange of Glasgow? Young men destined for learned professions were, it is true, generally sent to be educated in England; for others a private tutor was sometimes engaged; but in most cases the juvenile Virginians shouldered their satchels, and, picking up the wild grapes in their path, marched to the nearest hamlet to make the best of such tuition as it boasted of. Such, at all events, was the fortune of Washington. Under these disadvantageous circumstances, he pursued his simple studies with unusual vigor and exemplary diligence. At the age of thirteen, he strangely occupied much of his attention with the dry forms used in mercantile transactions. He practiced his skill in the writing of bonds, indentures, bills of exchange, and other deeds, compiled for his own use and guidance a code of rules for behavior in company and conversation, and transcribed such pieces of poetry as touched and charmed his fancy. From a boy, he was peculiarly careful to polish his manners, to cherish the heart's best affections, to do to others as he would be done to, and to exercise such a habitual control over himself, that he might restrain his constitutional ardor and hold his natural susceptibility in check. His early compositions were not, from the imperfect nature of his education, distinguished by grammatical correctness; but, by reading and perseverance, he gradually overcame these defects, and learned to express himself with force, clearness, and propriety. He had a decided turn for mathematical studies; and the last years of his school career were devoted to the mysteries of geometry, trigonometry, and surveying. For the last he felt a singular partiality; and he gratified the taste by measuring the neighboring fields and plantations, entering all the details and particulars in his note-books. This was done with systematic precision; he used his pen with the most scrupulous care, and acquired habits which were of inestimable value when he ascended to posts of peril and responsibility.

Meantime, his father had been cut off in the prime of life; but this early deprivation was, in Washington's case, almost counteracted by the character of his surviving parent, who, being a woman of sense, tenderness, vigilance, a strong mind, and prudent management, reared her family with the utmost discretion and success. She had the satisfaction of living to witness the splendid position to which the abilities, conduct, and energy of her son ultimately elevated him.

Washington went no longer to school after his sixteenth year. His relations had previously entertained the intention of entering him as a midshipman in the navy; and with this view had successfully exerted their influence to procure him a warrant. It appears that the future hero of a continent joyfully acquiesced in this scheme for his advancement in life; and had it been persisted in, he would no doubt have borne himself with credit and distinction. This was unquestionably a critical juncture in his career, and in the history of America; but it was terminated, imprudently in the opinion of his friends, by the interference of his widowed mother, who little relished the thought of her darling being sent "to rough it out at sea." She therefore authoritatively forbade his departure. Perhaps the incipient hero was not altogether disconsolate at the maternal veto being thus exercised; for about this date he proved himself not insensible to the magic power of female grace, and became vehemently enamored of some rural beauty. He celebrated her perfections in love-ditties, and confessed his pangs in letters to a confident; but, with a modesty surely rare under such circumstances, he ventured not to reveal the state of his agitated heart to the fair being whose image was stamped on its tablets.

At this period, Washington was fortunate enough to go on a visit to his eldest brother, Lawrence. That gentleman was intelligent and accomplished. He had served with honor in the expedition made, in 1740, against Carthagena; and secured the esteem and intimacy of the high-spirited Admiral Vernon. On returning home he had, in compliment to that gallant officer, named his property Mount Vernon; and they still continued in friendly communication. He had, moreover, become a member of the Colonial legislature, and connected himself by marriage with Lord Fairfax, who, having in earlier days proved his capacity by writing papers in the "Spectator," had just crossed the Atlantic to explore and examine the immense tract of land that belonged to him in the New World. Thus the company in which the elder Washington moved was by no means deficient in literary culture or patrician refinement; and his sagacious brother, in mixing with it, had opened up to his view aspects of society with which he might otherwise have remained unacquainted. He was too wise not to avail himself of the advantage in this way presented to his opening mind. Slow to speak, ready to hear, and anxious to understand, he used it to counterpoise the partial training his mental faculties had undergone, and thus laid the foundation of the mild dignity and scrupulous politeness which, in other days, made Sir Robert Liston declare, that he had never conversed with a better-bred sovereign in any court of Europe.

Lord Fairfax, on reaching his wild and uncultivated possessions, found that settlers were quietly making their way up the rivers, selecting the most valuable spots, and occupying them without leave or license. It was, therefore, deemed necessary that his seignorial rights should be asserted; and with that object he determined on having the lands properly lotted and measured, preparatory to claiming rents and giving titles. The destined victor in the War of Independence had already been presented to this clever, but eccentric, representative of the renowned Parliamentary general; a favorable opinion had, in consequence, been formed of the youth's merits and ability; and Washington being intrusted with the responsible duty, and attended by a kinsman of his lordship, sallied forth on his first surveying excursion in the beginning of 1748. The task was arduous and fatiguing; he was frequently obliged to pass whole nights under the cold sky, or in tents which afforded little shelter against the wintery wind and rain: but the expedition was not without beneficial results. He became conversant with localities then little known, but afterward the field of his military operations; he saw something of Indian life, witnessed an Indian war-dance, and acquired some acquaintance with the habits of the race upon which the spirit of civilization was bearing so hard. Besides, he executed his task with so much success, as not only to give complete satisfaction to his noble employer, but to establish his character as an excellent surveyor; a matter of considerable consequence, as there were then few in the district, and the emoluments were temptingly high. He therefore procured a commission, which gave authority to his operations, and entitled him to have their results entered in the provincial registers. By activity and diligence his occupation was rendered very lucrative; and on attaining the age of nineteen he had achieved so enviable a place in public esteem, that a most honorable military appointment was bestowed upon him by the Government on the approach of danger.

His taste for martial affairs had, indeed, been adhered to with resolution, and cultivated with assiduity. Since acting as a surveyor, he had resided chiefly with his brother, whose house was more conveniently situated for his exertions than was the home of his infancy; and he had, from this cause, been brought more into contact, than he would otherwise have been, with men versed in military matters. Under their instruction he had industriously practiced himself in sword exercise, and become not inexpert. Besides, he had eagerly studied books treating of the art of war. The early aspirations of great men are generally met with ridicule. "*Obsta principiis*" is too often the motto of jealous dunces. When the author of "Marmion" proposed in youth to compose his "War-Song of the Edinburgh Light Dragoons," the idea of his attempting such a thing raised coarse laughter, and was regarded as a piece of absurdity; and, in like manner, it is not difficult to imagine the brisk tittering excited by the efforts of the young colonial surveyor to initiate himself into handling the weapons and understanding the theory of war.

But however that may have been, it came to pass that, in 1751, when there appeared a prospect of encroachment on the part of the French, and it was deemed prudent to embody the militia to defend and protect the frontiers, Washington received a commission as Adjutant-General of one of the districts into which Virginia was divided. This entitled him to rank as major; and his duty was to assemble and exercise the local troops, inspect their arms, and maintain fitting discipline; no unworthy training for that military genius which subsequently accomplished so much for the land of his nativity. Then, as afterward, candor, sincerity, and straightforwardness were the characteristics of his noble mind. He had been eminently endowed by Nature with the qualities which form a ruler of men; and perhaps the training which he now underwent was, in reality, more favorable than any of a more regular and systematic kind would have been to the working out of his peculiar destiny.

About this period, Washington was withdrawn for a brief season from the sphere of his new duties. The health of his brother became so precarious, that medical advisers recommended an excursion to a different climate; and the company of some kind friend being required to cheer and sustain the invalid on his voyage, the fraternal affection of the boy-major prompted him to undertake the office. The atmosphere of a West India island being considered most likely to act as a restorative, Barbadoes was fixed upon. During the voyage thither, Washington busily occupied himself with making observations and increasing his knowledge; and on an October day they arrived at their destination.

Hardly could any prospect be more pleasing than that which arrested the eyes of the travelers, as, after being confined for five tedious weeks to the narrow limits of a trader, they anchored in the bay, the stillness of whose waters was only broken by the sailing of the dreaded shark, or by the tropical breeze which played lightly around, and gratefully modified the warmth of the sun, as it descended with merciless glow upon their strawy head-pieces. Before them lay the chief town, circling around the silver strand, and shrouded in palm trees that fringed the blue waters of the ocean. In the background, fields of the sugar-cane, planters' airy mansions, the tall windmills, and the negro-huts bosomed in the evergreen and luxuriant foliage of the tropics—having the appearance of scattered villages—presented a scene, picturesque, attractive, and promising delightful journeys to the curious stranger. Nor was Washington disappointed in that respect. Every thing came under his notice, and enlisted his sagacious reflection.

The soil, methods of culture, and the agricultural productions, engaged his attention no less than the manners of the inhabitants, their military force, their form of government, and their municipal institutions. While thus profitably employed he was laid prostrate by a sharp attack of small-pox, which confined him to the house for weeks; but with skillful medical treatment he was released from this doubly-dull durance, and enabled to resume his habits of gaining experience and collecting information.

Meantime the health of his brother had, at first, improved rapidly. Change of air and novelty of scene had produced a salutary impression; they invigorated his frame and revived his spirits: but the symptoms of decay speedily re-appearing he proceeded to Bermuda. Washington then embarked for Virginia, to execute the kindly duty of conducting his sister-in-law to her expiring husband; but ere arrangements could be made for that purpose, the latter was on the sea, and he soon after breathed his last under his own roof. The melancholy task of attending to the affairs of a departed relative, so near and dear, now devolved upon Washington, and for months he applied to the estate the sound sense and accurate investigation which ever characterized the great self-taught soldier and statesman in dealing with weightier affairs.

In the interval the sphere of his public duties had been enlarged and extended. The colony had, for purposes of defense, been divided into four grand districts; Washington's commission was then renewed, and the northern portion was confided to his steady care and untiring vigilance. This included several counties, each of which he had to visit periodically. The duties were quite in harmony with his taste and temper, and he discharged them with an energy and an enthusiasm which were not lost on those over whom he was appointed to exercise control, and among whom he had to insure discipline. Still he had not arrived even at that time of life when the generality of mortals are charitably supposed to have reached "years of discretion."

Events were now speeding to a crisis. Intelligence arrived that the French had crossed the lakes from Canada, and were preparing to establish posts and fortifications on the Ohio river. On receiving these alarming reports, the Virginian governor, having resolved to send an officer commissioned to inquire by what right they thus intruded on the English dominions, selected Washington, as peculiarly fitted to execute the duty with faith, discretion, and delicacy. Accordingly, about the close of 1753, he departed with suitable credentials and the requisite powers from Williamsburg, the seat of government; and with a retinue of eight persons, two of whom were to act as interpreters, he, after much toil and trouble, arrived at the French head-quarters. There he was courteously received and entertained by the commandant, a Knight of the Order of St. Louis. Immediate attention was promised to the subject of his mission, and in due time an answer, indicative of firmness and hostility, was granted to the remonstrance of his excellency the governor. Washington then retraced his steps, through trackless forests, over rugged mountains, and by swollen floods; making several hair-breadth escapes by land and water. During the expedition he had found frequent opportunities of extending his knowledge of Indian manners and customs; and he had been escorted to the French camp by an influential personage, bearing the title of "Half King." While returning, his journey was agreeably diversified by a visit to Queen Alliquippa, an Indian princess; no doubt, like the charming but hapless Yarico, appareled in beautiful shells, and possessed of wild graces. She maintained her state at the junction of two rivers, and had expressed her displeasure at the representative of the British king having failed to show her any proper mark of respect on his way out; but a polite apology and a substantial present soothed her wounded pride and ruffled dignity, and secured the young envoy a gracious dismissal. Twelve months later the dusky sovereign lady was under the necessity of placing herself and her son under his protection, when driven from her royal residence by the French troops.

After an absence of three months, Washington presented himself to the governor, and reported the result of his mission. In order to fire the patriotic enthusiasm of the colonists, the journal of his adventures was forthwith published. It appeared in all the provincial papers, and was reprinted in England by order of the government.

War was now imminent, and preparations were imperative upon the authorities. The governor was a wary Caledonian, and surrounded by a knot of his countrymen, who took care that in his appointments he did full justice to their claims; but, at the same time, he exhibited much zeal for the honor of the vice-regal office, and becoming ardor for the dignity of the British Crown. His schemes were, however, subject to be provokingly thwarted by the members of the local legislature, who manifested a republican spirit by no means agreeable to his loyal and patriotic sentiments. Hence he found considerable difficulty in making such arrangements for defense as he deemed necessary for the safety of English interests. Nevertheless, he succeeded in embodying a force to repel the invaders; and Washington having already, by his high courage and admirable conduct, proved his rare capacity for military business, was promoted to the rank of lieutenant-colonel, and nominated second in command. He immediately marched, with his new authority, to the Alleghany Mountains, and being joined by parties of those Indians who were favorable to the English, he commenced skirmishing with the enemy. In one sharp fray the leader of the hostile party was killed, and his men forced to yield. But in another encounter, at a place known as the Great Meadows, where he had thrown up an intrenchment, and called it Fort Necessity, Washington was, after a conflict of nine hours, obliged to capitulate. Then marching out, with flying colors and drums beating, he retreated to Williamsburg. His praiseworthy conduct during the campaign elicited high applause from the governor, and was rewarded with public thanks, conveyed through the House of Assembly. Next year he found himself in a somewhat awkward predicament. The forces being organized on a new system, he had to choose between being reduced to the rank of captain, and placed under officers whom he had previously commanded, or leaving the army. Without hesitation he resigned his commission, and spent the winter in retirement.

Early in the spring, however, he emerged from his retreat, and consented, while retaining his former rank, to accompany General Braddock as a volunteer. He was received with flattering respect, and prepared to take part in the expedition against Fort Duquesne; when, unfortunately, he was prostrated by a fever, which rendered his consignment to the baggage-wagon and the physician's care a matter of necessity: but he was sufficiently recovered in a fortnight to bear arms in the bloody battle of the Monongahela. Beautiful and impressive was the array of British troops on that memorable morning as the little army marched in order, with high hopes and ardent anticipations, the sun gleaming on their burnished arms. On one side was a flowing river, and on the other a shadowy forest. Suddenly, at noon, ere the rear had well crossed at a ford, they were attacked with fatal dexterity—the foe firing at a distance from behind trees, and practicing all the stratagems of Indian warfare. The general, disdaining to imitate such tactics, was mortally wounded; his two aides-de-camp were disabled; sixty-three out of eighty-six officers were killed and wounded; seven hundred private soldiers met with similar fates: but Washington seemed to have a charmed life. He rode about in all directions, and exerted himself with the utmost courage. He was a conspicuous mark for the enemy's sharp-shooters, and four bullets went through his coat; yet, though his companions fell in heaps around, he escaped unhurt. The nut-brown riflemen, old and young, singled him out; but with as little effect as, at Torquilstone, the arrows of the English archers had on the Milan steel of the bold leader of free lances. The idea of preternatural protection occurred to their superstitious imaginations; and as the Scottish Covenanters believed that General Dalziel possessed a diabolical charm against steel, and that Claverhouse was guaranteed against lead by the enemy of mankind, so the Indian warriors concluded that Washington was under the especial guardianship of the Great Spirit, and they ceased their efforts to slay him. Thus, although the day was most disastrous, he gained much praise by the valor, energy, and resolution he had exhibited throughout. He was instanced, even in pulpits, as preserved by a wise Providence to confer some signal benefit on his country; his public reputation rose high; the Legislature voted him a sum of money for his services; and when the local regiment was increased to sixteen companies, he was nominated their commander-in-chief. Being now intrusted with responsible functions, he devoted himself to the fulfillment of them with much care and foresight; and he procured the passing of a law to insure proper regularity and discipline. While thus gravely occupied, he had a dispute concerning precedence with an officer holding King George's commission; and in order to solve the difficulty, which was at once vexatious and perplexing, he had to undertake a journey to Boston, to obtain the opinion of General Shirley, commander of His Majesty's forces in America, who unhesitatingly decided the point in Washington's favor, and held serious and important conversation with him as to the plan of operations for the next campaign. Much curiosity was evinced, in the places through which he passed, to see the individual who had, at the early age of twenty-three, won so much renown for his bravery, and who was regarded as remarkable for the escape he had recently made. And there he was—a gallant and dignified cavalier, rather more than six feet in height, with long limbs, and a slender but erect and well-proportioned form—making an equestrian excursion of five hundred miles in the depth of winter, with two trusty comrades. He remained for some time at New York; and while there he had to encounter in a family circle—the most perilous of all arenas—a blooming damsel, whose charms, more effectual than the bullets of Indians, penetrated to his heart, and made so deep an impression that, after going to Boston, he returned and lingered till called away by the stern voice of duty. Doubtless reciprocal emotions fluttered in the gentle breast of the attractive nymph; but, as usual, the course of his love did not run quite smoothly: his hopes blossomed but to die. In a few months he was informed that a formidable rival was in the field, and the citadel in the utmost danger. Besides, it was intimated that, if he wished to save the coveted prize, he must make his appearance forthwith. Washington, absorbed with "the harsh duties of severe renown," or despairing of success, failed to comply with this friendly suggestion; the fair lady—a "cynosure of neighboring eyes"—did not, perhaps, excessively relish his apparent coolness; and his lucky competitor, being thus in undisputed possession of the ground, marched onward, with flying colors, to a connubial triumph.

Our hero, however, was not idle. If, like the rival of young Lochinvar, he had been "a laggard in love," he was no "dastard in war." The army had, on his return, received a considerable augmentation; and though the nature of his operations was unfavorable to the acquisition of much martial glory, he excited respect and admiration by the signal ability and ingenious resource he constantly displayed. Yet in modern, no less than in ancient times, abuse and calumny are essential parts of triumph; and they were now busy with the character and career of the successful young soldier. Some vituperative rumors were, it is stated, finally traced to the intrigues of the wily Scots, who clustered in ambitious expectancy, and in a "dark impenetrable ring," around their consanguineous governor. The excellent qualities of Washington's heart, his sensible modesty and honest frankness, were the best antidotes to the poison; but the labors attaching to his office were so arduous, that his health gave way; his physician insisted on a temporary retirement; and betaking himself to his estate, he underwent a feverish illness, which preyed upon him for months.

On recovering his strength, Washington resumed his military career. The accession of Mr. Pitt, afterward the great Earl of Chatham, to the English ministry, had inspired life and vigor into the struggle; a new expedition against Fort Duquesne was planned; and the place falling into the hands of the British troops, was named Fort Pitt, in honor of the mighty War Minister. When this happened, Washington resigned his command and returned to Virginia, as he had previously resolved to do in case of the enterprise being crowned with victory.

His affections, twice baffled in their objects, were now to find the peace and repose not seldom, even in the case of men of strong minds, essential to the achievement of great and memorable actions. Mrs. Custis, a widow lady, at this time resided in the vicinity of the provincial capital. She was still in the bloom of youth, gayety, and beauty, distinguished by wealth, affability, and attractions, and dignified with the maternity of two children. Besides, she possessed in rare perfection the domestic graces and accomplishments which, in the opinion of persons whom experience has divested of glowing romance, constitute the true fascination of woman. This flower of the female sex was, indeed, a being too captivating not to have wooers; and amidst social life and festive enjoyments few, perhaps, could have perused her various charms without admiration. Washington's noble bearing and sage conversation could hardly fail to make an impression on the gentle heart which her fair form enshrined. He came, saw, and conquered; and, in the beginning of 1759, they were happily united. Being now in possession of quiet leisure, Washington, with his matronly bride, settled at Mount Vernon, to which he had succeeded since the decease of his brother. The tranquil mansion-house was a most agreeable residence. In front was a spacious lawn, bounded by blossoming orchards and pleasant gardens, which reposed in the shade of thriving trees, and were watered by the broad and deep Potomac. The domestic habits of the owner of the domain were uniform, and characterized by a regularity from which he seldom deviated. He rose with the sun, and retired early to rest. His attention was chiefly given to agriculture, in which, in accordance with a strong natural inclination, he had always taken a lively interest. His land was devoted, for the most part, to the growth of tobacco, which he exported to be sold in the English markets. The life of an ordinary Virginia planter was, at that date, somewhat monotonous. He lived during the whole year on his own land, which, in most cases, lay so near some of the large rivers that ships sailed almost to his door, and received the produce of his farm to swell the imports into distant emporiums. In practicing hospitality, he was generally so profuse that inns were utterly useless. Weary wayfarers, even without introduction, had only to call at the nearest proprietor's house, with the certainty of being heartily welcomed and cheerfully entertained. He might not indeed be, and seldom was, rolling in wealth; but that point the guest would soon hear explained with emphasis. Every colonist availed himself of his privilege as a British subject to complain loudly that British merchants, by some process or other, contrived to appropriate the better part of his just profits; and even Washington, however different from his neighbors in other respects, scrutinized accounts with a sharpness which shows that he was not altogether without his suspicions.

The hospitality of the great colonial soldier was displayed on a scale of magnificence which must have tended to relieve the dullness; and when at home, he seldom allowed a day to pass without having visitors of intelligence and distinction. Moreover, he had a keen relish for field-sports. He hunted, at the proper season, twice or thrice a-week; was fond of the excitement and recreation which a fox-chase afforded; was familiar with the use of his fowling-piece; signalized his expertness against the game which abounded in his preserved grounds, and fought as courageously in an affray with poachers as he had ever done in a battle with the French. He was always eager to be useful, and took a particular interest in the affairs of his parish. He was recognized by the people in his neighborhood as a man of extraordinary candor and judgment; insomuch that when they became involved in quarrels, which there appeared no prospect of otherwise settling amicably, they were in the habit of resorting to him as a last appeal, and submitting the case to his reason, justice, and decision, just as his school-fellows had done in other days:

> "His doom contending neighbors sought—
> Content with equity unbought."

Indeed, his wish to act without fear, favor, or affection, when thus consulted, and to promote peace and concord, was so evident, that few uttered an audible murmur against his arbitration.

On relinquishing his military employment, he had been returned as a member of the House of Burgesses, and for a period of fifteen years was successful at each election. It was a rule with him through life to execute with unflinching diligence any duty he undertook; and as a representative his attendance was punctual and exemplary in the extreme. He seldom spoke; he had no longing for oratorical conflict, and altogether refrained from entering into stormy discussions; but his acute perception, earnest judgment, and sage prescience, gave him an influence in the assembly which his wordy, brawling, and disputatious compeers struggled and strove for in vain. He was in the habit of studying attentively, and forming opinions with scrupulous impartiality on the chief subjects under deliberation. In this respect, *Nunquam non paratus* might have been his motto. Thus, when the Stamp Act was imposed on the colonies by Mr. Grenville, he at once assumed a position of antagonism to the infliction, and concurred with firmness and determination in the measures of opposition adopted by America. From this, and his high reputation, he was chosen to command the independent companies of militia which the colonists had hitherto been privileged and encouraged to raise; he was sent as a delegate to the Virginia Convention, and afterward elected as a member of the general Congress, in whose proceedings he acted a prominent and influential part.

When the second Congress assembled, in 1775, it presented an array of "fierce faces threatening war." Blood had already been shed; at Lexington had commenced that contest which, with few intermissions, lasted for eight years. The English crown was, at a perilous crisis, found without competent advisers; Wisdom cried aloud in public places, without being regarded; and American senators openly and boisterously invoked the God of battles. Civil strife, fierce and bloody, was inevitable; and in this emergency Washington was chosen Commander-in-chief of the forces raised to carry on the momentous struggle. Yet it can not be supposed that this great man contemplated a separation from the mother-country without a pang. Even Jefferson, at this date, declared that in the whole empire there was no individual who more cordially loved the union with Great Britain than himself; and hardly any one competent to form an opinion on such a subject can conceive that Washington, who had given such tokens of patriotism, was less loyal in his sentiments. His forefathers had fought on famous fields, and in walled cities, for the crown of England; he himself had won his laurels under her lion-flag against her hereditary enemies; and he was, moreover, a man of faith, breeding, and refinement. With such a person, considerations of such a nature are not readily banished or suppressed, and there can be little doubt that his patriot soul was often tossed with contending emotions; like the Saxon nobles whom the Conqueror, with fire and sword, drove into the Scottish territory, who felt no respect for the Norman line of kings, but whose hearts lingered about the scenes where their progenitors had held sway and created civilization. The tastes and associations of Washington might well have led him, had an option been granted, to side with the imperial cause. But the course pursued by Lord North, who, as a statesman, ever displayed more wit than wisdom, and whom neither the sagacious warnings of Burke nor the vehement declamation of Chatham could awaken from a sleepy stupidity, left him no choice. He believed that his native plains must either be drenched in blood or inhabited by slaves; he regarded it as a sad alternative: but he did not falter or hesitate in his course. With engaging diffidence in his own powers he accepted the responsible position offered; and repairing to Cambridge, where the insurgent army lay, he proceeded to remodel and improve it to the best of his ability. In the interval Bunker's Hill had been fought. The victory remained with the Loyalists; but the engagement had convinced them that the foe was not to be despised. Subsequent events fully confirmed this opinion; and General Howe being under the necessity of abandoning Boston, Washington was received by the inhabitants with significant enthusiasm.

Soon after, the Declaration of Independence was published; but events inauspicious to the cause of the colonists now came onward in rapid succession. The defeat at Long Island filled their ranks with such dismay and consternation as put their general's invincible resolution to a severe test. New York was straightway relinquished by them, with considerable loss; a defeat was sustained at Chatterton's Hill; Fort Washington was lost; and General Lee was taken prisoner. This was a period to try the souls of those who had taken up arms against taxation without representation. Their operations had proved unexpectedly disastrous; their army had melted away till it seemed but a shadow of its former self; pardon had been proclaimed in the King's name to all who would return to their allegiance. Many persons of wealth, consideration, and respectability, especially yeomen of strength and substance, had accepted it on the offered terms; but Washington remained firm and decided. His fortitude might not inaptly be compared to that house against which the waves beat, and the rain came, and the winds blew, but which fell not, for it was founded on a rock. He calmly represented to Congress the plight to which he was reduced; and the crisis being such as to silence all querulous opposition, neither the whisper of envy nor the voice of discontent was heard. Even timidity was overcome by fear. Indeed the members appear to have been animated by views similar to those which the elder consul, "an ancient man and wise," is made to express when the thirty armies are described as on their way to Rome:

"In seasons of great peril'
Tis good that one bear sway;
Then choose we a Dictator,
Whom all men shall obey."

And, accordingly, Washington was wisely invested with supreme authority and dictatorial powers. The army was completely reorganized; and its dauntless, but firm and prudent leader, resolved to cross the Delaware, and attack the foes on their own ground. On a December night he assailed and defeated them at Trenton; and pursuing his advantage, he gained an important victory at Princeton. Next year, however, the fortune of war again changed, and Washington fought unsuccessfully at the fords of the Brandywine and at the village of Germantown. In the former of these actions Lafayette, inspired with burning zeal for the American cause, displayed his courage as a volunteer, and was wounded in the leg while dismounting to rally the retreating troops by his voice and example.

Ere long the French king recognized the independence of the United States by a formal treaty; a battle was fought at Monmouth with partial success; and a French squadron arrived to aid the new allies of the Bourbons. Nevertheless, an assault made by the combined forces on Rhode Island proved a failure; and a projected expedition against Canada came to naught. An intended attack on New York had a similar termination, and a mutiny among the troops filled the public mind with alarm and consternation. Still the clear spirit of Washington rose superior to adversity, and his deep determination was not to be shaken by disaster.

Affairs, indeed, seemed now to be hastening to a crisis; but as the year 1781 advanced, they began to wear a more favorable aspect. The cheering news was brought by a French frigate that powerful assistance might be calculated on; and a combined attack was planned against New York, but relinquished owing to intelligence in regard to the sailing of the promised auxiliaries from St. Domingo. When they at length arrived, York Town, in Virginia, was besieged by the allied forces, and Lord Cornwallis obliged to surrender.

It now became evident that the unhappy war was approaching its termination; and the American army, with a prospect of being disbanded, began to complain of grievances. Besides, many of the officers looked with so little favor on republican institutions, that, wishing for some more vigorous form of government, they deputed one of their number to convey to Washington the suggestion, that they were not averse to his thoughtful brow being begirt with a diadem. He rebuked the idea with stern indignation, and requested that it might never again be alluded to.

In the spring of 1783, intelligence arrived that a treaty of peace had been signed at Paris, and that the independence of the United States had been acknowledged by the British Government. Shortly afterward, a cessation of hostilities was announced, and arrangements were made for the evacuation of New York. On a November morning, the English troops finally embarked; a long procession, with Washington at its head, made formal entry and took possession of the city. At his side—followed by the provincial functionaries, officers, senators, and citizens—rode the governor, who closed the proceedings of the memorable day with a costly banquet. Yet, however flattering to their pride as a new nation, the ceremony was not altogether unsuggestive of melancholy considerations. The chief, the greatest, the most conspicuous actor in it, must have been conscious of mixed feelings; and it was natural that, a few days later, when parting with his warlike associates, his emotion should have been visible. He had conducted a great civil war; he had triumphed where the most sanguine might, without reproach have despaired; and he had throughout, without an interval, exhibited high mental dignity. He had earned the position of a prince, and the proud title of "Father of his country;" won for himself glorious renown, and achieved national independence for millions. But it was impossible to look for a moment to the future, enveloped as it then was in uncertainty, without recollecting—perhaps not without a sigh—that America was no longer a portion of that mighty empire on which the sun never sets; reared by Saxon sagacity, and sustained by Norman valor; constituted by the toil of the wise, and consecrated by the blood of the brave; and to whose immemorial institutions he had lately been as much attached as the inhabitants of Kent or Northumberland.

When Washington resigned the command of that army with which he had outmanœuvred the tactics of successive generals, and brought a war with the most powerful nation in the world to a triumphant issue, he was still in his fifty-first year; but he had a right to believe that his long and continuous services entitled him to repose. He had affluence and station; he did not covet power; and he looked forward to the enjoyment of calm, contemplative retirement, till, in God's appointed time, he should sleep with his fathers. He therefore went to Mount Vernon, devised schemes of internal navigation for developing the resources and extending the commerce of the country, and seems even to have indulged in prophetic visions of that vast trade which has since crowded the docks of Liverpool and stocked the warehouses of Manchester. It was then that he had the satisfaction of welcoming the visit of Lafayette, whose friendship he highly esteemed, and whose former services he duly appreciated. They parted with mutual regret; never to meet again.

While planting his grounds, pruning his fruit-trees, improving his property, receiving complimentary visits, answering courteous congratulations, and preparing peacefully to descend the pathway of life, under the shadow of his own vine and fig-tree—envious of none, and determined to be pleased with all—Washington became painfully aware that the system of government then existing did not meet the wishes and requirements of the American public. Indeed, some were so apprehensive of fatal consequences, that they were gradually inspired with the desire of receiving, from among the royal families of Europe, a prince who should wear a crown, exercise sovereign sway, and control the conflicting elements then making themselves felt for evil. To pour oil on the troubled waters, a Convention was appointed to devise a form of government calculated to give general satisfaction. Washington was chosen chairman; and, as such, affixed his name to the new constitution, which, though not coming up to the perfection of ideal theories, was ratified by the States and adopted by the people.

This scheme—in regard to which Franklin said, "I consent to it, because I expect no better, and because I am not sure it is not the best; the opinions I have of its errors I sacrifice to the public good"—provided for the election of a President. On this being known, all eyes were turned toward Washington, as the personage in every respect best qualified, by rank, station, and dignity, to occupy the eminence. His mind was, indeed, so tinged with the old leaven of aristocracy, that, in respect to military officers, he had requested that none but gentlemen should be considered qualified; but experience had taught him confidence in the aspirations of a free people. Every thing conspired to fit him to appear as the representative of various parties, to check the prevalence of extreme opinions, and to "stay the plague both ways." When the day appointed for the important business arrived, he was unanimously elected; and yielding with unfeigned reluctance to the public voice, he became the first President of the United States. In this trying situation, his singleness of purpose and stainless integrity shone forth with unparalleled lustre. He ruled in truth and sincerity—not to aggrandize himself, but to benefit his country. Though ungifted with the brilliant qualities which dazzle an ambitious people, and disdaining the demagogic arts too often employed to mislead them—his sound judgment, steady mind, and powerful understanding, enabled him to deal with the difficulties he had to encounter, and avoid or remove the obstacles that came in his way. He piloted the vessel he had launched through troublous times. With a firm hand and a bold heart he maintained the balance between the contending factions, exhibited a resolution not to be overcome or overawed, and in 1796 retired from the position to which he had imparted dignity with the respect, sympathy, and veneration of all parties and all nations.

This great, intrepid, and admirable man, went down to his grave in peace and honor in the year 1799, leaving to his country and mankind a glorious heritage, in a name unsullied by crime or rapacity, and an example to be held in everlasting remembrance by all future generations.

BURKE

The knowledge of Burke was of the most profound, various, and extensive kind; and his excellence in almost every species of prose composition conducted him to an eminent rank among writers. Moreover, his fame as an orator and statesman is not inferior to that of any man who ever appeared upon the theatre of political affairs; and he is justly entitled to the credit of having formed and sustained his vast reputation by genius, energy, and resolution. His own fearless pen has recorded, for the edification of posterity, that he possessed not one of the qualities, nor cultivated one of the arts, that recommend aspiring intellect to the favor of the powerful; he was not made for a minion or a tool; and he did not follow the trade of winning the hearts by imposing on the understandings of the people. At every step in his life he was traversed and opposed; and at every turnpike he was obliged to show his passport, and prove a title to the honor of serving his country. The memory of such a person surely merits a larger share of popular attention than it has hitherto received.

BURKE READING TO HIS MOTHER.

According to biographers, the family of Burke, which was ennobled in several of its branches, could boast of ancient lineage and a respectable position. His grandfather is stated to have been proprietor of a considerable estate, which was inherited and disposed of by the illustrious individual who made the name familiar to England and Europe. This fine old Irish gentleman resided near Limerick; but his son, having been educated to the profession of the law, carried on a very large business as an attorney in the city of Dublin. There, on the 1st of January, 1730, Edmund Burke entered upon his checkered and extraordinary existence; yet hardly any event could have appeared more improbable than that the child then born on Arran Quay should, as years rolled on, become "the philosopher of one era, and the prophet of the next."

From the circumstances of his birth Burke was not subjected to the disadvantage of a deficient education, nor to that of being destined for pursuits uncongenial to the bent of his mind. His academic course was, indeed, such as qualified him for the career he was appointed to run. Being of a delicate frame he was not sent to school at the usual early age, but taught to read by his mother, a woman of cultivated intellect. Ere long, country air being thought necessary for his health, he was removed from the Irish capital to the house of some relations at Castletown Roche; and there he was placed, for initiation into Latin, at the village seminary. In this situation he pursued his studies with juvenile enthusiasm for several years, and then went home for a brief period, during which he was under pedagogic rule. Perhaps, however, a residence under the paternal roof was not found excessively favorable to the mental development, and he was entered at a classical academy in the county of Kildare, kept by a worthy member of the Society of Friends, for whom, in the midst of all his subsequent triumphs, he retained a sincere and grateful respect. On one occasion, during a parliamentary debate, Burke, with becoming feeling, alluded to this old teacher as "an honor to his sect;" and, assuredly, it is no slight compliment to be spoken of in such terms by the greatest man of an age.

Meantime the youthful pupil applied himself to his books with much ardor and exemplary industry. He cared not to display his powers, but stored his mind with that multifarious learning which, in many an hour of oratorical conflict, furnished him with fine thoughts, lofty sentiments, and noble imagery. His superiority among the boys at the establishment appears to have been duly recognized, and was pleasingly exhibited in cases of emergency. Once, when the assizes were held at Carlow, he proved his natural versatility in a very amusing way. The master had, with laudable good-humor, allowed his scholars to have a holiday, on condition that the more advanced among them should write, in Latin verse, a description of the procession, and the impressions which the scene left on their minds. Burke executed the prescribed task with ability and fullness, and was, no doubt, congratulating himself on having acquitted himself with credit, when he was earnestly entreated to prepare a second account of the pageant for a less gifted class-fellow. Trusting to be supplied by his petitioner with some slight hints for guidance in this delicate and charitable effort at versification, the future fashioner of statesmen questioned his comrade in regard to what part of the ceremony had struck him as most remarkable.

"Sure," replied the Hibernian urchin, scratching his head, "I noticed nothing particular, but a fat piper in a brown coat."

Dexterously availing himself of the idea thus stupidly suggested, Burke, in a short time, produced a humorous doggerel rhyme, commencing with

"Piper erat fattus, qui brownum tegmen habebat."

Though his rare faculties were proudly appreciated by the learned Quaker, who foretold they would ultimately conduct their possessor to fame and fortune, it is worthy of remark that Burke's gay, witty, and vivacious brother, Richard, was generally regarded as the more brilliantly endowed of the active attorney's sons. The keen and anxious eye of their father, however, perceived the superior wisdom and energy that, even at that date, animated the glowing breast of the youth who was to stand forward as the terror of Indian oppressors, the champion of injured ladies, and the marvel of Christendom. Indeed, sparks of the peculiar sympathy for the poor and desolate, which breathes through his political discourses, already began to flash forth with promising brightness and warmth. A humble cottager having been compelled to pull down his little tenement at the mandate of an imperious road-surveyor, the young spirit of Burke, who indignantly witnessed the operation, broke out with vehement scorn, and he emphatically declared that, if ever he had authority in the realm, no man should, with impunity, so treat the obscure and defenseless. The boy is father to the man, and in after years, when his renown was at its height, he said that his object was not more to save the high from the blights and spoliations of envy and rapacity, than the lowly from the iron hand of oppression and the insolent spurn of contempt.

In the spring of 1744 Burke was entered as a pensioner at Trinity College, Dublin. Two years later he was elected a scholar of the house. To obtain the latter distinction a candidate had to go through a successful examination in the classics, before the provost and senior fellows, after which he was entitled to a small annuity, a vote for the representatives of the University, and free chambers and commons for a certain period. But it does not appear that Burke generally sought opportunities of proving the might of that genius which he must have felt to be in him. On the contrary, he silently hoarded up that universal information, which, in other days and in very different circumstances, he exhibited in forms so grand and magnificent. Thus, when the proper time arrived, he was able to speak or converse with eloquence and correctness on almost any subject that presented itself. He gave much attention to rhetoric, and improved his mind by perpetual and sagacious reflection. While at college his habits were quiet, his character unpretending, and his conduct marked by regularity.

Burke had, long before leaving the University, been enrolled as a student of law at the Middle Temple, but he was in no particular haste to keep his terms. It is even related that, while studying with zeal and earnestness at home to improve his capacity and extend his learning, he was induced to apply for the Logic chair at Glasgow, but too late to gain his object. At length, seeing no fair field for the exercise of his talents in the land of his birth, he resolved to betake himself to London, trusting to achieve for himself, by ability and industry, a position of honor and independence. He had already devoted much time to accomplish himself in composition, and written several essays to counteract the doctrines of a democratic Irish apothecary, whose daring lucubrations had won their author considerable local fame. Thus were exercised the rare strength and invincible courage in political controversy which afterward enabled him to trample many a potent and well-appointed adversary in the dust. It might have been that his success in this contest inspired him with the desire of signalizing his singular prowess in a wider field. At all events he repaired to the English metropolis.

His journey thither was not undertaken without feelings of sadness; and his eyes often filled with tears, as, after crossing the Channel, he was rolled through a country ornamented with pleasant mansions, neat cottages, and villages, whose cheerful and industrious appearance he could not help contrasting with the poverty of his native isle. Agriculture, he says, was his favorite science, and would have been his chosen pursuit if Providence had blessed his youth with acres. He was, therefore, highly interested in, and pleased with, its progress in the country he was now adopting.

At the time of his arrival in London, Burke was by no means unfitted, by knowledge or experience, to struggle with advantage. His classical and philosophical acquirements were enormous, and he had no slight conception of life and society. He was an eager observer of mankind, and had seen enough of the gay and fashionable while hanging on in Dublin to acquit himself with propriety in any company to which his marvelous conversational powers might procure him access. His stories and anecdotes were characterized by interest and variety. They did not lose any thing in effect by the look and manner with which they were set off, nor by the slight Irish accent, which to the last was perceptible, especially in his colloquial displays. Thus accomplished, he commenced his career of intellectual triumph by contributing to periodicals; thereby sharpening his wits and increasing his intelligence. The character of Englishmen immediately commanded his respect, and, celebrated as his birth-place ever has been for its display of female beauty, the graces of Englishwomen excited his enthusiastic admiration. He complained, indeed, that there was less regard paid to men of letters than he had been led to imagine, and that genius was in small danger of being enervated by the patronage of power. But he probably felt that his must in the end bear him upward, in spite of every obstacle: so he strove against discontent, and adhered steadfastly to habits of temperance, keeping his glorious intellect unobscured by the cloud which is certain to follow dissipation. The buildings in the wonderful city of which he was now an inhabitant, struck him as being very fine; and in good time, attracted, probably, by the descriptions of Addison, he visited the edifices of Westminster. He was deeply impressed with awe and veneration for the sacredness and solemnity of the place, and thought that sound and useful lessons might be learned from the monuments. Indeed, it is not difficult to conceive what fine thoughts and high imaginings must have crossed the mind and irradiated the brain of Burke, as, for the first time, he wandered through the venerable Abbey, and perambulated that historic Hall, which, in later days, was the scene of the most surpassing effort of his genius.

While earning a livelihood by literary labor, the income of the brilliant aspirant was no doubt small; but his industry was unceasing. He produced essays on various literary and political subjects for weekly and daily publications, and he studied with singular diligence. He usually read with a pen in his hand to make notes, extracts, and reflections. His apprehension was peculiarly quick, and his memory retentive; and he could thus travel with rapidity over a wide field. But it is impossible to work incessantly without impairing the health. A somewhat severe illness caused him to resort, for medical advice, to Dr. Nugent, a physician of skill and talent, who, considering that proper care and attention were more likely to prove beneficial than any medicine administered in the dust and solitude of the Temple, kindly invited the invalid to take up his quarters for a time under his roof. Burke wisely accepted the hospitality thus offered.

During the restoration of his patient to health and vigor, the Doctor found in his daughter an efficacious assistant; Burke found in her an amiable and agreeable companion, who soon made an impression on his heart. In such circumstances, even "the greatest philosopher in action the world ever saw" acted like other mortals; he told his enamored tale, and they were forthwith united. This step was most fortunate; the lady proved herself eminently worthy of his affection; and when years had brought trouble and anxiety in their train, her husband often declared, that all his racking cares departed whenever he crossed the threshold of his own house.

Burke had now a double motive to exertion. Animated by that love of fame—

> "Which the clear spirit doth raise
> To scorn delights, and live laborious days."

and at the same time by that sense of duty which is not the least laudable incitement to mental energy, he applied himself to the production of some work that might establish his name; and accordingly his "Vindication of Natural Society," in which the writer covertly, and with admirable effect, imitated the style and principles of Bolingbroke, made its appearance. The treatise exhibited much historical knowledge, versatility of genius, and sagacity of mind; but it failed to meet with the success or notice which its ingenious irony might have been expected to secure. It was published in the year 1756, and soon followed by his "Essay on the Sublime and Beautiful," which so much pleased and delighted the author's father, that a remittance of a hundred pounds was the consequence.

From this auspicious period Burke's celebrity and importance may be dated; and his reputation speedily secured him a worthy position among men of letters and eminence. Sir Joshua Reynolds sought his society; and at the hospitable mansion of the immortal painter he formed the acquaintance of Dr. Johnson, who declared his new friend to be the greatest man living. "Take up whatever topic you will," he was in the habit of saying, "Burke is ready to meet you. If he were to go into a stable and talk to the ostlers for a short time, they would venerate him as the wisest of human beings. No person of sense ever met him under a gateway to avoid a shower who did not go away convinced that he was the first man in England."

In the year 1764 Reynolds proposed the formation of a club, which met at the Turk's Head, and soon comprehended several of the most distinguished literary and political characters of whom Great Britain boasted. It long flourished without a name, but was at length recognized as the Literary Club. One of the nine original members was Oliver Goldsmith, who had been a college contemporary of Burke, and afterward gone to study medicine in Edinburgh. He had since traveled over much of the Continent, holding learned disputations at the different Universities that came in his way, where success entitled him to a dinner, a night's lodging, and a small sum of money. He had now thrown himself into the republic of letters, and much amused the brilliant circle at the Turk's Head by his strange eccentricities and ludicrous blunders.

At their meetings Burke was found fully a match for Johnson; and it was observed, that he was almost the only man living from whom the huge sage would bear contradiction. The subject of Bengal was sometimes under discussion; and Burke, even at that period, showed an extent and accuracy of information in regard to it rarely to be met with.

Burke had already projected and brought into operation the "Annual Register," which was for years carried on under his sagacious inspection; though political matters soon occupied so much of his attention that he had little leisure for literary pursuits not strictly connected with affairs of state: but his introduction to public life was gradual. In the year 1759 he became acquainted with *Singlespeech* Hamilton, son of a Scottish advocate who had come to England at the Union. This mysterious individual had, a short while previously, made the solitary but successful oratorical effort from which his nickname was derived, in a debate long remembered as one of the greatest in which the parliamentary personages of that generation had partaken. In 1761 he went to Ireland as Secretary to the Lord-lieutenant, and Burke accompanied him as a friend and adviser. For his services on this occasion the latter was granted a pension of £300 a year, which he sacrificed, after enjoying it for eighteen months, on his rupture with Hamilton.

Soon after making this sacrifice, which did not prevent him tendering his aid and drawing his purse to forward the interests of his whimsical countryman, Barry the painter, Burke had the gratification of playing a part in the political world. On the dismissal of George Grenville from the head of affairs, Lord Rockingham, chief of the Whig magnates, was intrusted with the duty of forming an administration. That nobleman, having been filled with admiration of Burke's occasional papers in the "Public Advertiser," was led to desire the acquaintance of the writer, who speedily became his private secretary, and member of parliament for Wendover. He was, not, however, "swaddled, rocked, and dandled into a legislator." He set himself studiously to comprehend official forms and parliamentary proceedings, used every means to accomplish himself in voice and action—with that view even frequenting the theatre to derive hints and instruction from the tones, looks, and gestures of Garrick. Both by solitary study and debating at a society, he prepared himself to take an active part in the business of the House of Commons. He made his first speech on the bill for repealing the American Stamp Act, with an eloquence which excited the admiration of all present, and evoked the valuable praise of the great Earl of Chatham. Sir John Hawkins expressed his amazement at the extraordinary eminence to which Burke had suddenly ascended; upon which Dr. Johnson said,

"Sir, there is nothing marvelous in it; we who know Burke feel sure that he will be one of the first men in the country."

On the fall of the Rockingham ministry, to which his genius had imparted some degree of dignity, Burke wrote and circulated a plain and simple defense of its measures. He soon after made an ironical reply to his own pamphlet in the form of a letter, signed "Whittington," and professing to be the production of a tallow-chandler, who aspired to the office of lord-mayor. In this epistle a severe attack was made on the cabinet which Lord Chatham had just put together.

By this time Burke, from his intimacy with patrician senators, was known and appreciated in the world of fashion, where his talents and acquirements qualified him to shine, in spite of those social demarcations whose lines are not always justly drawn. He was an especial favorite, and won golden opinions in the "blue-stocking" circles; and he was wisely careful not to mortify the vanity nor incur the wrath of learned ladies, by pointing out their errors or exposing their fallacies. His position in Parliament was soon ascertained and ere long recognized. On the very day when he broke ground in the House of Commons, the first Pitt addressed it for the last time, and men were in doubt which of them was the more splendid speaker. Ere two years had elapsed, Burke had established his oratorical supremacy.

About this period a tract of Grenville's exhibited so much ill-nature that the Rockingham party felt the necessity of retaliating. Accordingly, Burke published his "Observations on the Present State of the Nation." The popular error that a man of genius can not deal with practical matters as successfully as those who are less richly endowed by nature, was the consolation of mediocrity very much earlier than the days of Burke, and from him it now met with a signal refutation. He executed his task with complete triumph on every point of consequence, and proved his mastery over the dry, minute, financial, and statistical details, which were supposed to form the stronghold and peculiar province of his sharp but narrow-minded adversary.

Burke had, ere this, purchased a pleasant villa near Beaconsfield, in Buckinghamshire, where he could enjoy rural privacy and rest his eye on lawns, woods, meadows, and corn-fields. Attached to his residence was land worth about six hundred a-year, of which he retained the greater part in his own occupation, that he might indulge in the satisfaction of farming. Without adopting any expensive system, he proved himself one of the most successful agriculturists in the county. When living in town he had various articles of produce carted up with his own stout nags, which were employed one day to draw his carriage, and on the next to plow the soil. As a country gentleman he exerted himself to the utmost to ameliorate the condition of the peasantry among whom he lived; he was daily earning their blessings by the schemes he devised for their benefit. He planned various institutions for enabling mechanics and laborers to save something from their wages against the season of sickness, and his hand was ever open as day to the poor or distressed. Thus he won and enjoyed the respect and admiration of the neighborhood. To his numerous guests his hospitality was overflowing. He neither affected style nor studied display, but regaled them with substantial fare, and delighted them with cheerful and entertaining conversation. Among his visitors he counted Dr. Johnson, for whose talents and virtues he always expressed a sincere esteem, and by whose death-bed his voice faltered with grief and emotion.

As one of the freeholders of Bucks, Burke drew up a petition concerning the Middlesex election, which was approved of by a county meeting, and presented by him to Parliament. He likewise set forth his views and opinions of the political affairs of the day, in a treatise entitled "Thoughts on the Present Discontents," wherein he advocated the claims of the great Whig connection to the government of the empire. In the House of Commons he maintained their interests with unrivaled eloquence; he led their ranks, in opposition to Lord North, during the American War; and he was justly regarded as by far the most formidable assailant whom that minister had to encounter in the arena of debate. His magnificent speech on American taxation was considered one of the most extraordinary on record; but his fanciful flights and profound reasoning were often too little adapted to the taste of his audience to be relished or followed; and his contemporaries became careless of attending to orations which, nevertheless, will last as long as the English language. His own friends, who crept stealthily away to avoid listening to his rich effusions, were, on their publication, surprised at the delight experienced in perusing them. Such was their treatment of an orator who spoke for posterity.

A dissolution occurring in 1774, Burke was, without his knowledge, put in nomination as a candidate for the representation of Bristol. He had just been elected for Malton, in Yorkshire, when the intelligence of this unsought distinction arrived; and straightway he proceeded to the ancient city. There his eloquence was exerted with such force that it penetrated even the heads of the wealthy traders in rum and sugar, who, after a protracted contest, placed him at the top of the poll. An amusing anecdote is related of his colleague in the canvass—a colonial merchant. After one of the mighty orator's most glowing addresses to the inhabitants, the worthy individual feeling himself quite overpowered by the torrent, instead of attempting to explain his views to the audience as expected, exclaimed with grave but excited earnestness, "I say *ditto* to Mr. Burke! I say *ditto* to Mr. Burke!" It happened, however, that when the next general election took place, Burke had rendered himself so unpopular to the constituency by his support of the Catholic claims and of the Irish Trade Acts, that he judged it prudent to decline a contest; and he again took shelter in the borough of Malton, which he represented during the remainder of his parliamentary career.

The party, which Burke had all but created by his intellect and determination, had, meantime, been reinforced by an ally of rare prowess and extraordinary capacity. Charles James Fox, a younger son of that Lord Holland who had sprung into political life under the auspices of Sir Robert Walpole, and been ennobled for services rendered to Lord Bute, had entered the House before he was of legal age. For a while Fox held a subordinate appointment in the Government of Lord North, but was dismissed from it on account of some refractory votes. He then, in spite of his unfortunate gaming propensities, made himself one of the most accomplished debaters ever heard, by speaking every night but one during five sessions. He became the pupil of Burke, from whom he frankly avowed having learned more than from all other men and authors. Gradually he superseded his master in the leadership, and their united efforts forced Lord North from power.

The Marquis of Rockingham now returned to his former position, and Burke received the appointment of Paymaster-general, then one of the most lucrative in the state, and was admitted into the privy council. But, in defiance of all fairness and gratitude, he was excluded from the cabinet. The death of Lord Rockingham, in 1782, terminated his party's tenure of office; and Lord Shelburne being called on to undertake the duties of government, intrusted the lead of the Lower House to Pitt, then little more than twenty-three years of age. Upon this was formed the celebrated Fox and North coalition which speedily drove Lord Shelburne into retirement, though his youthful colleague had struggled with signal skill, dauntless courage, and commanding eloquence to baffle the efforts of the terrible foes ranged in fierce opposition. The Duke of Portland then became nominal premier; Fox and his ancient enemy, Lord North, were the principal secretaries of state; and Burke calmly went back to the Pay-office. But Pitt succeeded in defeating their East India Bill, and returned to power in the capacity of prime minister.

Burke on this set out on his crusade against the abuses and tyranny, which had long occupied his thoughts. Fourteen years previously the affairs of India had become à subject of Parliamentary deliberation and national interest; and Burke had proceeded to investigate the matter with restless energy. The East India Directors had proposed to send him out at the head of a commission for the reformation of abuses, with discretionary powers. He declined the offer, but applied himself with persevering industry to acquire a thorough knowledge of the question. The time had now arrived when it was to be turned to account; and forthwith commenced the long and fierce contest, in the course of which he shook the old oak roof of Westminster Hall with his denunciations of the great Eastern culprit.

Warren Hastings, originally sent out to India as a poor orphan, whom his guardian was glad to be rid of, landed in 1785 on the free soil of Britain, after having maintained and extended the English empire in the East, administered its affairs with singular capacity, and gathered a large fortune for himself. Burke believed him to be sullied with various crimes, and within a week of his triumphant arrival gave notice of a motion seriously affecting his character as a ruler. With fiery zeal, relentless animosity, and unflagging industry, he commenced and carried on the assault, till, in February 1788, the memorable trial began in Westminster Hall, which was gorgeously fitted up for the occasion. On the third day Burke addressed the court, and his opening speech occupied four sittings. The passion and energy of the orator were worked up to a pitch which overbore, for a time, the conviction of those who entertained friendly feelings for the accused. With all the ardor of his great soul, with all the powers of his splendid imagination, and with all the might of his marvelous intellect, he denounced in the loftiest language the misconduct with which Hastings stood charged. Ladies shrieked and fainted; men muttered and execrated the dark deeds his rich mind and brilliant fancy portrayed with all the eloquence of the highest genius; and even the feelings of the criminal were so carried away by the resistless flood, that he almost believed himself guilty. The effect, however, was evanescent; the ceremony proceeded languidly; and years after it was brought to a termination by the acquittal of the Governor-general. Meantime, on the breaking out of the French Revolution, Burke, indignant at the removal of ancient landmarks, took a most gloomy view of its tendency, and was thus separated in opinion from his former associates, who did not hesitate to express their satisfaction at the event, and their admiration of the principles that had produced it. A party rupture was the consequence; and in 1791, during a Canadian debate, Burke, who had previously declared that he and Sheridan had parted forever, solemnly renounced all political and private friendship with Fox. "My separation," he stated, "is a principle, and not a passion. I hold it my sacred duty to confirm what I have said and written by this sacrifice. And to what purpose would be the reunion of a moment? Henceforth I can have no delight with him, nor he with me." Even when on his death-bed, he adhered sternly and steadfastly to this resolution, and declined an interview with his old friend and pupil. He had already published his "Reflections on the French Revolution," which soon overshadowed and agitated Europe. Dublin University conferred on him the degree of LL.D. for the wondrous power with which he had pleaded for established governments; and Oxford communicated to him an address of thanks. Though long exposed to multitudinous annoyances, and irritated by inferior men, his intellect had not suffered in the slightest degree. Doubtless, his counsels in regard to Continental affairs were somewhat fierce, arbitrary, and impracticable, as was not unnatural at a time when blood was flowing like water. But his genius and knowledge were still gloriously conspicuous; and this crowning effort of his powers as a writer was more than equal in strength, ability, and imagination to the splendid achievements of his earlier and more vigorous years.

In 1795 a pension was bestowed upon him for his long and faithful services to the State. This, although the slightest reward which a grateful monarch could have bestowed on his most gifted subject for labors on which Englishmen, to the latest generations, will look back with pride, as they profit by his burning sentences and words of wisdom, brought upon him most rancorous attacks. He was still mourning the loss of his only son, a youth of great promise; but, nevertheless, produced an answer characterized by his tried ability and scornful sarcasm. But no defense was necessary; and he who had sacrificed his repose, pleasures, and satisfactions to what he considered his duty to the country, and who had ever, without fear, favor, or affection, obeyed the dictates of conscience and the promptings of patriotism, need have cared little for the puny assailants who now crawled forth with their ragged mops to bespatter the wide and broad mirror that reflected his unrivaled greatness to an admiring world.

At length, in 1797, his bodily health began, rapidly to decline, though his mental faculties continued unimpaired to the last. On the 8th of July in that year he expired, after a brief struggle, and was buried in Beaconsfield church, where a plain mural tablet has been erected to his immortal memory.

NECKER

Ardent admirers of such mental and imaginative power as was displayed by the marvelous man whose career has just been sketched, will be unable to discover any striking signs of that sublime quality in Necker. Yet history hardly presents a more impressive and agreeable instance of moderate talents honestly exercised, and resolute industry unflinchingly practiced, conducting an obscure individual—in spite of countless obstacles—to boundless wealth and supreme distinction, in an exclusive country of which he could not even boast of being a native. His example is, therefore, of peculiar value to youth, and eminently worthy of attentive consideration, as showing what may be achieved by integrity and perseverance against all disadvantages.

The forefathers of this celebrated person whose name justly occupies so conspicuous a place in the political annals of continental Europe, are stated to have been Irish Protestants, at a time when there was particularly little personal safety to those holding the doctrines of the reformed faith. At a troublous period they fled from persecution, and sought refuge in Prussia, whence another generation found their way into Switzerland. Thus it happened that Necker was born in Geneva, on the 3d of September, 1732, where his parents were in respectable circumstances, and where his father held the Professorship of Public Law. The boy was doubtless educated with care in his native city, whose beautiful situation on the Rhône and at the end of Lake Leman, with its fine walks and pleasant prospects, furnished a fitting scene wherein to indulge his youthful and ambitious aspirations after fame and fortune. But at the same time the manners and customs of the place conveyed to him impressions still more salutary, and predisposed him in favor of those habits of rigid virtue on which he subsequently built his high power and enviable reputation, as also those sound religious principles which, in after life, distinguished him and his house from those among whom his lot was cast.

The opinion that the true genius is a mind of large general powers, determined by accident to some particular direction, is rather confirmed than otherwise by the instance of Necker. His natural bent was toward political and philosophical studies, and had they been encouraged and pursued, he might have become a fanciful and brilliant thinker; but his parents did not regard his prepossessions with satisfaction. On the contrary, they deemed it better that his time should be devoted to the lucrative labor which fortune supplies to a votary of activity, energy, and intellect. While commerce fills the purse it clogs the brain; and, though highly favored in his efforts, Necker was not luckier than others in this respect. In earlier years he is said to have written two comedies; but the extraordinary struggle which must have been required to metamorphose a friendless clerk into one of the richest men of his time would naturally tend to crush and destroy any of the more precious particles of talent and enthusiasm with which he had been endowed by nature. His uncompromising virtue, rare amiability, common sense, amazing industry, and well-proved philanthropy, are the claims which his name possesses to the respect and gratitude of posterity.

Regarding the wishes of his parents as law, Necker sacrificed his own inclinations, and was sent at the age of fifteen to acquire a knowledge of mercantile affairs in the establishment of Vernet, a banker in Paris. Notwithstanding his aspiring vein, it would, indeed, have been difficult at that critical period of his existence for any one to imagine the possibility of the young Genevan adventurer rising to be first minister of royal France—figuring as the centre of literary society in the most polished of European capitals, and exercising a mighty influence on the destinies of the world.

Nevertheless his ability and industry were soon proved, and brought him into notice; his employers duly considering, of course, that it was their interest to do so, afforded him such assistance as was likely to redound to their own profit and advantage. His perseverance was encouraged; he rapidly ascended to a place of trust and confidence in the banking-house, and thus laid the foundation of that character for care and aptitude in business which, as years passed on, made him Chairman of the French East India Company—the highest of his commercial distinctions.

The reputation, however, on which he rose to political eminence had to be created by unflinching assiduity, and the exhibition of intellect. Female inspiration was essential to its proper formation in the capital on the Seine; and presently an influence of no unworthy kind was present to nerve the hand, elevate the mind, and fire the soul of the young banker's clerk, struggling, though unaided, to make a name and form a reputation.

As has been well observed, "Women are the priestesses of predestination. It is the spirit of man that says, I will be great; but it is the sympathy of women that usually makes him so." That influence, in a very pure and elevating degree, it was ere long Necker's good fortune to find. While in the employment of Thelusson, a rich banker, he was in the habit of visiting at the house of Madame de Vermenoux, who had just engaged a remarkably learned and accomplished Swiss governess, of captivating appearance, to teach Latin to her son. This foreign instructress, though young, had run no ordinary career. She had encountered and borne up against troubles and disappointments with heroic courage and dauntless energy. In the gay days of girlhood she had been wooed, won, and sighed for by no less eminent a person than the embryo historian of the Roman empire. In obedience to the mandate of his family, who relished not the idea of so strange a match, Gibbon philosophically abandoned, though he could not altogether forget, the learned and beautiful object of his attachment. The death of her father, the venerable pastor of a mountain village, left her quite unprovided for; but, far from sinking under the circumstances, she conveyed her surviving parent to Geneva, where the liberal education she had received enabled her to maintain both by teaching young females. On the death of her mother she had been induced to remove to Paris, and thus met the man whose aspirations she was to guide and whose ambition she was to direct. Necker was immediately impressed by the charms and accomplishments of the erudite damsel, and, on becoming better acquainted, her grave style of beauty and noble character of mind threw over him a potent spell, and produced upon his heart an effect of no ordinary kind. Then, however, he could offer nothing but a devoted heart, with such worldly prospects as the enthusiasm of youth, especially in such circumstances, can readily conjure up. Thus, in consequence of their mutual poverty, they were under the harsh necessity of submitting to the delay of years. Soon, however, did the hero of this somewhat romantic engagement emerge from that chill obscurity which aspiring spirits like his can ill brook. He became a partner of the flourishing banking-house in which he was employed, and hailed the sun of fortune's better day all the more eagerly that it gave him the power of completing their union without any violation of prudential considerations. Madame Necker's ardent desire for honorable fame speedily exercised an effect on her husband. It quickened his efforts after distinction, and prompted him to apply his intellect to huge adventures and important speculations. By his transactions in corn he realized an immense fortune, which was employed and increased by large financial operations with the Government.

Meantime he was steadily advancing in social favor, to which his amiability and uprightness highly recommended him, and he was chosen envoy for the republic of Geneva at the court of Versailles. When that State was, in some crisis, contemplating the appointment of an embassador to Paris, the Minister of the Crown assured Necker that such an envoy was altogether unnecessary. "I will have nothing to do with any one in this affair but yourself, Monsieur Necker," he said. This office opened up a passage for him to aristocratic circles, where his known wealth and accurate information secured him a tolerable degree of respect. As he rose to affluence and social importance, his natural inclination began to assert its dormant claim; he withdrew from active business, and devoted much attention to the pursuits toward which his heart had originally been turned. He had studied finance with singular determination; and his extensive knowledge of that subject, as shown in several pamphlets written at this period, excited much interest, and won him considerable praise.

In 1773 he carried off the prize at the Academy, with his *Eloge de Colbert*; and soon after won even greater distinction by his able essay, entitled *La Législation et le Commerce des Grains*. His information was extensive, and his views of questions as intelligent and comprehensive as his training and education admitted of their being. His regular and precise habits were, doubtless, rare as the conjugal devotion which raised the wonder of sneering skeptics and gay courtiers. His conversation, though a little pedantic, was lively, refined, and instructive, and his manner characterized by the courage of honesty.

Indeed the time had now arrived when the upright character, financial skill, and approved ability of the Swiss adventurer, rendered him a personage whom the Government could not overlook. His disposition was so amiable that it inspired love and esteem in those who were best acquainted with him; while his generosity and munificence had fascinated the masses, and won him popular applause. Besides, his intellect had impressed itself on public feeling, and on the national mind. He enunciated the doctrine, not under all circumstances agreeable, that no new tax was lawful till all the resources of economy had been tried; and he held opinions in favor of retrenchment before the idea was in fashion with the multitude. Such a man was unquestionably of no small value in the administration of affairs. The finances were in all but hopeless disorder, and war was apparently approaching. Therefore, though he was, as a foreigner, distasteful to the nobles, and as a Protestant an object of aversion—not unmingled, perhaps, with dread—to the clergy, urgent necessity overbore considerations which might not have yielded to a less imperious monitor, and he was nominated Director-general of the Finances. To allay the foolish murmurs of the privileged classes, he was not admitted to a seat in the cabinet; and to the complaints of the clergy, who naturally remonstrated against a Protestant being intrusted with an office of such importance, the prime minister of the day used this very significant and conclusive argument: "I will give him up to you, if you will pay the debts of the State."

Having thus placed his foot on the ladder of power, Necker speedily made his influence beneficially felt. Various reforms, great and small, in the administration of the national finances, testified that a strong hand and a clear head were enlisted in the service of a country that much required them. He commenced his official career by prudently declining to receive the emoluments pertaining to the post he occupied, and forthwith signalized his accession to office by suppressing some six hundred places about the Court and Treasury. His early education had strongly impressed him in favor of free institutions; and his system of government was essentially popular. His plan was, to render as public as possible the national accounts and expenditure, and to form provincial assemblies, in which local affairs and taxation might be discussed and debated. His schemes, however, were not in any respect agreeable to the courtiers, and he was assailed by a continuous shower of pamphlets from the members of the Parliament of Paris. Under these untoward circumstances he deemed a place in the Council requisite, that he might be in a proper position to defend his measures when they were under the deliberation of that body.

"What! you in the Council, and you do not go to mass!" exclaimed the First Minister of the Crown, with every feature of his countenance marked with surprise.

"Sully did not go to mass, and yet he was admitted to the Council," replied the Swiss financier, with becoming dignity; but in vain. The minister offered to comply with his request, if he would become a Roman Catholic; but, as in duty bound, Necker resolutely refused to sacrifice his religious convictions to political advancement, and sent in his resignation to the king. His majesty, painfully aware of the value of the services he was thus about to lose, accepted it mournfully; and those who had coalesced to overthrow the obnoxious statesman rejoiced for a brief season over the triumph they had, for their misfortune, achieved.

Meantime Necker had made a noble and philanthropic use of the influence he possessed, and of the immense wealth which he had amassed by his talents and industry. His private character was so unexceptionable, and his morality so unimpeachable, as to contrast remarkably with those among whom he acted so prominent a part; and, with the assistance of his precious wife, he had done much to relieve and alleviate the wants and distresses of the poor and indigent. Madame Necker had expressed a wish to devote her talents to literature, but her husband hinted his objection to such a course being pursued; and she betook herself to those acts of charity and beneficence, to which he proudly appealed in a day of darkness and gloom. Thus, at a great cost of time, labor, and money, they had founded the hospital in Paris which still bears their name; and there, in contemplating the good effected by their exertions, they found consolation in times of trouble. On the day preceding his resignation, they went thither; and the Sisters of Mercy who attended the patients sang portions of the Psalms—the only poetry with which they were acquainted—and loudly extolled the Neckers as the helpers and benefactors of the poor and needy. The fallen minister was, perhaps, much more moved with such demonstrations of affection than by all his trials, and felt a pang at losing a position which gave him the power of conferring blessings on his less-favored fellow-creatures.

Necker now retired to St. Omer, a short distance from Paris, where he soon had conclusive proofs of his wide popularity. He received hundreds of communications from people of the highest rank and importance, regretting his removal from office: the road between his residence and the city was crowded with the carriages of persons who went to pay their respects to him in his retreat; and ere long he had it in his power to decline the proposals of three foreign sovereigns, who each hastened to offer him the management of their exchequers.

In 1787 he published his celebrated attack on Calonne, then presiding over the financial department; and so bitter did the controversy become, that the king judged it necessary to banish the ex-minister twenty leagues from Paris. Next year, however, the feeling against his successor became so strong, the monetary embarrassments so perplexing, and the public excitement so great, that there appeared no other politic course than to recall Necker from his retirement. Accordingly he was privately applied to by the queen, through the Austrian embassador, to resume his former functions; but he declined doing so without possessing complete control. He was, therefore, recalled, as a kind of financial dictator. His return was a triumph of the most brilliant description. He was welcomed along the road from Bale with expressions of joy, gratitude, and admiration, by the inhabitants of the district. The day of his entry into Paris was kept as a festive holiday, and the popular enthusiasm manifested itself in shouts of applause: but he came too late to be permanently of service to the disordered and agitated state. Few men have ever met with so hearty a reception from their fellow-subjects; and Necker had sufficient ambition and vanity not to be altogether insensible to the glowing triumphs of such an hour. Yet, when congratulated on his recall, under circumstances so flattering, he regretfully remarked—"Ah, would that I could recall the last fifteen months!"

Nevertheless, his influence was, as anticipated, speedily and beneficially felt in the restoration of public credit, and the relief of the capital from the famine which had threatened and terrified its inhabitants. Events had, indeed, arrived at a crisis which baffled the strength of his guiding-hand and the resources of his busy brain; and he soon found questions arising which the public excitement prevented him from dealing with, or settling, to advantage. The wearisome and invidious duty of being responsible for proceedings over which he had no control, was his for a brief period; and he, unfortunately, lacked the qualities which enable a public man to stand and save himself and others in an age of revolution. His popularity vanished as the storm approached; and, at length, on the 4th of September, 1790, sick at heart, and tired of contending with difficulties which no human power could have subdued, he finally resigned the high office which, in ordinary times, he was capable of filling with so much honor to himself, and so much advantage to the country, disappeared from the stage, and was quickly forgotten amid the excitement and bloodshed of a revolutionary tempest. He betook himself to Coppet, and felt his banishment from the moving world less than most men who have been compelled to relinquish power. He had that admiration of his learned, virtuous, and amiable wife, which swallowed up such considerations. Her influence over his heart was as unlimited as was her devotion to his wishes. Though she was somewhat cold, formal, and precise, in his eyes she seemed perfect, and he had ever regarded her with a feeling approaching to idolatry; and in days of adversity she shone forth, and exhibited domestic love, noble truth, and high-souled purity. On her death, in 1794, Necker was solaced by the affection and friendship of their accomplished daughter, Madame de Staël, since generally recognized as one of the most distinguished women who ever lived. In 1800 he was visited by Bonaparte, when marching to Marengo. Necker expired in the year 1803, and was buried in the grounds at Coppet, by the side of his departed spouse.

This famous man was not endowed with that splendid genius which has elevated many from obscure situations to positions of power and dignity; but his industry was untiring, and his integrity beyond question. He rose with credit, by habits of steady and incessant exertion and independence, which were transferred from one sphere to another, adhered to with resolution, and might have proved successful in raising the land of his adoption to a condition of enviable wealth and prosperity, but for the mighty event which tortured the foresight of the most sagacious, and defied the valor of the bravest.

PITT

The name and memory of a great statesman, who has led and ruled senates by the might of eloquence, carried measures beneficial to millions, or impressed immortal principles on public conviction, are generally, in spite of political disputes and disagreements, regarded by a free and favored people with feelings of respect, admiration, and gratitude. They are associated in the mind of a community with periods of peril or prosperity, and recalled by each succeeding generation with national pride. "Great men," said Burke, "are the guide-posts and land-marks of the state;" and, assuredly, history presents few more spotless or splendid reputations than that of the son of Chatham, who came forth and signalized his prowess as a ripe politician, accomplished debater, and skillful tactician, prepared for the work and warfare of the senate by his comprehensive views in what have been termed the proper sciences of a statesman—those of government, politics, commerce, economics, history, and human nature—at an age when many are making their first and last crude efforts at public speaking, or expending their faculties in frivolous dissipation and enervating luxury.

Doubtless the name which Chatham had made immortal was a tower of strength; and his brilliant example could hardly fail to inspire with a love of kindred fame the son on whom his fondest hopes rested. Indeed, there were both interest and curiosity experienced as to whether the power of the Pitt family would be increased or diminished. And, moreover, there was not wanting that encouragement to noble and patriotic exertion which is usually given by a generous public to the sons of great and popular ministers of state. It may, therefore, be truly said, that

> "With prospects bright upon the world he came,
> Pure love of virtue, strong desire of fame;
> Men marked the lofty path his mind would take,
> And all foretold the progress he should make."

The family to which this illustrious man belonged was rich and respectable, though not patrician in origin or descent. The Pitts were for ages settled in Dorsetshire, but at length one of them became Governor of Madras, and brought home from the East that celebrated diamond, the largest then known to be in existence, which was sold to the Regent Orleans for more than three millions of livres, and took its place as the most precious of the crown jewels of France. The son of this fortunate functionary was a gentleman of Cornwall, and hereditary patron of some boroughs; for one of which, Old Sarum, his second son, a cornet in the Blues, was returned to Parliament. The talents of the latter were speedily exerted in such a way as to give offense to Sir Robert Walpole, who manifested the annoyance he felt by dismissing him from the army: but nothing could restrain the course of that terrible eloquence, which, in reality, was hardly under its possessor's control. Instead of depending, as others had done, on oligarchies and "pocket-lists," he relied for support on the middle classes, then struggling into importance, and, with their aid, ere long became the greatest war-minister who ever presided over the destinies of England. He married a daughter of the political house of Grenville, whose members played so conspicuous a part in the affairs of the eighteenth century, and had several children, of whom William Pitt, the second son, was born at Hayes, in the county of Kent, on the 28th of May, 1759.

The boy destined to exhibit so wonderful an instance of precocious statesmanship received the rudiments of his education under the paternal roof; and, although so delicate in health that he could only devote half the wonted time to study, his progress was remarkably rapid, and his talents evident to all who knew him. When eight years old, he was seen by the mother of Fox, who instinctively prognosticated the rivalry between her distinguished son and the young prodigy. The contention which had long existed between their sires no doubt suggested this idea to the anxious parent; and when she marked the singular cleverness of the little boy, and observed the wonderful propriety of his behavior, the maternal solicitude sharpening her penetration, enabled her to augur the fierce and bitter strife which was to shake senates and shatter parties. Lord Chatham was justly proud of his son, and predicted that he would add honor to the name; nay, more, he expressed a belief that he would some day be one of the first men in Parliament; and, if a minister of state, that he would arrive at the highest dignity. He therefore gave his utmost assistance in forming the future premier's mind, and incited him to lofty and laudable aspirations. These labors were not in vain; and the Great Earl lived long enough to feel assured that a useful and brilliant career lay before the object of his tender care.

One evening a member of Parliament proposed to take the veteran statesman's two boys to hear a debate in the House of Commons; but he refused to allow the younger to go. "If William," he is reported to have said, "heard any arguments of which he did not approve he would rise to controvert them; and, young as he is, he has not even in that assembly many equals in knowledge, reasoning, and eloquence." He must indeed have been a "marvelous boy," to be spoken of even by a fond father, at such an age and in such circumstances. At this date he is stated to have had a turn for poetry, and to have composed, along with his brothers and sisters, a play in rhyme, which was acted by them before some friends of the family. He subsequently, while at college, produced a tragedy, which, when at the head of public affairs he calmly committed to the flames in presence of a friend, by whom this emanation of his poetic faculty had just been eagerly perused and spoken of in terms of high admiration; though perhaps the merits of the piece might not altogether have justified the praise.

Pitt's earlier education was conducted by a tutor, but, as has been stated, under the vigilant superintendence of his father, who noted his progress, and rejoiced at the constant indications he gave of superior endowments. Haughty, vehement, and despotic in his nature as that extraordinary minister—the pride of England and the terror of her enemies—was to foes and friends in public life, no such characteristics were allowed to interfere with the quiet and happiness of his domestic circle.

In his fourteenth year, young Pitt was sent to the University of Cambridge, and entered at Pembroke Hall, where Dr. Prettyman, afterward Bishop of Lincoln, was his tutor. In age and appearance, indeed, he was a mere boy; but he was by no means boyish in mind or intellect. His acquirements were wonderful, and he could converse on various subjects with all the seriousness of manhood. He was much liked by his youthful compeers for his lively and amiable disposition; and at the same time esteemed by the tutors on account of his decorum in conduct and diligence in study. His manners in private life were then, as ever, frank, easy, agreeable, and utterly devoid of the cold arrogance and unbending demeanor he exhibited in his senatorial capacity.

Lord Chatham had desired and intended that Pitt should become a candidate for academical honors, but the gifted youth was prevented by weak health from keeping the requisite terms. Nevertheless, he obtained the degree of A.M. in compliment to his illustrious parentage, without any public examination. His juvenile contemporaries on the occasion testified their approval of his being thus distinguished by interrupting the public orator with loud and vehement acclamations. One of his warmly-attached college friends was Wilberforce, who entered upon public life about the same date as himself.

When Pitt left Cambridge, he was accomplished in no ordinary degree. In Latin authors he rarely encountered a difficulty; and he had, even at his entrance, been capable of translating pages of Thucydides with scarcely an error. He was intimately acquainted with the beauties and defects of the works he had perused. Indeed those who observed the ease with which at first sight he read obscure books, state, that his facility would have appeared beyond the compass of human intellect, if they had not actually witnessed it. During his residence at college his diligence in learning was exemplary, and his success remarkable. His education was conducted with a view to the struggles of the bar as well as the conflicts of the senate; his attention to study was of the strictest kind; and he displayed eminent qualifications for entering on either path of life. He made himself intimately acquainted with the legal history of the country, studied the policy of modern nations as well as their constitutions and forms of government, and acquired much knowledge of the origin, prosperity, and decline of states that had existed and been influential in remote times. His peculiar quickness of conception rendered his progress in these branches of information comparatively easy; and when he left college, after an unusually long residence, his mind was as perfectly formed as mere theory could make it. He long retained his love for ancient learning; and even amid the bustle of politics and the devising of budgets and subsidies, was seldom without some work from which to refresh his mind with classical lore.

Lord Chatham's letters written to his son about this period overflow with parental affection and judicious advice. After the too eager and ambitious youth had recovered from a severe illness, he was thus touchingly addressed by his justly gratified father:

"How happy the task, my noble, amiable boy, to caution you only against pursuing too much all those liberal and praiseworthy things to which less happy natures have perpetually to be spurred and driven. I will not tease you with too long a lecture in favor of inaction and a competent stupidity—your two best tutors and companions at present. You have time to spare; consider, there is but the Encyclopedia. And when you have mastered all that, what will remain? You will want, like Alexander, another world to conquer."

After removing from the University the younger Pitt repaired to the Continent, and spent some time at Rheims, still resolutely pursuing his studies and adding to his stores of knowledge.

In 1778 his famous father died, under circumstances which rendered him dearer than ever to the country, of whose honor and interest he was ever so vigilant a guardian, and whose name he made so great, and dreaded among the nations of the earth. Pitt, who had been present when Lord Chatham fell down in the House of Lords while raising his enfeebled voice to cheer the drooping spirits of Englishmen, appeared at the public funeral as chief mourner, and ere long proved the inheritor of his father's popularity. Between them had existed the strongest affection and the most complete confidence.

Having duly kept his terms at Lincoln's Inn, Pitt was called to the bar in 1780, and went the western circuit with sufficient encouragement to justify expectations of success in his legal pursuits. Lord Mansfield, indeed, declared, that if he persevered in the profession he would be regarded as one of its chief ornaments. But it was perfectly natural that he should rather aspire to parliamentary distinction; and accordingly he engaged in an unsuccessful contest for the representation of Cambridge University. It was, however, for Appleby, a borough under the influence of the Lowthers, that he was first, through the friendship of the Duke of Rutland, returned to that house, which was so often stilled into silence as he rose to speak, delighted as his grand voice swelled in every ear, and filled with thunders of applause as he, with a coolness and self-possession unfelt by all listeners, resumed his place with a look of lofty contempt for his foes.

Pitt was not in any way bound by the political tenets of the patron of the constituency which he represented. He was free to act on his own convictions. He took his seat in January 1781, and next month made his first speech to the House, in support of Burke's motion for an economical reform in the Civil List. He was eminently successful, and displayed an ease, fluency, and accuracy of language which riveted attention and sustained public hope. It is related, that when he had accomplished this his first parliamentary success, Fox hurried up to express his warm congratulations. As they were conversing, an honorable, gallant, and experienced member passed them, and remarked, "You may well praise his speech, for, excepting yourself, no man in the House could have made such another; and, old as I am, I expect to see you both battling it within these walls, as I've seen your fathers before you." Fox looked rather sheepish and disconcerted at this somewhat blunt and embarrassing compliment; but Pitt answered with happy promptitude, "I've no doubt, General, you would like to live to the age of Methuselah."

At the close of the session some one having remarked to Fox that Pitt promised to be one of the first orators ever heard in the House, that great man unhesitatingly answered, "He is so already."

Pitt still continued to practice his industry and exercise his intellect at the bar, and was highly complimented for his ability by more than one legal sage; while in Parliament he was receiving the highest marks of admiration for his speeches against the ministers of the day, and their conduct in regard to the American War. At length Lord North was compelled to retreat from power, and Lord Rockingham empowered to form an administration. Pitt would have been a valuable auxiliary; but, from not belonging to what Lord Chatham had called "the Great Revolution families," he was disqualified, like Burke, from sitting in the cabinet, and prudently declined taking office. He soon after submitted his motion for an inquiry into the representative system, with the view of lessening the influence of the dominant aristocracy. His efforts in this respect were unsuccessful, and he afterward endeavored circuitously to accomplish his object by creating a host of plebeian peers. Whatever opinions he may have subsequently entertained in regard to the necessity of Parliamentary Reform, were rendered vain and impracticable by the startling events which speedily changed the face of Europe. Meantime his family rapidly increased; he was described as a greater orator even than his father, and as possessing the full vigor of youth, with the wisdom and experience of the maturest age. Gaming—the vice of the period—he resolutely refrained from.

On the death of Lord Rockingham his administration fell to pieces; and Lord Shelburne became First Minister of the Crown. The latter nobleman was eminent for his intelligence, knowledge, and variety of information; a great linguist, fond of science and letters, and actuated by popular principles. He appointed Pitt Chancellor of the Exchequer, and intrusted him with the management of the House of Commons, within eighteen months of the young statesman's having obtained a seat in Parliament. In this most responsible position he displayed consummate powers in debate, and proved himself entirely worthy of the confidence reposed in his ability and discretion. The opposition leaders conceived that they had been injured by Lord Shelburne, and showed no mercy to his chief colleague, either on account of his youth or hereditary claims to public respect; but Pitt faced their embattled host with haughty defiance. It certainly required no ordinary courage to do so.

Burke's great soul was at that time heavy; he was not insensible of the humiliation he had recently experienced; and, like the Northumbrian Hotspur before breakfast, he was ready to vent his hoarded wrath on any one who appeared as an antagonist. Besides, he little relished the spectacle of the assembly, whose brightest ornament he was, being ruled by a lad who had not donned manly garments, when he was achieving conversational triumphs over Dr. Johnson, and contesting the palm of eloquence with "the great Commoner." Sheridan even went the length of comparing the ministerial leader to one of Ben Jonson's characters, "the angry boy in the 'Alchymist;'" and Fox relentlessly poured forth against him the terrible torrent of his stirring and impetuous eloquence.

There is something touching in the idea of a struggle against such men having been maintained by a youth of twenty-three. It must, indeed, have been a marvelous sight to mark that young minister, with his plumes thus scattering on the Parliamentary gale, rise from the Treasury bench to do battle against his puissant foes. His form was tall, thin, and stately; his eyes blue, but bright with pride and intelligence; and on his wide brow, and in his disdainful air, were legibly written that proud and lofty scorn which had deeply struck its root in his imperial mind. Facing the Opposition with a glance of stern indignation, he gravely rebuked the untimely levity of the sage champion of oppressed India, and declared that he could not approve of the indiscretion which so unseasonably ran away with good sense and sober judgment. Then he chilled the spirit of the defiant author of the "School for Scandal," by a contemptuous allusion to his theatrical pursuits, than which, perhaps, no thrust would have been more likely to tell with the gifted, but graceless and eccentric, senator's patrician coadjutors. And ere his enemies had recovered from their surprise at a stroke, which the extreme and peculiar difficulty of his situation alone could justify, he turned indignantly upon the eminent rival of his life, branded him with sarcastic reprobation, and defended his noble colleague in another place from the strictures passed upon him. Then rising, for a time, above party strife and personal considerations, he denounced the coalition which was being formed as an event stretching to a point of political apostasy, that not only astonished so young a man as he was, but amazed and confounded the most veteran observers of the human heart; and he exclaimed with glowing eloquence and fervent patriotism, "If this baneful alliance is not already formed, if this ill-omened marriage is not already solemnized, I know a just and lawful impediment; and, in the name of the public safety, I here forbid the bans." His high spirit sustained him in all attacks; and he delivered one of his most splendid orations at this period. But all his efforts were in vain; the Shelburne ministry had been weak from its formation; and it fell, after a brief but not inglorious tenure of power, during which Pitt had been gratified with the opportunity of proving his capacity for administration, and the power to defend what he did. Indeed, so clearly had his talent for government been shown, that the king was desirous that he should himself undertake the duties of prime-minister; but feeling that the strength of the party to which he belonged was as yet unequal to sustain him in the fierce struggle which, in such a case, would inevitably have ensued, he wisely refrained from grasping prematurely at a prize so flattering and fascinating to young ambition. However, it came into his hands much sooner than he could have contemplated. Having declined to lend his support to the administration of Lord North and Mr. Fox, and suffered a second defeat at Cambridge, he spent several months in France, and returned with the intention of resuming his legal pursuits. But events soon occurred which led him to abandon this resolution. His rivals had incurred much unpopularity; and their India bill was regarded with such dislike and apprehension, that the Peers thought fit to reject it, and by their vote terminate the official existence of its authors. On this taking place, Pitt was again requested to assume the reins of power; and he bravely consented. The position was arduous and difficult in the extreme; and he had scarcely completed his twenty-fifth year. He had to encounter, almost single-handed, an opposition conducted by men whose powers, genius, and eloquence might well have daunted the heart of the boldest, and appalled the imagination of the most experienced ministers; and they were supported by a party infinitely superior in numbers to that which followed him. Though they had formerly sought his services with eagerness, yet when a motion was made for the issue of a writ on his acceptance of the premiership, they met it with a loud and general shout of derisive laughter and provoking ridicule; many, who might otherwise have hastened to proffer their support, hesitated to enlist under a leader so young and inexperienced in affairs of state; and they confidently predicted his immediate fall from the dangerous eminence to which he had ascended at so early an age. Under such circumstances, Pitt was not upheld by the family or political connection which other ministers had used; but he had much confidence in his own resources, and in the support of the crown and people, who, whenever an opportunity was presented, proved that he had not erred in his calculations. His opponents it must be admitted, had no slight reason to predict his speedy retirement and his inability to conduct the public business; for in a House of Commons decidedly hostile to his pretensions, he had not a single ally capable of making himself formidable, with the exception of his chosen friend Dundas, better known as Lord Melville. With such aid as that skillful and sagacious debater could render, the tall, slender, stern, and dauntless minister, struggled with credit through a session against an enraged majority and a host of terrible foes, panting for a swift revenge. Their desire, however, was not destined to be gratified. Several resolutions, declaratory of the incompetence of ministers to conduct the business of the realm, were, indeed, carried; their speedy resignation frequently seemed inevitable; but the king encouraged them to persevere against the difficulties with which they were encompassed; the country, on being appealed to, ejected a hundred and sixty of Pitt's opponents from their seats; and he received the thanks and the freedom of the city of London for the uprightness and disinterestedness he had exhibited. Pitt was, as he might well be, proud of, and emboldened by, his immense popularity; and when the new Parliament assembled in the month of May, 1784, he had to encounter an opposition so numerically feeble, that his arduous duties were entered upon with some degree of satisfaction. He was now in a position to maintain his ground; and that he could do so against the fierce and unsparing attacks of such potent adversaries as Burke, Fox, and Sheridan, amply proves the care, attention, and industry with which, by hard and continuous study, he had fitted and prepared himself to enact so great and heroic a part.

Pitt, as has been stated, was the pupil of Lord Shelburne, first Marquis of Lansdowne; and at that distinguished nobleman's house he became acquainted with Dr. Price, a clever Dissenting Minister, who furnished him, among other suggestions, with his original scheme of redeeming the National Debt by means of a Sinking Fund, which, in 1786, he developed and submitted to the House, in a speech of six hours' duration; and it was accepted without a division.

But the aspiring and ambitious statesman, however austere and absorbed he might be, had other arrangements to make, besides re-organizing a party, and, as the head of it, devising vast financial operations. It was necessary to find fair and bewitching ladies of rank to smile upon his efforts, and render his side attractive; and there can be no doubt that in this important respect Fox was much more propitiously situated. He had also to countervail the advantage which his great antagonist derived from troops of aristocratic friends, by arraying under his banner the adventurous genius and rising intellect of the country. His bearing in public was peculiar, and certainly not such as to attract the affectionate sympathies of his contemporaries; he displayed little of "the soft green of the soul," and his manner was utterly unbending. Yet so enormous was his influence out of doors at this early period that he was solicited to represent numerous constituencies; but he preferred being returned, by a large majority, for the University of Cambridge, which had twice previously shut the door in his face, and of which he was afterward chosen High Steward.

On entering the House, he was in the habit of stalking along to the Treasury bench with a severe aspect and a scornful air, scarcely acknowledging the presence of even his most intimate friends and devoted adherents. When he rose to speak every tongue was hushed; his tones were lofty and arrogant; his sentences rolled forth fluently, and swelled with delightful harmony; and every word was heard with amazing distinctness. His speech delivered in 1791, on the slave-trade, is stated to have been the finest effort of his oratorical faculties; and his unreported war-speech, in 1803, was so surprisingly excellent that Fox, in replying, said that the orators of antiquity would have heard it with admiration, probably with envy. He had the power of speaking with the utmost clearness, though when the process of mystification was necessary no one could perform it with more skill or effect. That eloquence of which Lord Chatham had been too often the slave seems to have been completely under the control of his favorite son.

In private life Pitt was, as has been already stated, amiable in disposition, buoyant in spirits, and warm in friendship. He was not insensible to the charms of female grace, but office was "the pride of his heart and the pleasure of his life." When a match between him and Mademoiselle Necker was proposed by her father, he is said to have answered, half jestingly, that he was already wedded to his country.

The schemes of Pitt for raising Great Britain to a state of high material prosperity were frustrated by the outbreak of the French Revolution, whose causes appear to have baffled the comprehension of the most sagacious, and whose consequences defied the foresight of the most prophetic. His entrance upon official life had been signalized by a treaty of peace, and his policy was founded on its maintenance; but he was urged by his new allies, who followed Burke and Windham, to support the war against France, and thus gratify the propensity of "an old and haughty nation, proud in arms." The philosophy of Burke threw a halo around ancient institutions, and Pitt formed the great league for their defense. The spirit of Englishmen was roused; they clamored for war; and forthwith that long, terrible, and momentous contest, which was brought to a glorious close on the field of Waterloo, was entered upon.

Pitt continued to administer the affairs of the empire till 1801. He had been successful in accomplishing the Union with Ireland, and was anxious to carry a measure for the relief of the Roman Catholics of that country. However, he was foiled in this intention by the determination of the king and the feelings of the public. He then, suddenly and unexpectedly, retired from the helm of the state, and gave a guarded support to the ministry of his successor, who had formerly filled the Speaker's chair, and who was subsequently raised to the peerage as Lord Sidmouth. That personage and his colleagues concluded, in 1802, the Peace of Amiens, which was of short duration; and they, being found inadequate to the functions they had, at a dark, awful, and perilous period, undertaken, were forced to retire in 1804. Then Pitt returned to power, and "bade the conqueror go forth," nor in vain; but his situation was perplexing in the extreme. With shattered health and depressed spirits he was exposed to attack from every species of assailant, though unaided, except by the ardent genius of Canning—his most gifted, eloquent, and distinguished disciple. He was not destined much longer to endure the struggle. The news of the defeat of the allied armies at Austerlitz came with a most crushing effect upon his great and proud soul, and he sunk with rapidity. He was cheered in his last hours by the intelligence of the glorious victory at Trafalgar, but all hopes of recovery had passed away. His old tutor, who had now been promoted to the bishopric of Lincoln, attended his dying couch, and solicited him to join in devotional prayer. Then answered the expiring statesman, with that voice that had often thrilled listening audiences, and taught them that they were in presence of a ruler of mankind—"I fear that I have, like many others, neglected my religious duties too much to have any ground to hope that they can be efficacious on my death-bed. But," he added, with fervor, "I throw myself entirely on the mercy of God." He then joined in religious exercises with piety, calmness, and humility. On the morning of the 23d of January, 1806, he breathed his last, at his residence on Putney Heath.

A public funeral to his mortal remains, a national monument to his memory, and a sum of money to discharge the debts contracted by him while toiling in the service of the state, were voted; and he was interred in that corner of Westminster Abbey where the ashes of so many famous statesmen, who have shaken senates with the fierce conflict of oratory, repose in peace together. He was, indeed, well worthy of every token of respect which a great and enlightened nation could thus bestow; for though men may and do differ as to his genius for legislation, his success in administration, and the propriety and effects of his achievements, there are few who can contemplate without admiration his high talents, his majestic eloquence, and the zeal he ever manifested to serve the country which he loved so well, without reference to pecuniary gain or the gratification of mere vulgar ambition.

LORD ERSKINE

Among the great men and accomplished orators who, during Pitt's long and arduous tenure of office, strove energetically to curb his will, humble his pride, and exalt his celebrated rival, none was more conspicuous for ability and eloquence than the immortal Erskine, though it was not in a senatorial capacity that he displayed, to their full extent, those vast powers, or achieved the oratorical triumphs which added lustre to an ancestral name, and formed a reputation so splendid.

Thomas Erskine, unquestionably one of the most brilliant, courageous, and irresistible advocates who ever appeared at the English, or indeed at any, bar, was born on the 10th of January, 1750, in the ancient and historic city of Edinburgh. He was the third son of the Earl of Buchan, a Scottish nobleman of long and illustrious descent, but in circumstances so reduced and different from those enjoyed by the race for many centuries, that his yearly income was less than is now obtained, with ease, by not a few banker's clerks. Some small portion of the family estate still remained, and on it an old castellated residence, probably in as ruinous a condition as the famous Wolf's Crag, and, therefore, uninhabited by its proprietor. Had the Caledonian thane been a single man, and unblessed by connubial ties, he might have run a career similar to that of the great novelist's proud, haughty, and restless hero, "the last Lord of Ravenswood." But he had prudently married the daughter of a Lothian baronet, who speedily brought him several children: so he passed his life in chill poverty, and died in the odor of sanctity while at Bath, seeking consolation in the eloquent preaching of Whitefield, which was said to make sinners tremble as if a lion were roaring among them.

Although it is likely that this exemplary earl was a justice of the peace, and rather more than probable that there were lawsuits in the family, it does not appear that, previous to the chancellor's birth, the repose of the noble countess was disturbed or agitated by such dreams as heralded the Spectator's introduction into existence. However, that patrician matron was held in esteem as a woman of pious character and aspirations. She took pains to bring up her sons in the way they should go, and instruct them in the rudiments of education. She grounded them thoroughly in the Presbyterian catechism, and so imbued their young minds with the spirit of religion that Erskine, in after life, was in the habit of devoutly ascribing each piece of good fortune to a special interposition of an over-ruling Providence.

At an early age he was placed at the High School of the Scottish metropolis, then the most approved seminary north of the Tweed; and there he remained for several years. His natural talents shone forth; he distinguished himself sufficiently to be generally at the top of his class; and no doubt, also, he proved his courage and prowess in the boyish exploits undertaken in the neighborhood, and the juvenile warfare daily earned on in the play-ground. It was well for him to be exposed to such an ordeal, for the path that lay before him was not gaily strewed with roses, but thickly "beset with thorns and briers:" so also, though in a less degree, was that of his witty, cheerful, and able brother, Harry, afterward Lord Advocate for Scotland and Dean of Faculty.

When Erskine had reached the age of twelve, his high-born parents removed to St. Andrew's, with the view of adopting a style of living more in accordance with their narrow finances than could be pursued by people of "note and quality" even in the Scottish capital. At St. Andrew's he attended the grammar-school for a while, and subsequently took advantage of some classes in the college of the old town; though it appears that his opportunities of profiting by that ancient institution were extremely limited. Nevertheless, his talent appeared; he manifested a strong love of books, and he derived from those within his reach a considerable amount of miscellaneous information, which opened up his mind and fired his ambition. Bright dreams of future eminence began to illumine his young heart, and, feeling the urgent and paramount necessity of doing something for his support and advancement in life, he expressed a decided preference for the learned professions, and a desire to have his time and energies employed in the pursuit of one of them.

The requisite means, however, were wanting to gratify his inclination in this respect; and his parents were compelled to state, that the best thing they could do to promote his interest was to have him placed in some man-of-war as a midshipman. The prospect of donning a blue jacket and cocked hat, and of the consequent adventures—generally so pleasing to the juvenile imagination—was by no means so fascinating to the clever, studious, and intellectual young "honorable" as might have been expected; but, after some ineffectual efforts to make matters more to his liking, he felt himself bound to endure what he regarded as a hard fate, and was accordingly embarked about the completion of his fourteenth year. Doubtless the usual parting-scene was enacted with all due formality. Gil Blas is made to state that, when he left home, his parents made him a present of their blessing, which was all that he had ventured to expect, for the very competent reason that they had nothing else to bestow; and, no doubt, Erskine was similarly favored. Perhaps, also, the noble earl would gravely admonish the young sailor not to trifle or hurt himself with his sword; his mother would give him a last embrace; and his sisters would, with tears, give evidence of their grief.

The next few years of Erskine's life were passed on board ship, where, however uncongenial the service, he gave all due attention to discipline, and besides found time for improving his mind and increasing his stores of knowledge. When ashore, he made a point of seeing something of life in the various places where he happened to be; and those who recollect his fine and beautiful passage about the Indian chief, in his speech for Stockdale, will hardly question the use he at this period made of his rare faculties. Having probably drawn his ideas of naval life from the interesting descriptions in the pages of "Roderick Random," it is not wonderful that he found his situation more tolerable than he had been led to anticipate. He particularly enjoyed himself while stationed at Jamaica, relished its picturesque scenery, and experienced the delightful novelty of dancing at dignity balls with quadroon damsels, who chattered in broken English, exhibited grinning rows of ivory teeth, and whose white dresses contrasted strangely with their colored skins and their dark rolling eyes, which gave evidence rather of their African than their European descent.

Though unfortunately, as it then seemed, engaged in pursuits for which he had no real vocation, the aspiring Scot struggled manfully onward in his profession. Nor did he fail in after life to make judges and juries aware that he had profited largely by his naval experience, when engaged in cases connected with marine affairs, as he frequently was from his knowledge of technical phrases and other matters. Meantime he, at length, had the comfort of being appointed acting-lieutenant in the "Tartar," and of making a voyage homeward in that capacity; but on arrival in England, finding that the ship was to be paid off, and that he would, from this circumstance, be reduced to his original rank, he desperately resolved to tempt the seas no more.

About this period his father's earthly existence terminated; and Erskine, who appeared as one of the mourners, was much impressed with the solemnity of the funeral obsequies. Having abandoned all thoughts of a naval career, he turned his thoughts to a military life, and had sufficient influence to obtain an ensign's commission in the 1st Regiment of Foot, with which he straightway went to Minorca. His commission had cost all the money he possessed, and an application for a small allowance had been refused by his eldest brother, the eccentric Earl of Buchan, who afterward, on this ground, boasted that the future chancellor owed every thing to him. Yet, under these inauspicious circumstances, he contracted a romantic marriage with a young lady of respectable parentage, which luckily proved more propitious than is usual with unions formed under circumstances so forbidding.

While stationed in Minorca, though there appeared little prospect indeed of his acquirements ever being turned to account, he devoted himself with remarkable assiduity to the cultivation of his mind, by a profound and earnest attention to the English classics. In this way, by long and deep study, he became most familiar with the works of Shakspeare and Milton; so that, with a very slight knowledge of Latin authors, and almost none of Greek, he—a native of the north—rendered himself a consummate master of the English tongue. His tastes were thoroughly intellectual, and he even indulged them by officiating as temporary chaplain to the regiment; to which he not only read prayers, but preached two sermons from the drumhead, with no small measure of success.

On returning to England, Erskine obtained six months' leave of absence, part of which he spent in London. While there he had the advantage of meeting, conversing with, and encountering in discussion, no less eminent a person than Dr. Johnson, attended by his faithful dog and biographer. This was at the house of Sir Alexander Macdonald; and the "young officer in the regimentals of the Scots Royals," attracted much attention by the fluency, precision, and vivacity of his discourse. At the same date Erskine appeared to advantage as the author of a pamphlet on the abuses of the British army, which had an extensive circulation, and procured him some fame. Soon after this he was promoted to a lieutenancy, and for some time longer endured the disagreeable process of marching with the regiment from one place to another. His family and his dissatisfaction gradually increasing, a gloomy cloud seemed to hang over his existence; and there was ever before him the dismal prospect of his life proving a long series of imaginings never to be realized, and of aspirations never to be gratified.

Under such circumstances, while he was quartered in a provincial town, a great thought was born within him. One day, to drive away care, dispel annoyance, and perhaps to gratify a rational curiosity, he strolled into the assize court, where the great Lord Mansfield was presiding, with his wonted serene and impenetrable dignity. Perhaps birds of Erskine's feather were rarely seen in such haunts. At all events, his regimentals quickly attracted the eye of the veteran judge, who, struck, no doubt, by the peculiarly elegant and aristocratic appearance of the singularly intelligent-looking officer, even condescended to inquire who he was. On being informed that he was a younger son of the late Earl of Buchan, and very much in the same position in which the noble, learned, and influential Chief Justice might have found himself, but for the good fortune which had early led him to fatten and flourish in the pastures of the South, the latter kindly accommodated the lieutenant of foot with a place beside him on the bench, and courteously explained the case that was being tried. Thus seated by a man who had raised himself, by his genius, from the oatmeal porridge and aristocratic poverty of Scone Palace to wealth and an illustrious position, it struck the aspiring and discontented subaltern that here was a sphere in which his intellect might be exercised with advantage and renown. He therefore availed himself of his distinguished countryman's politeness, which took the shape of an invitation to dinner, to state the hardship of his lot, and explain his views. So truly great a man as Lord Mansfield would hardly, at such a moment, forget his own early trials and struggles. In any case, his young acquaintance was rewarded with some slight encouragement, and the sage advice to consult his friends. Erskine's surviving parent readily approved of the plan; and, between jest and earnest, she said he must be Lord Chancellor. Accordingly, having formed his plans, he was admitted as a student of law at Lincoln's Inn, and, at the same time, entered himself as a fellow-commoner of Trinity College, Cambridge, where in spite of narrow means, his wit and talent soon brought him into notice. The sale of his military commission produced him a serviceable sum of money; and, divesting himself of scarlet uniform, he proceeded to accomplish himself in the composition of English. An amusing specimen of his skill in versifying is a parody of Gray's "Bard," which gained him some applause. It was produced on the occasion of his being detained from dinner at the College hall by the tardiness of his hair-dresser, and begins with this not very complimentary stanza:

"Ruin seize thee, scoundrel Coe!
Confusion on thy frizzing wait!
Hadst thou the only comb below,
Thou never more should'st touch my pate.
Club, nor queue, nor twisted tail,
Nor e'en thy chatt'ring, barber, shall avail,
To save thy horse-whipped back from daily fears,
From Cantab's curse, from Cantab's tears!"

Having taken the honorary degree of A.M. in 1778, the future defender of Lord George Gordon was called to the bar in the same year. When settled in London, he practiced his oratorical powers at debating-clubs, and pursued his legal studies in the chambers of a special pleader; yet it does not appear that his knowledge of the law was ever very profound, notwithstanding his possessing, in some measure, a legal intellect. His domestic arrangements were on the most economical principle; there is even a tradition to the effect that his honorable spouse was under the necessity of acting as washerwoman for their family. His fare was of the humblest description; his dress was remarkable only for its shabbiness; he frequently found it no easy matter to provide the necessaries of life for the passing day; and he was heard thanking God that, out of his own family, he did not know a lord. It appears that his acquaintance with attorneys was still more limited in extent. Being complimented on his health and spirits, he answered sportively that he ought to look well, having nothing else to do, as had been remarked of somebody's trees.

But a man with the blood of a long line of earls in his veins, and with the consciousness of already having given proof of superior endowments, was not likely, while enduring galling poverty, to be wanting in aspirations after fame, or to lose an opportunity of winning a name and bettering his circumstances. Erskine felt within him both the stirrings of ambition and the capacity to do and dare with success, if an occasion were presented. His affairs were probably at the worst, when accident threw Captain Baillie in his way.

That brave and gallant officer had, as Lieutenant-governor of Greenwich Hospital, written and published a statement of abuses existing in the establishment, reflecting with particular acerbity on Lord Sandwich, first lord of the Admiralty. For this pamphlet Baillie was forthwith suspended by the Board, and a prosecution commenced against him by some of the less important individuals, whom he had assailed in pursuance of what he regarded as the performance of his duty. While the case was in prospect of being tried, Erskine happened to meet the redoubted captain at a dinner-party, and, without being aware of his presence, expatiated on the subject of the prosecution with so much warmth and animation, that though they were not introduced on that occasion, the ex-lieutenant-governor declared that the briefless barrister should be one of his counsel; but as there were to be four seniors, the latter naturally despaired of receiving any attention. However, at a consultation, when the others were inclined to consent to a favorable compromise, Erskine respectfully dissented, and advised them to stand the hazard of a trial; whereupon the captain swore a round oath, and cried, as he caught the future occupier of "the marble chair" in his strong arms, "You are the man for me!" When the case came on, the seniors were heard at great length on behalf of Captain Baillie; and the last of them, Mr. Hargrave, being in some way indisposed, was obliged to retire several times during his lengthened argument, and thus so protracted the proceedings, that on his concluding Lord Mansfield said that the remaining counsel should be heard next morning. This was precisely what Erskine desired, and indeed appeared almost providential, as it afforded him time to arrange during the night the heads of what he was to say. Besides, he had the advantage of addressing the court with refreshed energies and revived faculties. When the judges took their places next morning, he rose from the back row, and delivered a speech of such marvelous ability, that it has since been regarded by sagacious critics as the most brilliant forensic display ever witnessed under similar circumstances. As he left the hall attorneys flocked around to congratulate him on his extraordinary triumph, and from that memorable day business flowed in upon him. Being asked how he could so boldly face a venerable judge like Lord Mansfield—the very type and figure of justice—his feeling reply was, that he fancied his children were tugging at his gown, and saying, "Now is the time to get us bread!"

Erskine was next selected, on account of his naval intelligence, to draw up the defense to be spoken by Admiral Keppel, on his trial. This he did with much success; and the admiral, on being acquitted, presented him with bank-notes to the amount of a thousand pounds, which he flourished in triumph before his friends, exclaiming, with the almost boyish and mirthful fancy, ever freely indulged in private, "*Voilà* the nonsuit of cow-beef!"

The skill, dexterity, and eloquence, together with the complete devotion to the interests of his client, which he displayed in the conduct of cases, led to an extensive and lucrative practice; and in 1781 he was retained as counsel for the silly but then enthusiastically Protestant Lord George Gordon, whom he defended with brilliant power and signal success. In 1783, though having then been only five years at the bar, and delivered for a still briefer space from the horrors of "cow-beef" and threadbare garments, it was thought advisable to confer on him a patent of precedency. This gave him the privilege of donning a silk gown and sitting within the bar. It was likewise deemed prudent to have him brought into Parliament, and he was returned to the House of Commons as member for Portsmouth, to try his skill as a debater among the giants who then ruled the Legislature. The result was by no means gratifying to his numerous friends and admirers, who really seem to have entertained the unreasonable expectation that he was to trample Pitt in the dust as easily and proudly as he had done the nameless creatures of Lord Sandwich. In fact, his acquaintance with political matters was limited, from the keen and earnest attention which he had given to his professional pursuits; and his new position was so utterly different from that to which he had been accustomed, as to render him somewhat like a fish out of the water. In Westminster Hall, his ardor, his enthusiasm, the sparkle of his piercing glance, the grace and nobleness of his figure, the freedom and celerity of his movements, the clearness and flexibility of his voice, the surpassing beauty of his diction, the correct taste with which he conceived and the singular felicity with which he executed most difficult flights, and his figures of speech characterized by a boldness which unexceptional success alone could redeem from the charge of temerity, had fascinated juries, startled dignified sages of the law out of their propriety, and commanded the admiration of experienced advocates. But in the House of Commons his ardent spirit was chilled, his enthusiastic temperament damped, and his eloquent tongue made to falter by the scornful stare, the contemptuous indifference, and the cold sarcasm of the dread son of Chatham.

ERSKINE'S FIRST SUCCESSES.

Meantime his fame at the bar ascended rapidly.His powerful memory, wakeful vigilance, and knowledge of those with whom he had to deal, enabled him to conduct cases with wonderful skill. He defended the Dean of Asaph in a speech of much merit and high courage; and in 1786 was appointed Attorney-general to the Prince of Wales, an office of which he was deprived for appearing, with dauntless determination, on behalf of the notorious Thomas Paine, author of "the Rights of Man," in spite of the threatening frowns of royal power and the suggestive warnings of northern craft.

Though bold and conscientious above all others in the performance of his duty, Erskine had good reason to say to his admirers, "Gentlemen, I am but a man." He had, indeed, a considerable amount of vanity in his nature, and even in his best days liked well, after the case had been called, to keep a crowded and impatient audience waiting in court for a few minutes till he should make his appearance with something like stage effect. When he entered, to conduct some most important case on which, perhaps, he believed "the last and best gift of God to his creatures" depended, it was a little too apparent to intelligent spectators that his new yellow gloves and carefully-dressed wig were recognized by him as essential parts of the solemn proceedings. But if he did too assiduously cultivate popular favor he can not be justly accused of having shrunk from fear of court proscription, even when his fortunes hung trembling in the balance.

The period of the state trials was that of Erskine's greatest triumph and highest popularity. His grave, sturdy, and sensible-looking antagonist, on that occasion, was Sir John Scott, afterward Lord Eldon, who had worthily risen to distinction by "living like a hermit and working like a horse." He was then attorney-general, and his duty, as public prosecutor, could hardly have been very agreeable. Indeed, he seemed at times to have been in no small danger from the excitement of the mob, who daily bestowed upon Erskine frenzied applause. After the acquittal of Hardy, the ringleaders insisted upon taking the horses out of the brilliant counsel's carriage, that they might draw him to his house in triumph. Years after, when he was relating this circumstance in presence of Lord Eldon, that distinguished personage managed to turn the laugh against his old opponent by adding, with quiet humor, "Yes, and I believe you never saw more of them."

In 1802 Erskine visited Paris, and was presented to the Emperor Napoleon, then First Consul, who, however, only honored him with the single question, "*Êtes vous légiste?*" On returning home, he was restored to his office of Attorney-general to the Prince of Wales, who revived in his favor the dormant functions of Chancellor to the Duchy of Cornwall.

On the death of Pitt, Lord Grenville, who had previously left the party of his illustrious relative and former colleague, formed, in conjunction with Fox and Addington, the ministry of "All the Talents." Erskine was nominated to the woolsack, and being advanced to the peerage became Lord Chancellor; thus fulfilling his mother's jocular prediction. He resigned, with his political friends, in 1807, and shortly after made his celebrated speech in the House of Lords against the Jesuit's Bark Bill; but henceforth he ceased to play a prominent or influential part in public affairs. In 1815 the Prince Regent bestowed on him the Order of the Thistle. He is reported to have regretted that, from having been Lord Chancellor, he was prevented from pleading at the bar, where had been won his crown of fame; and to have remarked frequently to his friends, that the only reason he had for accepting the great seal and a peerage at the time, was to place the maternal prophecy beyond all hazard of breaking down. However, he consoled himself for the loss of his position in the forum by reciprocating compliments with his friend Dr. Parr. When the great scholar once promised to write the ex-chancellor's epitaph, Erskine replied, "Such an intention on your part is almost enough to make one commit suicide."

Dr. Johnson said that every man has a lurking wish to appear considerable in his native place, and no doubt Erskine was actuated by this natural feeling; yet it was somewhat late in life before he turned his steps toward the land of his fathers. There, however, his reception was so flattering that he conceived a strong desire to revisit it in 1823. He insisted upon going by sea, as being an old and experienced sailor, and was so unfavorably affected by the voyage that he never recovered the shock.

He expired at Almondale, near Edinburgh, on the 17th of November, 1823, and was buried, in accordance with the fashions and customs of the country, in the family vault at Uphall, in West Lothian.

LORD COLLINGWOOD

The ancestors of this noble-hearted and patriotic Englishman were "dreaded in battle and loved in hall." Their courage has been recorded in history, and their courtesy celebrated in song. Yet it is less than probable that any mailed warriors of the knightly race possessed these attributes in greater perfection than did this gallant and heroic admiral, who, in the nineteenth century, on that boundless empire which his countrymen claim as their heritage, made the ancient name he bore so widely and gloriously known in Europe and the world. The Collingwoods were for several centuries planted in the proud and extensive county of Northumberland. There they owned large territorial estates, held a high social position, and formed distinguished matrimonial alliances. Their prowess and valor were displayed in the perpetual conflicts which, previous to the auspicious period when King James united the crowns of the two realms upon his learned forehead, laid waste and impoverished the wild and unruly borders. When the Civil Wars occurred, being staunch and fearless cavaliers, they adhered to the cause of the first Charles, and lost much land in the gloomy and disastrous struggle for the prerogatives of that ill-fated Prince. In later days the chief of the name—being a friend and companion of the popular, munificent, and deeply-lamented Lord Derwentwater—engaged in the hapless insurrection of 1715, had his estates forfeited to the crown, and was called upon to lay his head on the block for that royal house, against whose subjects the Collingwoods of another age had ever been ready to fight to the death. From these and other causes a representative of the family, in the middle of last century, appears to have found himself in a position the reverse of convenient, and in circumstances by no means affluent. In any case he settled at Newcastle, married a lady of Westmoreland and was blessed with several children.

Cuthbert Collingwood, who inherited little beside the Christian and surnames, described by the old ballad-maker as being "so worthy to put in verse," and the stainless courage of "that courteous knight," taken prisoner at Redswire, was the eldest of his parents' three sons, and born on the 26th of Sept. 1750. No doubt he sported, during childhood, on the banks of the Tyne, regarded the shipping in the port with a curious eye, and was carried on fine afternoons, like other juvenile inhabitants of Newcastle, to buy shortcake in the neighboring village of Chester-le-Street.

In due time he was sent to the Grammar School, and there trained to fear God, serve his country, and honor the king. The master of the institution at that time was the Rev. Hugh Moises, a most worthy and successful teacher of the old stamp, who never spared the rod when the application of it was likely to promote the improvement and welfare of his pupils; nor refrained from bestowing the meed of praise which they had fairly earned by meritorious conduct. By such means, in all probability, Collingwood—a pretty, gentle, and generous boy—was taught those wholesome lessons of obedience and self-respect which he afterward knew so well how to practice himself and to inculcate on others, at once with the benevolence of a philanthropist and the firmness of a despot. At this educational establishment religious exercises were regularly attended to; and, perhaps, in the sentiments there instilled into his mind may be traced the origin of those habits of practical, unpretending piety, which characterized his illustrious career. Among the youths who were there being instructed by Mr. Moises, who marched to church under his auspices on Sundays, feared his chastening birch on week-days, and who in after years acknowledged the benefit they had derived from his tuition, were the two Scotts, sons of a wealthy coalfitter in the place, and destined to arrive at the highest rewards and honors of the branches of the legal profession to which their time and talents were devoted. The younger of them, who ere long occupied so high a position, and exercised so much influence as Lord Eldon, was Collingwood's class-fellow, and used to state, somewhat unnecessarily, that both of them were placed at the time-honored seminary because their fathers could not conveniently afford to have them educated elsewhere. The fame which they worthily attained in different spheres proves that they lay under no considerable disadvantages on that account. When Collingwood's dispatch narrating the battle of Trafalgar arrived, the king expressed his extreme surprise that a naval officer, who had spent so much of his life at sea, should write in so admirable a style. But on being informed that his brave and patriotic subject had been a scholar of Moises, his majesty considered that fact sufficient to explain the excellence shown.

In subsequent life, when experience had sharpened his powerful faculties, it was Collingwood's opinion that a boy intended for the sea should be early placed at a mathematical school, and carefully initiated into the science of navigation; as otherwise there is little likelihood of his achieving much progress on board a man-of-war. We are told of Lord St. Vincent, that the only instruction he ever received was from a considerate old sailing-master, whom he encountered while stationed at Jamaica; but it does not appear where Collingwood acquired his theoretic knowledge on this subject. It is probable, however, that he enjoyed the advantage of being grounded by the celebrated Hutton, who, just as Collingwood attained his tenth year, commenced a mathematical class in the town, and was, in some capacity, connected with instructing the mischievous imps under the sternly just sway of Moises. At the age of eleven Collingwood was dedicated to the profession of which he became so useful a member, and so bright an ornament.

The circumstances which have led to our great naval heroes first going to sea are sometimes peculiarly interesting, and even romantic. Take, for instance, the case of the Hoods—sons of a vicar in Somersetshire. A gallant captain was spending his time ashore in traveling about the country, and in passing through the quiet village of Butleigh, his carriage happened to break down. He looked around for an inn in which to stay while it underwent the necessary repairs, but there was no public place of accommodation to be had. The stranger, with some reason, seemed a little disconcerted; but matters were presently cleared up by the appearance of the worthy parson, who invited him to his house with hearty good will, and entertained him hospitably. Next morning the guest, before leaving, said, "Sir, you have two sons, would either of them like to go with me to sea?" They availed themselves of the frank offer,—both entered the service, and one became Lord Hood, the other Viscount Bridport. Jervis, the son of a barrister, was intended to follow his father's steps; but the groom persuaded him that all lawyers were rogues, and the little fellow, running away from school, insisted on being a sailor. After entering the navy he experienced hardship and poverty, but he struggled upward, with manly spirit, to wealth, fame, distinctions, and an earldom. Nelson's father was a clergyman in Norfolk, but his maternal uncle, a captain in the navy, promised to provide for one of the boys. Horatio was so slender in frame, that he was thought incapable of roughing it out at sea; yet he earnestly requested to be sent. Accordingly he was packed off alone in the coach to join the ship, but had the mortification of pacing the deck in wretchedness for a whole day before being taken notice of, while swelled in his young breast all the germs of the genius that recognized no fear, and the eccentricity—more valuable than the wisdom of others—which ultimately rendered him the dread of foes and the admiration of friends.

A relationship, similar to that which influenced the fortunes of his mighty compeer, seems to have guided Collingwood in his selection of a career. Captain Braithwaite, who afterward rose to the rank of admiral, had married the boy's aunt. That officer then commanded the "Shannon," and it was resolved to place the young aspirant under his care and protection. A touching and interesting glimpse of his earliest experience on board is afforded as he sat on the deck, sad at heart, and with tears in his eyes, which flowed more rapidly as he gazed through them at the shore. The first lieutenant observing the comely little sailor in so downcast a mood, and perhaps remembering his own feelings on a like occasion, was touched with compassion, and addressed him in language of sympathy and encouragement. Whereupon Collingwood felt so grateful that he led the kind-hearted officer to his box, and offered him a large piece of plum-cake, which his anxious and affectionate mother had given him at parting.

COLLINGWOOD'S JUVENILE GENEROSITY.

Collingwood experienced much kind treatment from the kinsman under whose protection he embarked on his career of duty and renown. He afterward confessed the obligations he owed to Admiral Braithwaite in the acquirement of professional knowledge. But the sage, meditative, and energetic seaman, was far from trusting to the aid or inspiration of others in his triumphant struggle. He thought earnestly, and labored diligently, for himself. He steadily practiced that self-culture which he ever strongly and perseveringly recommended to others. Besides perusing treatises on naval affairs, he read extensively, and with no small profit, in historical works; he obtained books relating to the places to which he happened to sail, and exercised his intellectual faculties by comparing these descriptions with his own impressions of the localities and scenery. Moreover, he embraced and acted on the opinion that a man should, before arriving at his twenty-fifth year, establish for himself a character and reputation of such a kind as he would have no cause to be ashamed of throughout life.

In the ordinary course of events Collingwood parted from his gallant relative, and sailed for some time with another officer. Between these two services thirteen years were consumed, and during that period he made the acquaintance of Nelson. At its termination he went to Boston with Admiral Graves, and was thus present at the battle of Bunker's Hill, in command of a party of seamen to assist and supply the troops, who, under General Gage, encountered the insurgent colonists. After that event he was advanced to the rank of lieutenant; and in 1775 joining the "Hornet" sloop, in that capacity he sailed to the West Indies. The ship in which Nelson was lieutenant came to the same station; and with the immortal hero Collingwood renewed the feelings of friendship, which, cemented in the interval by many high aspirations and bright dreams, were strikingly and glowingly displayed on another and more glorious day.

Meantime Collingwood had the good fortune to succeed his friend as commander of the "Badger," and, subsequently, as a post-captain in the "Hinchenbroke" frigate, with which he was ordered to proceed to the Spanish Main, and employed on the expedition sent up the river San Juan. The climate to which he was now exposed was in the highest degree pestilential; the majority of his crew fell victims to its excessive insalubrity; and in this perilous situation he was sustained and saved from sharing their fate by a remarkably strong constitution. Right glad, however, with all his powers of endurance, must he have been when relieved in the autumn from this scene of woe and suffering. He was then appointed to the command of the "Pelican." With that frigate, of twenty-four guns, he captured a French vessel, recovered from the enemy a richly-laden Glasgow merchantman, and was soon after wrecked among the rocks of the Morant Keys. He next obtained the command of the "Sampson," a ship of sixty-four guns, which was paid off at the peace of 1783. Then he was dispatched, in the "Mediator," to the West Indies, where he and his younger brother, a naval officer of great promise, who filled an untimely grave, actively aided Nelson in enforcing the provisions of the Navigation Act against the encroachments of the Americans.

In 1786 this brave and manly sailor arrived in England, and joyfully turned his face homeward. He spent the next four years among his Northumbrian relatives, of whom he had hitherto seen much less than he could have wished. At the termination of that period an armament was preparing against Spain, and he was immediately nominated to a command;

but the differences which had led to this step being speedily accommodated without going to war, and there appearing no prospect of active service, he again repaired to the frontier county; all the more readily, perhaps, that he had already surrendered to a lady in that northern province the exquisitely tender heart, which no prolonged service nor scenes of bloodshed could ever harden, or render indifferent to the welfare or sufferings of others. He was forthwith married, and there appearing no probability of his professional abilities being in requisition, he looked forward to a long season of that domestic peace and happiness which he was eminently fitted by nature to create and enjoy. However, his expectations in this respect proved vain; the French war broke out, he was under the necessity of sacrificing his cherished wishes to his country's good, and he returned, with characteristic courage and resolution, to arduous and indefatigable exertion on that element which, almost without interruption, was his sphere for the remainder of his earthly existence.

> "Calm thoughts that dwelt like hermits in his soul,
> Fair shapes that slept in fascinating bowers,
> Hopes and delights—he parted with them all."

Collingwood was, without delay, appointed to the "Prince," Admiral Bowyer's flag-ship, and served with that officer in the action of the 1st of June, 1794, in which Lord Howe accomplished a signal victory. He displayed his wonted vigilance and energy, in watching for the enemy and preparing for strife and wounds. But even then his thoughts strayed often to a gentler scene—to the home of his family, to green woodlands, and "mountains blue." Even on the eve of battle his fancy heard the ringing of the village bells, and his imagination conjured up the form of his fair spouse as she walked to church, not unmindful of her absent hero. The conflict was sharp, and soon over; and in it Collingwood behaved with much gallantry. Nevertheless, his services were unacknowledged by Lord Howe; and in the distribution of medals he was passed over, much to the surprise of the fleet, and of some officers with whom he had fought side by side, and by whom his bravery had been duly appreciated. "If Collingwood has not deserved a medal," remarked Captain Packenham, of the "Invincible," "neither have I; for we were together the whole day."

Collingwood was a man of too much pride and propriety to waste words on such a subject; but he was, at the same time, actuated by that sentiment of self-respect which forbade him to overlook such an injustice. Ere long an occasion of vindicating his independence and reputation was presented: this happened when the great victory off St. Vincent was happily achieved in 1797. The hero of that day, Sir John Jervis, when writing to the

Admiralty, expressed the highest praise and admiration of Collingwood's conduct, which, in the "Excellent," had been conspicuously meritorious; and he announced that the Northumbrian captain was to be rewarded with one of the medals distributed in commemoration of the glorious event. Collingwood could now speak out without loss of dignity; and he stated, with feeling and firmness, that he must decline receiving this mark of distinction while the former one was withheld.

"I feel," he said, as his slender, well-formed person, seemed to swell with emotion, and as his full dark eye flashed with chivalrous pride, and the consciousness of a heart that feared no foe: "I *feel* that I was then improperly passed over; and to receive such a distinction in this case would be to acknowledge the propriety of that injustice."

"That," replied Lord St. Vincent, with evident admiration, "is precisely the answer I expected from you, Captain Collingwood."

Shortly after this conversation took place, Collingwood experienced the gratification of having the two medals transmitted to him from the Admiralty, with a civil apology for the earlier one having been so long kept back. He was now instructed to assist in what he considered as the humiliating office of blockading the enemy's ports; and, after a brief interval of repose in the society of his friends and relatives, he was promoted to the rank of Rear-admiral of the White; when, hoisting his flag in the "Triumph," he proceeded to the Channel fleet, which was under the command of Lord Bridport. He was soon after detached with a reinforcement of twelve sail of the line, and sent to join Lord Keith in the Mediterranean, where the Brest fleet, with the principal naval force of France and Spain, then lay. He subsequently shifted his flag to the "Barfleur;" and in the beginning of 1801 became Rear-admiral of the Red.

The events of 1802 afforded Collingwood the satisfaction of returning for a while to his home at Morpeth, in the north of England. He arrived in the merry month of May, and greatly relished his quiet and repose. He was fond of company, and among his friends showed much lively humor and no inconsiderable knowledge of books. His tastes were plain and simple, and his inclination averse to display. He gratified his paternal feelings by superintending the education of his daughters. He pursued his own studies with more than youthful enthusiasm, improved his style of composition by making extracts from the various works he perused, and indulged his natural fondness for drawing. His garden was situated on the banks of the beautiful Wansback—a river alluded to in "Marmion"—which flows through a succession of fertile valleys; and there he passed many agreeable hours. Indeed he seems, like Lord Bacon, to have looked upon gardening as "the purest of all pleasures, and the greatest refreshment to the spirits of man." One day, a naval officer coming to visit Collingwood in his happy and tranquil retirement, sought him in vain about the grounds, and was inclined to give up the search, when he suddenly discovered the admiral, along with his old and trusty gardener, busily occupied in digging with vigor at the bottom of a deep trench. The affairs of his domain ever formed an interesting subject of inquiry; nor did distance diminish the respect which he entertained for his faithful horticultural henchman.

In the beginning of 1803, when a renewal of hostilities between England and France occurred, Collingwood was summoned from weeding the oaks in his cheerful northern retreat, which he was never blessed with an opportunity of revisiting; though he often sadly and fondly luxuriated in the anticipation of resuming a place by his own fireside, never more to leave it.

Meantime he was sent, in the "Venerable," to the squadron off Brest, Admiral Cornwallis joyfully exclaiming on his arrival, "Here comes Collingwood—the last to leave and the first to rejoin me!" In the April of 1803 he was advanced to the rank of Vice-admiral of the Blue, and next year engaged in the blockade of Cadiz, until compelled to retire by the appearance of the combined fleets of France and Spain. He soon resumed his station, where he remained till the following autumn; when thither came that terrible English sea-captain who had already driven the French fleet before him, "from hemisphere to hemisphere," and performed the vow, long before made, that he would teach Bonaparte to respect the British navy. On the 21st of October, 1805, Trafalgar was fought and won; though the brilliancy was at first, in some degree, clouded and overcast by the fall of the conquering hero, in whose breast patriotism had so long glowed with fierce ardor. On that glorious and ever-memorable day, Collingwood nobly did his duty. In the morning, he arrayed himself for the coming strife with extraordinary care and precision. Meeting with Lieutenant Clavell, whom he had long regarded as "his right hand," the brave admiral, with his accustomed mental equanimity, said, "You had better put off your boots, and put on silk stockings; as, if one should get a shot in the leg, they would be so much more manageable for the surgeon." Then, going on deck, he encouraged the men in performing their duty, and asked the officers to do something which the world might talk of in time to come. Nor, when the hour of encounter arrived—when the successes of his great comrade-in-arms were to be crowned with an imperishable triumph—did he fail to sustain his old reputation for prowess and courage. He led the British squadrons into action, and with his single ship, the "Royal Sovereign," advanced gallantly into the midst of the enemy's forces. It was then, as he was keenly pressing onward, that Nelson, standing on board the "Victory," decorated with all his stars and honors, and prepared for death and glory, exclaimed, as the remnant of his right arm moved with excitement, "See how that noble fellow, Collingwood, takes his ship into action!" At the same time Collingwood, knowing what thoughts would be passing through his heroic friend's mind, remarked to Clavell, with a smile, "What would Nelson give to be here!" It is singular that his spirit of economy should have manifested itself under such circumstances; as when he saw the gallant-studding-sail hanging over the gangway, he requested his lieutenant to assist him in taking it in, and observed that they should live to want it again some other day. Having poured a broadside and a half into the stern of the "Santa Anna," the two vessels were soon so close that their lower yards were locked together. Another was placed on the lee-quarter of Collingwood's ship, while three bore on her bow; but England expected every man to do his duty that day, and it was nobly done. As for the "Santa Anna," she was soon compelled to strike; and the Spanish captain coming on board to surrender his sword, was told that the name of the ship was the "Royal Sovereign."

"I think she should be called the 'Royal Devil,'" he exclaimed in broken English, as he patted one of the guns with his hand.

When his illustrious friend fell mortally wounded, the chief command devolved on Collingwood, who, for his brave exploits and signal services on this and former occasions, was created a peer, honored with the thanks of Parliament, and rewarded with a pension and the freedom of several cities. On the day following the victory he issued an order for a general thanksgiving to Almighty God, for having mercifully crowned the exertions of the fleet with success. His position now became peculiarly arduous and difficult. He had the responsible task of managing the political relations of England with the countries bordering on the Mediterranean, in addition to discharging the duties appertaining to his naval command. He encountered them with an unremitting industry, which speedily brought on a disease fatal to his health. Yet believing that it was his duty to do so, and that he might live once more to meet the French, he remained at his post, shattering his frame with toil, fatigue, and exposure, and racking his mind with perpetual care and thought. At length his body began to swell and his legs to shrink; so that his removal to England was represented as indispensable. He accordingly surrendered his command, and embarked; but he was not destined to set foot on the soil whose freedom and sacredness he had spent his strength in guarding. On the 7th of March, 1810, he expired at sea, in his sixtieth year.

His end was calm, peaceful, and resigned; as his life had been just, exemplary, and benevolent. Throughout he had been sincerely religious, and most regular in his attendance at divine worship. Even on Sundays, when the weather was such that the crew could not assemble on deck, he was in the habit of retiring to his cabin, and reading the service for the day. His piety was utterly without pretense; his acts of charity were frequent; and his ear was never shut against a representation of real distress. He was strictly scrupulous in his respect for inferiors, and particularly anxious for the interests of those over whom he had authority. His disposition was most repugnant to the exercise of severity; and though no man was better qualified by nature to enforce proper discipline, his humanity and refined sentiment rendered him averse to doing so by extreme means. He looked up to his Creator with devotion and gratitude, and he regarded the lowly with kindness and generosity.

On their arrival in England, the bones of this brave and worthy admiral were consigned to the dust in St. Paul's Cathedral, hard by the spot where the ashes of Nelson repose. A monument has since been erected to his memory by a grateful public; and his services well deserved such a recognition from a free people. He lived, in deed and in truth, not for himself, but for his country; and he knew no fear but the fear of God. He had, indeed, nobly done his duty to the last, sacrificing all personal considerations, with patriotic disinterestedness. Domestic enjoyment, quiet, health, life itself, were in his eyes nothing compared with the preservation of our shores and liberties from the great, skillful, and mighty foe, who planned earnestly and labored anxiously for their conquest and destruction.

LORD TEIGNMOUTH

This estimable and religious man was not endowed with any of the splendid intellect of Pitt, nor with any portion of the brilliant genius of Burke; yet his abilities were such, and so sufficiently recognized, that the former, when in the pride of place and power, thought prudent to nominate him for a trust hardly less important than his own, though without family influence or connections; and the latter, when denouncing the administration of affairs in the East, to protest against the appointment with feelings of which contempt assuredly formed not one of the ingredients. Indeed, his career, so remarkably successful and extraordinary, presents a pleasing and inciting example of a person ungifted with any marvelous capacity raising himself to become the peaceful and spotless ruler of millions of human beings.

The family from which he derived descent was of considerable antiquity in the county of Derby; and in former days several of its members had been returned to the House of Commons. Being connected, as times changed, with India by a matrimonial alliance, one of the race became a captain in the Company's marine; and his son, while in the enjoyment of a lucrative situation as supercargo, married, for the second time, the daughter of an officer belonging to the same service, and had two sons; of whom John Shore, destined to fill one of the most splendid places on the face of the earth, was born in London, on the 5th of October, 1751. He was subsequently removed into Essex, where his parents usually resided; and there the infancy of the future Governor-general of India, was passed, much like that of other boys of his age and condition.

These were the good old-fashioned days, when parents were not nervously apprehensive of any fatal effects from dressing their sons in garments befitting their sex, and allowing them that degree of liberty consistent with a proper attention to order. Accordingly, at a very early age, Shore availed himself of the license afforded him, and contrived, by hook or by crook, to find his way to the roof of a very high barn, the most elevated part of which he bestrode with an utter and lucky unconsciousness of the extreme danger to which he was exposed. Fortunately he was rescued from this perilous resting-place without any mishap; and, probably with a view of keeping him out of such mischief in future, he was mounted every morning on one of the coach-horses, before his father's serving-man, and in this fashion rode to a school in the vicinity; to be initiated into learning at this rustic establishment, and into the ways of the world as understood by the juveniles who attended it. He was in good time removed to a seminary at Tottenham; and about the same date he lost his much-respected father: but the surviving parent was a woman of highly estimable character, polished manners, and with such an annual income as enabled her to give her two sons a liberal education.

Shortly after the melancholy event alluded to, John Shore was destined to the service of the East India Company, while he was yet a little boy, with a spare frame, but sinewy, and such as fitted him to take part in, and enjoy puerile sports and pastimes. This arrangement was brought about by an old friend of the family, who was perhaps glad to secure for the Company the prospective services of so thorough-bred an aspirant as the son of a supercargo and the grandson of a captain in their marine, unquestionably, might claim to be. The offer of a writership was thus made, and, as a matter of course, promptly accepted. This affair being satisfactorily settled, Shore was removed to a school at Hertford, where he delighted in being admitted to an excellent library to improve his mind and extend his information. He, moreover, gratified a natural taste for poetical compositions by rising early in the morning to feast his spirit on Pope's "Homer;" and he perused books of travel till his imagination had been taken captive with the idea of such adventure, that he longed, with as much enthusiasm as he was capable of, to go on some expedition of discovery. Such a desire would, in all probability, be rather heightened than otherwise by the prospect of ere long sunning himself beneath an Eastern sky; and apparently his general interest in such matters did not soon expire, from the anxiety he afterward manifested to possess some account of Sir Joseph Banks's voyage round the world, which otherwise would have been of little moment to a youth exercising judicial functions in India at the age of twenty, or thereabouts. While at Hertford, Shore had what he considered a miraculous escape from drowning, and which he ever afterward ascribed to a special interposition of Providence in his behalf. Along with a young companion, he had gone to bathe in a river in the neighborhood of the school; and, in their haste and carelessness, they had mistaken a deep pool for the place where they usually immersed themselves. They were just on the point of plunging in when a voice called on them to wait, and, at the moment, an equestrian appeared at their side, quite as suddenly and opportunely as the two strange horsemen did at Lake Regillus. He demanded if they could swim, and on being answered in the negative, threatened them with a sharp castigation unless they walked off immediately. Thus menaced, and considering that they were at the moment liable to be lashed with peculiar facility and effect, the gentle youths clutched up their raiment, and, in fear and trembling, fled from the spot.

While encouraging and cultivating his turn for general literature, Shore had not lagged behind his fellows in the proper studies of the school; and in the course of time he was sent to Harrow, then flourishing under the auspices of Dr. Sumner. There he was placed on the fifth form, between Sheridan and Halhead; Dr. Parr being tutor of the three. Shore applied himself to his classic studies, and showed so keen a sense of their beauties that he became a great favorite with the learned and fastidious head-master; though it was augured, that of the three leading boys, Halhead was the one destined to immortal distinction. And while events were proving the fallacy of this prognostication, Harrovian prophets were preparing another proof of the vanity of human anticipations by assigning to Sir George Sinclair the prospective triumphal crown in preference to Lord Byron and Sir Robert Peel. Shore left when on the point of succeeding to the captaincy of the school. When Warren Hastings, at once the ablest and most unscrupulous governor whom India ever saw, obtained a writership and was shipped off to Bengal, his withdrawal from studies which seemed likely to make so clever a youth one of the first scholars of the age not only elicited an indignant remonstrance from the master of Westminster, but even prompted that worthy individual to make the generous and disinterested offer of sending so promising a pupil to Oxford at his own expense; but it does not appear that the fate of the future friend, associate, and successor of Hastings, excited equal interest or pity in the breast of Dr. Sumner. However, their intimacy had become such that a correspondence was commenced between them, which did not cease till death put a period to it.

When Shore left Harrow, it was found that, however accomplished his education had rendered him generally, he was by no means possessed of a kind of knowledge which the Company required their servants to be perfect in,—namely, the keeping of accounts with correctness. In order, therefore, to qualify himself for the post to which he had been nominated, Shore was placed for a few months at an academy at Hoxton, where he was initiated into the mysteries of arithmetic and book-keeping, and fitted to enter upon and pursue his duties, and return with a fortune, if he escaped Asiatic tigers and the yellow fever. The seminary, strangely enough, contained a young nobleman, destined, like Shore, to enact the part of Governor-general of India, namely, the Marquis of Hastings, whom, half a century later, he had an opportunity of reminding of their early acquaintance, when the stately peer was on the point of embarking on the administration of the affairs of that empire which had been preserved and rendered durable by the vigor and courage of his great namesake.

Toward the close of 1768 Shore sailed from England, in company with about a dozen of writers and cadets, who proved a most disorderly set; and about the middle of the next year he set foot in Calcutta, which then consisted of tenements, whose appearance promised any thing rather than comfort to the weary and storm-tossed voyager. Nothing aspiring even to the dignity of a brick house was to be seen, however inelegant such a structure may be thought; and the town was rendered unhealthy by exposure to open drains, which emitted smells little resembling those of rose-water or meadow hay. This was no agreeable place of residence for a lad whose health was so impaired that the companions of his voyage almost gave him up as lost. Nevertheless, he bore up against all disadvantages, though scarcely having a single letter of introduction; and was, soon after his arrival, consigned for twelve months to a desk in the secret political department, where he labored with exemplary industry at the records. Though his income was fearfully small, he practiced the most stern economy rather than rely on his mother for assistance; while so rare and rigid was his integrity, in an age when Indian officials did not scruple to help themselves, and thus make up for their limited salaries, that he won the meritorious appellation of "honest John;" which in subsequent life, and in the midst of multitudinous temptations, he never was guilty of forfeiting.

In 1770 Shore was nominated assistant to the Provincial Council at Moorshedabad, where, deprived of all real power, the Nabob of Bengal still resided, with princely magnificence, and played at government. While holding this office, the young writer had the unexpected good fortune to be elevated to the responsible position of a judge, at the immature age of nineteen. The fact of his being invested with large and important juridical functions, furnishes a pretty strong illustration of the remark of Hastings, as to "the boys of the service" being "the sovereigns of the country." But this charge, so far from overwhelming Shore, called forth the innate steadiness and perseverance of his character; and he discharged the duties with so much success, that, though he decided no fewer than six hundred cases in a single year, there were not more than two appeals against the justice of his adjudication. Meanwhile his leisure hours were diligently devoted to the improvement of his mind, and to preparation for climbing the steep ascent that yet lay, enveloped in shadow, between him and the height he was destined to reach with honor and security. Perceiving what profit might arise from an acquaintance with the Oriental languages, his industry was immediately aroused to the undertaking; and he strove for proficiency in the Arabic, Persian, and Hindostanee tongues. He did not neglect his former learning, but kept a journal in Latin, that the language might remain fresh in his memory, and read from several Greek authors with a similar object. Still he imagined that the road to fortune and affluence was daily narrowing, and complained that hope, patience, and perseverance, were all he had left; though most people would be inclined to consider such qualities very sufficient capital for an intelligent youth who had hardly arrived at legal age. He was still regretting that he had left England, when, after employing his knowledge of Oriental languages before the Provincial Council at Moorshedabad, he was appointed a member of the Board of Revenue, and thus plunged into that long quarrel which was, as years rolled on, transferred from the council-chamber of Calcutta to Westminster Hall. He owed this promotion to the opponents of Hastings, and was, besides, inclined to sympathize in their opinions; but he could not regard the distracted state of affairs in British India without dreading the influence it might have on his personal fortunes. He felt the extreme difficulty that there was of taking any course without endangering his prospects, and he looked to the future with a gloomy eye. At this crisis his good angel appeared, in the shape of a sagacious old gentleman; who, after listening to his expressions of doubt and anxiety, said, "Young man, make yourself useful, and you will succeed." Shore, luckily for his own interests, accepted the maxim as the rule of his life and conduct,—frequently repeated it to, and inculcated it on, others; and he found the system it enjoined wonderfully efficacious in promoting his interests under divers circumstances. His opinions and feelings were avowedly hostile to the supremacy of Hastings; and he was employed to revise one of the bitter philippics launched by the vain and rancorous Francis against the dread governor, when the star of the latter was thought to have fallen. Add to this, that Shore lent his pen to prepare a memorial against the Supreme Court of Judicature, and its chief-justice, Sir Elijah Impey, the former school-fellow, and now unprincipled tool, of Hastings. These matters he managed with all the skill and dexterity possible in the position of affairs; yet when Francis, baffled and utterly routed, beat a retreat, it was with no small reason that Shore conceived himself in danger of being consigned to adversity. But his efforts to "make himself useful" had been so apparent, that his services were deemed well worth securing.

The now triumphant governor, however, bore no good-will to Shore. He did not forget that the latter had been among the allies of his adversaries; and his nature, though in some respects great, and even heroic, was not forgiving, any more than righteous or merciful. Yet when he abolished the provincial councils, and instituted the Supreme Council of Four, the first man whom he appointed to a seat in it recommended that Shore should have the second. Hastings expressed much astonishment at such a proposal: but his adviser answered, "Appoint Mr. Shore, and in six weeks you and he will have formed a friendship." The prediction proved perfectly true;

Shore held his position thus conferred for years, and frequently had to appear as chief of the Board during the absence of Hastings from the seat of government. He remained in India till Hastings quitted it, in 1785, with triumphal honors. They sailed for England in the same ship, and, during the voyage, Hastings addressed to Shore an imitation of an ode of Horace—an occupation of time which might not have occurred had he scented the fiery tempest that was awaiting his arrival.

When separated from the delightful companion of his voyage, whose conversation had been so pleasing, Shore, the ever-prosperous hero of one maxim, had, unfortunately, no opportunity of practicing it. His mother had died the year before, and he was thus deprived of the pleasure which he had often looked forward to enjoying in her society. He felt dull and solitary: he had been absent from the country for more than sixteen years, and, doubtless, many of the old friends who had watched his youthful career with interest and satisfaction, had sunk into the grave. His confirmed Indian habits were not quite convenient; he felt the want of sympathy; and, perhaps, he began to make the appalling discovery that it is not good for man to be alone, and that a helpmate would be particularly acceptable. At all events, as fortune had hitherto bestowed upon him success in life, chance now threw a little romance in his way.

His younger brother had been educated to the clerical profession, and was at this time residing with his wife near Exeter. Thither Shore—tired of himself, of his London friends, and of walks over Westminster bridge before breakfast in cold November mornings—bent his way. On arrival he found that his brother and sister-in-law were from home; but he found full and complete consolation for their absence. A snow-storm had detained at the house a young lady of great personal attractions, by whom he had the felicity of being courteously received and entertained. Their interview was fatal to any dreams of celibacy in which Shore might have indulged. Suddenly crept around his heart a flame which would have seemed more natural in the gay and gallant inhabitants of places where Italian maidens lean on marble balconies on warm nights, and listen to lovers' tales, than in the sage and reflecting descendant of the ancient couple, in whose memory "the Shore trees," sung of by Wordsworth, were planted on the summit of the Oker Hill; and who, moreover, had just exchanged his dwelling amidst the garden-houses of Eastern nabobs for the frost and sleet of an English winter. But if his love was as sudden and inspiring as Romeo's, it was destined to be more happy in its results. Before the sun had gone down his affections were engaged; he retired to rest, doubtless pondering on what a day may bring forth; he was now as resolute in cultivating his charmer's favor, as he had formerly been in making himself useful: ere three months had gone over she was his wife; and, during half a century, they had cause to be grateful for the Providential snow-storm.

Within the fortnight after his marriage, Shore, perhaps for the first time in his life, found it extremely difficult to act on the principle which had hitherto proved so advantageous. He was offered a seat in the Supreme Council of Three, established under Pitt's India bill, and requested to return to the East, where it was anticipated that his experience would be of infinite value to Lord Cornwallis, the newly-appointed governor. His situation was a little perplexing; but at length he consented to forego the blessings of home for the sake of advancing his fortunes, which were of greater consequence since he was no longer single. He accordingly sailed from Portsmouth, and sought refuge from his dark and distressing thoughts in a perusal of the Company's records. He had again abundant opportunities of proving his industry and usefulness; and particularly employed himself in the settlement of the revenues of Bengal, Behar, and Oresa; and in 1789, with increased reputation but impaired health, set his foot once more on his native soil. He took up his residence in the county where his infancy had been spent, and appeared as a witness at the trial of Hastings, of whose conduct he did not wholly approve; though he thought himself bound to treat it with indulgence.

The adventures of John Shore were not yet ended. He was called upon once more to "make himself useful," and to reap the fruits of having done so in times past. He had gone to Devonshire to take a long lease of a house there, when intelligence reached him that Lord Cornwallis had resigned his high office, and that the succession to it was within his grasp. Pitt wished to introduce into the English empire in the East the pacific system which he had led Parliament to enjoin, and rightly conjectured that Shore was the man to do so with effect. The offer, however, was so unexpected and undesired, that he at first resolved on declining the high distinction, and hurried to London to explain his reasons for taking such a course. On returning home and announcing this refusal to his wife, she disinterestedly begged him to sacrifice all domestic consideration; and thus persuaded, he declared he saw that he must be a great man in spite of his teeth, and received the splendid and lucrative appointment. Burke immediately protested against the office being filled by one who had been connected with Hastings; but the Court of Directors answered, that Shore was regarded by their body as one of the ablest and most upright servants of the Company. Having been previously created a baronet, he set sail in the autumn of 1792, and after a long voyage reached, in the brilliant capacity of Governor-general, the same town which he had once entered, apparently in a dying state, to write for an annual salary of twelve pounds a year, to pay an exorbitant rate for a wretched and unwholesome lodging, and to endure poverty with the consoling assurance that if he made himself useful he would succeed.

Soon after the arrival of Sir John Shore in India, the celebrated Sir William Jones died; and Shore, who afterward became the biographer of the great scholar, succeeded him in the presidency of the Asiatic Society. On taking the chair he paid an eloquent tribute to the virtues of his deceased friend. He took measures for the advancement of true religion in Bengal, and was corresponding with several eminent men on the subject when he was plunged into a war with the Rohillas—the sequel to that sanguinary contest upon which Hastings had entered under circumstances so unjustifiable. A single battle, however, settled the matter.

In 1796, Sir John Shore had introduced to him no less famous a personage than the future illustrious hero of Waterloo. On that occasion he remarked, that if Colonel Wellesley ever had an opportunity of distinguishing himself, he would do it greatly. It appears that Sir John was successful in such prophetic efforts; for he is related to have expressed a similar prediction in reference to Sir Robert Peel, when that eminent politician was entering upon his eventful and mutable career.

In 1797, Shore had the honor of an Irish peerage bestowed upon him; and next year relinquished his office, and sailed for England, when he was succeeded by the Marquis of Wellesley. The peaceful policy he had pursued then went out of fashion; it was condemned by his successors; and he took little concern in Indian affairs, though nominally a member of the Board of Control, and a privy-councilor of Indian appeals.

Long after returning to his native land for the third time, after a long, arduous, and successful career, when gliding quietly down the stream of life, Lord Teignmouth was nominated President of the British and Foreign Bible Society on its formation, a dignity, the duties of which he was well fitted to discharge. He was a man of the utmost philanthropy; and the spread of divine truth and light among nations and people sitting in darkness was an enterprise into which he was calculated to enter with an ardor assuredly not exhibited in his worldly pursuits, nor displayed in his poetic effusions.

The remainder of Lord Teignmouth's private life was that of a refined and well-educated English gentleman. He appeared to his neighbors an amiable, estimable, and religious man, who could hardly have cared much for the pomp and power to which his usefulness had conducted him. He died in peace and honor, in 1833, leaving a name which is associated with industry, excellence, integrity, and humanity; not with high genius, indeed, but with all those qualities of heart and soul which give a man comfort and happiness during the days of his earthly pilgrimage, and impart consolation to his spirit in the hour when the lamp of life is flickering and about to expire.

DEAN MILNER

In the middle of the last century, hard by a church dedicated to St. Mary—on a spot at that time considered somewhat rural in appearance, but since absorbed by the even then very populous town of Leeds—stood an humble, unornamented cottage, the outer door of which was studded with nails, like that of an ancient peel or a modern prison-house; and there a Yorkshire weaver, of the name of Milner, lived in comparative poverty. He is stated to have been characterized by sagacity, industry, and self-denial, but nevertheless had not proved particularly successful in the trade he followed; having besides, like many persons of a higher rank, suffered severely from the effects of the rebellion of 1745. Though not blessed with much intellectual culture, he had, as is common with his class, a full appreciation of the manifold advantages of a sound education; and vowed that he would not shrink from personal sacrifices that his children might at all events enjoy that invaluable possession. He was already the father of two boys, one of whom afterward attained worthy celebrity, when, on the 11th of January, 1750, Isaac Milner, the third of the family, first saw the light.

So many of those famous personages whose illustrious footprints have been traced in the foregoing pages, with a view to the encouragement of youths aspiring to excellence, could boast of gentle lineage and hereditary associations, that it is impossible not to experience something like a sensation of relief, and to feel the charm of variety, in turning to the career of a man without any such pretensions—not incited by the ambition of adding to a name that had been feared or respected in another day, and whose position in early life was not rendered easy by wealth, or "shone upon from the past." Cradled under the roof of a cottage, apprenticed during seven years as a factory boy, and clutched from the loom by fraternal partiality, to be employed as usher in a provincial school, he raised himself by intellectual vigor and perseverance to places of honor and importance; and he was extolled among his great, learned, and reverend contemporaries, in his various characters of academic, historian, divine, and philosopher.

From infancy, or, in any case, as far back as his memory would go, Milner was animated by a strong affection for his elder brother, author of the well-known "Church History," who, in pursuance of their sensible parents' laudable resolution, had been placed at the grammar-school of the town. Doubtless, by one so closely united to him in bonds of tenderness and relationship, the future dean would in childhood be taught to read, and inspired with that restless and singular love of knowledge which rendered him, in later days, so peculiarly eager and ardent in the pursuit, acquisition, and investigation of any subject which circumstances brought under his notice or chance cast in his way, no matter how unconnected ordinary mortals might deem it with the regular duties and avocations pertaining to the station he occupied. The elder brother, originally intended to pursue his father's trade, soon became so distinguished in the school, that one of the teachers was in the habit of recommending his pupils to apply to Joseph Milner's memory in regard to questions of history and mythology, observing that he was more easily consulted than dictionaries, or the Pantheon, and quite as much to be relied on. The natives of the hamlet speedily began to gaze at him as a "marvelous boy," and testified their respect by calling him "the learned lad." Nor at the fireside of the family cottage did he lack encouragement. The earnest artisan manifested the utmost desire that the young scholar should have every aid within their reach to promote his improvement in learning, and one Saturday night astonished the little circle by the tidings that he had just spent the money which ought to have purchased a joint of meat on a Greek book for his son, being unable to procure both out of the slender earnings of the week. The brothers forced their way together through great difficulties; each arrived at distinction in his sphere of labor; and perhaps few more pleasing instances of brotherly love continuing could be cited than that which they, from first to last, exhibited. As early as his sixth year, little Isaac was led by the hand of his future benefactor to school, whither he continued to trudge daily for some years under the same guidance and protection. His progress in juvenile studies was most rapid and satisfactory: he soon learned to translate Ovid and Sallust with tolerable correctness; and he, in due time, commenced taking lessons in Greek, under auspices which must have delighted his father's heart, and tempted his imagination, however calm, to indulge in visions of a golden future for the hopeful boy.

In the ninth year of his age, Milner's young mind had the advantage of being opened and impressed by a visit to the mighty metropolis, though how, at that date, he happened to be taken on such a journey unfortunately does not appear. However, he is related to have been in London when news of the capture of Quebec by General Wolfe arrived. It was bawled through the streets by watchmen at the midnight hour, and bonfires blazed in triumph; and then he was told, for the first time, about grim-visaged war and the odious French. Assuredly he heard enough of them before the close of his long life, in that age of great and portentous events.

About this period the father of the Milners was cut off amidst his efforts to educate his offspring and promote their welfare; and thus seemed to be defeated all the wishes and hopes which the cleverness of the traveled little lads had created in the bosoms of their friends. It was necessary, indeed, to make the best of matters; and the elder brother being otherwise disposed of, it was deemed prudent to put Isaac out to a trade. The town being one of the greatest markets for woolen cloth in the kingdom, the inhabitants of the surrounding villages were employed in the manufacture. Accordingly, Milner was sent to work at and be initiated into the mysteries of a factory, which, in his case, must have been sadly against the grain. Kirke White, when placed in a situation somewhat similar, complained of being most unhappy, and of wanting something to occupy his brain. And Milner, doubtless, had little more relish than the boy-poet of "Clifton Grove," who perished in his youthful fame, for the trade to which he was now apparently doomed for life. To a youth conscious of great abilities, and whose extraordinary faculties had been already recognized by teachers, such an occupation must have been almost worse than the labor of a slave; for, praiseworthy as aspirations after success, arising from the practice of such honest industry, may generally be, they were not of the kind to call forth those talents which subsequently made their possessor president of a college, vice-chancellor of a university, professor in the chair that had been occupied by Newton, dean of a cathedral, and one of the most fascinating conversers of his generation in the country that produced him, and also one of the most celebrated mathematicians and philosophers of his day. He studied, during hours not devoted to work, Greek and Latin books; probably perused on Sundays the "Pilgrim's Progress," which was always a source of real pleasure to his spirit; and perhaps even gained some acquaintance with the works of Shakspeare, Milton, and other great English authors, with which he was familiar in his advanced years. He was soon to have larger opportunities and a fitter scene for the refreshment and cultivation of his powerful mind, thirsting for knowledge.

MILNER RESCUED FROM THE LOOM.

The rector of the grammar-school had manifested much interest in the young Milners; and they were not quite unaided in their hour of need. By the generous exertions of several kind friends, and the well-timed liberality of others, Joseph, the elder brother, had been sent to Cambridge, and had there so conducted and distinguished himself, that when he left the university the head-mastership of the Hull grammar-school was conferred upon him, principally by the influence of the grandfather of Wilberforce, an appointment which led to a friendship not unimportant in its results to the gentle philanthropist, and to the success of the views he held. And now the heart of Joseph Milner was turned toward the prospects of his brother, and he pondered what could be done to promote his welfare and happiness. He therefore requested one of the clergymen in Leeds to examine the lad, in order to ascertain and report as to his qualifications for becoming usher in the school. The reverend gentleman thus commissioned proceeded to the factory, where he found Milner seated at work with a classical author on each side. An examination fully proved, that though removed for a considerable time from school, his diligence and love of learning had, in the mean time, amply supplied the place of instruction, and that he was quite competent to undertake with propriety, and discharge with credit, the tutorial duties in question. There still remained the important part of the business, which consisted in obtaining to the youth's leaving the factory the consent of the owner, who, however, does not appear to have been so severe a taskmaster as the imaginary Wodgate Bishop. In any case, after a brief negotiation, he agreed to forego the remaining years of the apprenticeship; and entering the work-place, he made the heart of young Milner leap with joy and rejoice at the magic words, "Isaac, lad, thou art off!" In after years, he did not forget the comrades by whose side he had toiled and spun. He was ever really and unaffectedly humble; ready to acknowledge his original companions, and to minister to their necessities if they were poor. He was never ashamed of his juvenile employment, nor had he reason to be so; and when he encountered those who had known or labored with him in obscurity, it was with the same frankness, courtesy, and cordiality, but at the same time with the shrewdness, animation, and intrepidity, with which he met lordly guests at Rose or Lowther Castle. In this way he showed his rare nobility of soul.

Being happily freed from the manual labor which was unsuited to his abilities, Milner repaired straightway to Hull, and proved a most efficient assistant in the institution presided over by his brother. His department in the establishment was the instruction of the younger pupils, among whom he found Wilberforce, who was a lad of spirit, though delicate, and considered so remarkable for his powers of elocution, that it was customary to place him on a table and make him read aloud for the benefit of the other boys. Milner had, years before, besides constructing a sundial, given evidence of a decided bias toward mathematical studies; and he was now, while striving to accomplish himself in the classics, formally initiated into the elements of the science with so much profit, that when the scholars were engaged with lessons in algebra, and any difficulty occurred, the usher was immediately called upon to solve the problem, which he usually did with a promptness and facility not unworthy of one destined to be seated in the Lucasian chair. Joseph Milner had no cause to repent of having saved the talents of his brother from being lost amid the dust, noise, and wheels connected with the preparation of woolen cloth for Russian and German merchants; and he acted toward his gifted relative with exemplary and beneficent kindness. The keen and steady energy with which the latter pursued any object of inquiry that was presented to his attention—a characteristic that sometimes even exposed him to ridicule—was calculated to impart confidence to any attempt made toward his promotion in life; and it was determined that he should, in the year 1770, go to the university at which the reputation of his brother had been formed.

It seems that the elder Milner accompanied the embryo President of Queen's College to his destination. Their circumstances, as well as economical considerations, led them to adopt, on their long journey, that mode of traveling much more pleasant to contemplate than experience, with which we are in some degree familiar, from the descriptions of those great novelists who flourished in the reign of the second George, and who left such interesting pictures of life and manners as exhibited at the period. They accomplished the distance from Hull to Cambridge on foot, with occasional lifts by the way in a wagon, to recover from fatigue. On their arrival, Isaac was entered at Queen's College as a sizar, at a time when the privilege, in a pecuniary point of view, which he enjoyed as such, entailed the disagreeable necessity of performing various menial but by no means humiliating duties. Among these was ringing the chapel bell, and serving up the first dish to the fellows at dinner. On one occasion, when so busied, he was luckless enough to overturn a mess of soup on the floor, instead of placing it on the board, and was sharply rebuked for his awkward clumsiness; whereupon he excited much derisive laughter by exclaiming, in the dialect of his native country—"When I get into power, I'll do away with this nuisance!" The threat, thus expressed on the spur of the moment by the modest and diffident sizar, was more religiously executed than most promises uttered in such a frame of mind; and when raised to academic dignity, he altogether abolished the services of which that he had been rendering formed so irksome and invidious a part.

Notwithstanding the ungrateful and troublesome tasks thus devolved upon him, Milner's success at the University was great. He enjoyed one advantage—not always granted to men springing from so humble an origin—in a personal appearance which could not fail to prepossess beholders. His form, above the usual height, was cast in admirable proportions, and his presence striking; and his regular and handsome features expressed the talent of his brain, the benevolence of his mind, the kindness of his heart, the serenity of his temper, and the frankness of his disposition. His mental faculties were, as time passed on, placed beyond question by the brilliant success he achieved; and the fulness and variety of his colloquial powers rendered him the soul of the circles he frequented, either in Cambridge or London, and his listening audiences comparatively subservient. His mind became so marvelously comprehensive in its grasp, that it could master the details of any subject; and so universal was his information, that there were few trades on which he could not enlighten those who made them the business of their lives. He was, perhaps, a little more zealous than discreet in collecting his vast stores, and he was in the habit of reflecting from them with a pen in hand to take notes.

One very singular instance is given of his zeal in the acquirement of apparently uncongenial knowledge. Late in life, when his portrait, by Kerrick, was engraved, and his friends were anxious to have his coat-of-arms on the print, the then dean, on being applied to, at once declared that he had, of course, no armorial bearings, but he entertained no objection to be furnished with such as had nothing ridiculous about them. It was, however, a constant maxim with him that any knowledge which comes in one's way is worth gathering, and his attention being thus attracted toward heraldry, he procured books, and succeeded in gaining much curious information on the subject in which he had no natural interest.

Throughout his earthly existence, Milner was distinguished by piety, purity, and integrity; and though ready enough to converse on other subjects with sportive levity, he never alluded to that of religion without the utmost sincerity and the most becoming seriousness. On entering the University he studied indefatigably, and with a result which must have been highly gratifying to his anxious relatives. In 1774 he took the degree of Bachelor of Arts, and that year the moderators not only assigned him the dignity of senior wrangler, but likewise the title of *Incomparabilis*. On attaining this distinction, Milner ran off, in the pride of his heart and intellect, to indulge in the extravagance of ordering a seal, with the head of his immortal predecessor, Sir Isaac Newton, engraved on it.

He was now admitted as a member of the Hyson club, which had been formed in 1758, and could boast of several names known to fame. About the same period, the appointment of tutor to a Polish prince was placed within his acceptance, but declined; and his reputation as a mathematician was so unquestioned, that the papers he made out for the use of his pupils were much prized; and there even occurred an instance of a bed-maker being bribed to procure some of them by stealth, to be copied by a student belonging to another college. Yet it was not merely with mathematics that his attention was now occupied. Various philosophical subjects were subjected to his learned faculties; his intellectual performances had secured him friends, and he had shown the independence of spirit by standing alone, among the students of the college, in a refusal to attach his name to a petition against subscription to the Articles of the Church. To this fact he referred with satisfaction in later days, in his encounter with the Bishop of Peterborough, whose denunciation of the sin and danger of giving people the Bible to read, unaccompanied by the Prayer-book, had brought him into the controversial arena.

At the age of twenty-six Milner was ordained deacon, and next year was admitted to priests' orders, having in the interval been elected a fellow of his college, of which he became tutor in 1777. At that date he took the degree of Master of Arts. He got into the habit of now and then assisting his friends by officiating in country churches in the neighborhood; and he was presented to the rectory of the parish of St. Botolph. Milner had already contributed several papers to the "Transactions of the Royal Society," of which he, in due time, became a fellow; and he was led to embark, with all the ardor which characterized him, on the study of chemistry. Eminently successful in this pursuit, he proceeded to deliver public lectures on the science. It appears, however, that the experiments he made considerably impaired his health; and this unfortunate circumstance prevented him from undertaking much public labor in his clerical capacity; but he studied scripture and theology with critical interest, and thus laid the foundation of his extensive knowledge of divinity. He was in the habit of going to spend part of the Cambridge long vacation with his brother, in whose house now resided their aged mother, a woman of mental vigor and activity, and to whose shrewd and talkative humor several amusing anecdotes bear witness. When at Hull, in this way, Milner disdained not to return to his duties as usher. To the boys he could be gay and frolicsome, and they relished alike his playful manner and the clearness with which he explained what they could not understand without such assistance.

In 1784, Milner was chosen Jacksonian Professor of Natural and Experimental Philosophy; and in the same year took part in the institution of a society for the advancement of philosophy and general literature, which only enjoyed a brief existence.

When Wilberforce was living in the house of an aunt, who held Methodistical views of religion, and was suspected of being impressed with such doctrines, his rich and sapient grandsire delivered himself of this alarming and oracular saying: "Billy shall travel with Milner when he is of age; but if Billy turns Methodist, he shall not have a sixpence of mine." It did come to pass that, after Wilberforce was elected member for his native shire, and his acquaintance with Milner was renewed, he requested the company of his former instructor on a Continental tour. Accordingly they started on their excursion in the autumn of 1784, accompanied by the young, wealthy, and eloquent senator's female relatives. It is related that, during this expedition, the travelers being on one occasion in imminent danger of being dashed over the brink of a precipice, from the weight of their vehicle overpowering the horses, Milner leaped out, and, grasping the wheels, exerted his great physical strength so effectually, that the danger was obviated. During their wayfarings they met, in Switzerland, the celebrated Lavater, in whose conversation Milner was much interested. Shortly afterward Milner visited his friend at Bath, when "the volatile representative of the county of York" was attacked by a serious illness, and subsequently at his temporary residence in Westmoreland, which being filled with guests of distinction, furnished the divine with a fair field for the display of his wonderful power and versatility. He held conversations with his host on religious subjects, and exercised no slight influence on the mind and opinions of the great philanthropist, in whose schemes for the freedom and welfare of the human race he warmly sympathized.

In the year 1786 Milner took his degree of Bachelor of Divinity, and about the same time was an active member of the Board of Longitude, instituted for the purpose of considering and reporting to government any discoveries calculated to mitigate the perils of navigation. He was regarded as one of the most talented men at Cambridge, where he was considered as an excellent lecturer. As Jacksonian professor he gave alternate courses on chemistry and experimental philosophy, the former of which were especially well attended; and he continued to occupy the chair till his preferment to ecclesiastical dignity.

About his thirty-eighth year he was elected President of Queen's College; and in this capacity he is reported to have aimed at affording encouragement to learned men belonging to the foundation, and introducing such improvements in the reformation of abuses, and other means, as were calculated to conduce to the welfare of the students, and the honor of the university. Four years later he took the degree of Doctor of Divinity, on being appointed to the deanery of Carlisle, of which he took formal possession by reading prayers in the cathedral. As a preacher he was most effective: his voice, in which he took pride, was sonorous and magnificent; his eloquence was, on the whole, dignified and impressive; and when it was known that he was to preach, as he was in the habit of doing almost every Sunday during his periodic residence, in the cathedral of the ancient city, the aisles and every part of the building were thronged with people of all religious persuasions. Indeed it was remarked, that on such occasions you might walk on the heads of the crowd; and even those who did not entirely agree with his doctrines, admitted the ability with which they were urged, and the striking light in which they were placed. Nor did he court popularity by the brevity of his discourses; for we read, that on an Ash Wednesday he preached to a thronging congregation in the chapel of Whitehall, on "the one thing needful," for no shorter space than an hour and twenty minutes.

Milner's presentation to the deanery was closely followed by his election to the Vice-chancellorship of the University, of which he was so distinguished a resident; and in 1809 he was unexpectedly re-elected to the office: having, in the mean time, been called to fill the mathematical chair, which a century earlier had been occupied by the ever-illustrious Newton.

The ties which, amidst all his triumphs, had hitherto been instrumental in binding the Dean of Carlisle to the world, were about this period weakened by domestic losses. His mother had already gone to her grave; and in 1797 his brother, who had just been appointed to the vicarage of Hull, breathed his last. The latter bereavement touched Milner's heart to the core; he began to feel less concern with earthly affairs, to exhibit greater earnestness in his professional duties, and to set his affections more steadfastly on things above. His life, indeed, was far from being without its enjoyments and consolations. He looked upon his summer residence at Carlisle as, in some measure, a period of relaxation, associated on terms of intimacy with the families in the vicinity, and derived pleasure from the hospitalities that were practiced, and the company that assembled at the mansions of Lord Lonsdale and the bishop of the diocese. He was prepared to converse with those whom he met on the subjects with which they were most familiar, in a style joyous, jocund, or grandiloquent. "He talked, also, to his chosen and intimate friends," it has been said, with power, "but not in the same fitful strain. To them, from the abundance of the heart, he spoke on the theme which engages the latest thoughts of all men, the retrospect and the prospect; the mystery within, and the dread presence without; the struggle, and the triumph, and the fearful vengeance; and whatever else is involved in the relations which subsist between mortal man and the eternal source of his existence. To search into those relations, and into the duties, and hopes, and fears flowing from them, was the end which Isaac Milner still proposed to himself, under all his own ever-varying moods."

Milner, with affectionate devotion to the memory of his deceased brother, repaid the essential obligations which in youth he had incurred, by editing and improving the "Church History," written to disseminate the theological views he held; and added thereto a biographical sketch of the author. Nor, in the midst of affluence and reputation, did he forget the wants of his more humble relatives; to whose necessities, as to those of the poor of his native place, he ministered with a bountiful hand. In Carlisle, also, he contributed toward the various objects of public charity; he was ever anxious to serve those who, in private, applied to him for assistance; and he subscribed liberally toward the erection of the new churches, which were rendered necessary by the large population of the old Border city.

In 1819, having previously been introduced to Dr. Chalmers, Milner wrote to the magistrates of Edinburgh, urging the claims to the Professorship of Natural Philosophy in their gift, and then vacant, of that eminent Scottish divine, whom he described as "a man of great genius, varied talents, and sound principles, both religious and civil."

After attaining the age of threescore and ten years, this distinguished man died on the 1st of April, 1820, and was buried in the chapel of that college of which by intellectual industry he had risen to be the head.

DAVID HUME

Though any attempt to excuse or palliate Hume's erroneous views and opinions in regard to religion—the dissemination of which he is said to have regretted—would be little less than high treason against Christianity and civilization, his example, in other respects, is of infinite value. His career was characterized by resolution, independence, and self-command, at a time when these qualities were not much in fashion; and his life is a lasting protest against the idea, that the habits of a literary man are necessarily lax in respect to pecuniary affairs. Moreover, he must be acknowledged as prince among the historians of England. He still retains his ascendency after the lapse of an eventful century; and his great work is looked to as the natural source of information on the subject of which it treats. The intelligent reader is animated by feelings of admiration after perusing its inimitable pages; while the less informed goes to it for guidance and instruction. Yet much of this mighty memorial of his great intellect was composed in the face of a reception so galling to a proud spirit, and so discouraging to a heart panting for fame, that most men would, under the circumstances, have thrown down the pen in blank dismay; but Hume, notwithstanding his temporary disgust, had courage and genius fully equal to the occasion. He felt how glorious was the prize at stake, and pushed bravely forward to snatch it. And it is, indeed, impossible too highly to admire the calm, intrepid, unshrinking perseverance he displayed in thus consummating, in spite of all the clamor that the earliest volumes elicited, a work which he ere long had the consolation of knowing the world would not willingly let die. Such, doubtless, has often been the lot of those who write for immortality!

The pedigree of this illustrious personage, who frankly confessed to the charm of an ancient name, was such as might satisfy the most exacting genealogist. Indeed, it is traced in the books of heralds, through potent barons and mighty earls, to the Saxon conquerors of Britain; though it does not appear that he was fully aware of a fact, which, to say the least, would have been reflected on with complacency. But as the subject is not altogether uninteresting to many, it may be here adverted to with brevity.

When the Norman Conquest took place, a Northumbrian prince—whose grandmother was daughter of an English king, and whose brother became, by marriage with the heiress of the Nevilles, progenitor of those barons slain on the field of Barnet—was driven to seek refuge on the north side of the Tweed, where he founded that powerful feudal connection known as the house of Dunbar, which fell in the fifteenth century. One of its branches, and the inheritor of much of its power, was the baronial family of Home, whose chiefs bestowed such lands as came into their possession on their younger sons. One of these cadets—the historian's ancestor—was thus gifted with Tyninghame, a fertile estate in Lothian; but being, unlike his remote descendant, an irreclaimable spendthrift, he totally dissipated this paternal grant. It happened, however, that his son, a youth of promise, was received into favor by the head of the clan, and planted at the Ninewells, on the pleasant banks of the Whitadder, where his successors, whose names no minstrel has sung, vegetated for three hundred years. In fact, though residing close to the Border, they do not appear to have fought in the wars which desolated the vicinity, nor even to have speculated in the precarious trade of cattle-lifting. They seem neither to have been puissant knights nor "rank reivers;" nor were they in request when a charter was to be attested, or an eldest son served heir to his father. But they paid a species of "black mail" to the English captain of Berwick, received protection, lived in peace, speared salmon, and cultivated their fruitful lands. In the reign of Queen Anne, one of these lairds, whose sire's heart's blood seems to have stained the blade of an exasperated sheriff, went in youth to the Scottish capital, and was in due time called to the bar; but without pursuing the legal profession further. He was considered a man of attainments, and took to wife, in 1708, the daughter of Sir David Falconer, Lord President of the College of Justice. By this lady he had two sons and a daughter, of whom David Hume was born, at Edinburgh, on the 26th of April, 1711.

The consideration of a distinguished lineage certainly imparted to Hume's heart a calm satisfaction and colored, though in the slightest degree, his writings; but as he was deficient in sympathy with the past, it could not infringe on his philosophic mind, perplex his clear intelligence, or influence his serene judgment. The political sentiments in which he was nurtured were destined to exercise a much greater effect on his life and works. His father's residence was situated in a district where the lords of the soil were, with rare exceptions, deeply tinged with Jacobite principles. Their interest and inclination alike prompted an adherence to the cause of the ancient line of kings; and at the very time when the future historian first saw the light, the accession to power of a Tory ministry had conveyed hope and animation to their breasts. Thus when he began to creep about and lisp forth inarticulate sounds, complaints of real injuries and imaginary insults sustained by his relatives since the Revolution would greet his childish ears, and perhaps enter into his young soul. In his fourth year, these restless worthies proposed to hold a public meeting with a view of obtaining a redress of their grievances; but as the authorities deemed that it might prove a cause of embarrassment to the newly-established government, it was sternly interdicted, and precautions were taken to repress any attempt to disobey the official mandate. David's fierce clansmen bit their gloves, shook their heads, and vowed revenge. Several of them risked and lost all in the insurrection of 1715; his chief and a near kinsman were committed to the Castle of Edinburgh for their devotion to the house of Stuart; and amidst scenes of tumult, disorder, and confiscation, the first few years of Hume's life passed over. Perhaps, indeed, to his brother and himself having been minors at the time may be ascribed their not having assumed the white cockade, and that the acres held for centuries by their ancestors were not appropriated by some intriguing agent for forfeited estates, or seized by a factor with few scruples of conscience and sufficient dexterity in arithmetical mystification.

At an early age—indeed almost in infancy—Hume lost his father; and his widowed mother, though young and handsome enough to have aspired with success to a second husband, devoted her whole time and attention to the rearing and education of her children. David soon began to manifest an ardent love for his books. As a boy he was particularly docile, well behaved, and attentive to his studies, without being remarkable for the display of precocious talents. The family property had, of course, gone to his elder brother; and as the portion of a second son was not such as to encourage for a moment the idea of passing his life without labor, he felt under the necessity of bringing his abilities into active operation. With this view he was sent to fit himself for exertion by completing his education at the university of his native city, where he went through the usual academic course with comparative credit and success.

His extraordinary ability at this period is beyond all question, for a letter written to a youthful intimate at the age of sixteen proves that his marvelous talent was then exhibiting itself. Having been fired with that enthusiasm for literature which continued to be his ruling passion and chief delight, he impressed his guardians with a high opinion of his studious disposition; and they, taking into account his steadiness of conduct and sobriety of demeanor, arrived at the conclusion, that the Scottish bar would be a proper sphere for the exercise of that intellectual industry of which he daily gave signal proofs. His tastes, however, were rather unsuited to pursuing the profession successfully; and he states that he was generally engaged in devouring Cicero and Virgil while he was supposed to be occupied with the more practical studies of Voet and Vinnius. At eighteen the law appeared utterly nauseous to him, and his aversion to it as the business of life became extreme. He pondered and reflected; he could think of no other method to push his way in the world than as a scholar and philosopher, and this prospect pleased him infinitely for a season; but his health giving way under the pressure of severe mental application, a reaction came, and his ardor quite expired. He abandoned all thoughts of the law as a profession, and removed to the residence of his brother. The change of air and scene had a beneficial influence, and the young philosopher applied to the family doctor to restore his health and spirits. The latter laughed at his patient's imaginary ailments; but, at the same time, accompanied his unwelcome raillery by the extremely palatable advice to drink a pint of claret a day, and take plenty of equestrian exercise. Hume attended to the prescription, daily swallowed a proper quantity of the grateful beverage, and rode some ten or twelve miles on horseback. Though caring little for rural pleasures, pursuits, or recreations, he seems to have really enjoyed himself at this period: he soon gathered strength from his exercise in the open air; and, from being a tall, lean, and raw-boned lad, he passed to the other extreme—his complexion became ruddy and his countenance cheerful. His pursuits seem to have been diversified. He studied Latin, English, French, and Italian. He read books of morality, and was captivated with their beautiful representations of virtue and philosophy; and he listened, not without gratification, to stories about the fortunes of their race from some knightly clansman or old freeholder. The traditionary lore and local associations were apparently, it must be confessed, quite lost upon him: he was without local ambition; and the scenes of his boyhood, when he has occasion to mention them, are alluded to with the same cold dignity with which he writes of places which he had never seen. His intellect was so severely original, that it disdained to draw one particle of inspiration from buildings and battle-plains which have since been invested with so pleasing a charm, and made the subject of glowing verse. There is no sign of his having viewed Norham Castle, Flodden Field, and Halidon Hill, or ridden through "the rich Merse," and perambulated the ancient capital of the eastern marshes, or gazed on the "desolate grandeur" of Home, with romantic enthusiasm, poetic perception, or provincial pride. While accumulating information in regard to distant countries with industry and rapidity, he altogether neglected or scorned the precious metals which lay in his way; and while contemplating the perfections of Roman poets, he had not a thought to spare to the Border ballad-makers, whose verses Scott toiled to preserve and restore. He had therefore small temptation to linger amidst the fields, meadows, and woods through which he had roamed in his thoughtful childhood. He felt, indeed, that such an expenditure of time was by no means in harmony with his circumstances; and, believing that business and diversion would give him peace of mind and relief from anxiety, he resolved to betake himself to a more active life, and entered on a course, of all others, at variance with his natural bent toward studious retirement and philosophic reflection—that of commerce. In doing so, he confessed that he could never wholly give up his pretensions in learning but with his latest breath. He merely laid them aside for the time, with a view of resuming them to greater advantage. In reality, he was actuated by an ardent and consuming passion to achieve literary fame and found a philosophical reputation when he formed his determination—a most inauspicious frame of mind, assuredly, with which to enter upon the harsh duties of mercantile existence!

About the beginning of March, 1734, Hume started for Bristol. He visited London in his way, and then traveled onward. He had obtained introductions to several leading merchants in the place; and on reaching his destination established himself in the counting-house of one of them, in the hope of forgetting the past, preparing for the future, and enriching himself by commerce. But the petty cares, the perpetual bustle, and the perennial annoyances of such a career, were found, as might have been anticipated, utterly intolerable to a person to whom legal studies had appeared irksome and unattractive; and, after a few months' trial, he relinquished his new situation, with all its coarse, uncongenial duties, and those prospects of remuneration which are so seldom realized.

Hume had already, according to his own statement, collected materials for many volumes. He, therefore, passed over to France, with the view of prosecuting his studies in some rural retreat. No doubt he could have done so at the time-honored mansion of his fathers, but circumstances had occurred since he left which rendered it impossible to return there with any feeling of comfort; so he made a short stay in Paris, and then repaired to Rheims, in the north of France, where he spent some months in literary retirement. "I there," he writes, "laid that plan of life which I have steadily and successfully pursued. I resolved to make a very rigid frugality supply my deficiency of fortune, to maintain unimpaired my independency, and to regard every object as contemptible except the improvement of my talents in literature."

Having formed this wise and prudent determination, he removed to La Flèche, in Anjou, where he prepared his "Treatise on Human Nature;" and then he returned to London, to superintend the publication, and endure the suspense. Being issued in 1738, the work, to use his own expression, fell still-born from the press; though when subsequently published in separate essays, it was a little more successful.

Having thus, at the age of twenty-seven, embarked and made an inauspicious voyage on the uncertain sea of literature, Hume, without even waiting to know the fate of his work—for which a publisher had given the sum of fifty pounds—turned his face northward; and, perhaps, with some slight regret that he had relinquished the profession of the law, and deserted the merchant's desk, sought the agreeable seclusion of his family's fair domain, which he found his brother laudably occupied in improving and enhancing in value. Among its old trees, pleasantly shading the gentle acclivity whence burst the nine fountains which gave a name to the place, and with which the argent lion on his ancestral shield was charged, Hume experienced so much satisfactory enjoyment in "retirement, rural quiet, friendship, books," that, though the ideas and tastes of his relatives could not have harmonized very readily or easily with his own, he would, in all probability, had other matters been equal, have chosen to pass his life there. But the ambition for literary fame continued strongly to animate and influence him; and his time was chiefly spent in grave reading, deep meditation, in restoring his knowledge of the Greek language, and in corresponding, among others, with his friend Henry Home, afterward celebrated as Lord Kames.

Such was his position, when the last Marquis of Annandale, a Scottish nobleman, whose eccentricity took the form of lunacy, having read some of the hapless essays, was so charmed with something he saw in them, that he conceived a passionate wish to obtain the services of the learned author as his tutor. Hume was induced, by the temptation of an ample salary, to accept the office of companion to this weak-minded man, and had his temper severely tested in consequence. After holding the luckless and invidious post for a year, during which the marquis seems to have written a novel, relating to some events and love affairs in his own life, Hume's patience and placidity gave way, and, throwing up the situation, he became candidate for the Professorship of Moral Philosophy at Edinburgh, which, although powerfully supported, he was unable to obtain, on account of his well-known sentiments on religious subjects.

Matters, however, ere long, began to assume a pleasanter aspect. An honorable appointment, as private secretary to General St. Clair, uncle of Lord-chancellor Loughborough, was almost immediately bestowed on him, as if by way of solace for his depressing defeat. The General had originally been destined for an important expedition to Canada, which somehow ended—or, rather was metamorphosed—into an incursion on the coast of France. On returning, Hume retreated to country quarters, and wrote a defense of the expedition, which has since been printed; and shortly afterward he accompanied General St. Clair on an embassy to the courts of Turin and Vienna, in the double capacity of secretary and aid-de-camp, wearing the uniform of an officer. His time, while in this position, was passed agreeably, in good company, and with considerable profit in a pecuniary point of view.

Meantime his "Inquiry concerning the Human Understanding," being the substance of his former work in a new shape, was published in London, but with scarcely greater success than the original; any interest it excited being merely of a temporary character. However, his natural cheerfulness bore him up against his repeated literary disappointments; and he returned to Scotland to delight his kinsfolk and acquaintances with narrations of his adventures in lands beyond the sea, and to digest the frustration of his hopes as well as he could. Still resolute of purpose, he wrote, during a two-years' retirement, his "Political Discourses," which were given to the world in 1752, and excited interest and attention both at home and abroad. Indeed, though in some measure overshadowed by the celebrated work which his friend Adam Smith produced fourteen years later, they unfold and enforce those views of economical science which are now recognized and adopted, for better or for worse, by all English statesmen. Moreover, they have, in the highest degree, the merit of originality; and their style is so admirable, that they can be perused by general readers at once with profit and pleasure. At the same time he composed his "Inquiry concerning the Principles of Morals," which, notwithstanding his own high estimate of its comparative merits, was little noticed or regarded. The former emanations of his great intellect were now beginning to attract observation, and he was gratified by finding that answers antagonistic to the views they maintained were gradually appearing; but he discreetly formed the resolution of not being drawn into controversy by such effusions, and inflexibly kept his purpose in this respect.

Hume had now attained the age of forty, and, though there certainly exists evidence which makes one suspect that he had not always proved that rare impenetrability to female blandishments for which his biographers have given him credit, there was, at this time of life, small chance of his being betrayed into a matrimonial alliance. His brother, therefore, aroused himself to the duty of transmitting the name, and continuing the succession, and, in 1751, wedded the daughter of a neighboring family. This country gentleman was a person of retired habits; he had a strong aversion to every thing savoring, or even having the appearance, of vanity; and he was so extremely prudent in his actions, that, with the exception of his marriage, he never took any step without having previously calculated the consequences to his satisfaction. When the latter momentous event occurred, the philosopher felt a natural longing to have a tenement of his own. His mother, whom he describes as a woman of singular merit, and whom he had in her lifetime treated with much filial kindness and affection, had been in her grave for years; and he proposed "to take up house in Berwickshire" with his sister; but duly weighing and deliberately considering the matter, he came to the conclusion that a town was "the true scene for a man of letters;" and, removing to Edinburgh, he exercised so much frugality in disposing of his slender income that he was enabled to live in comfort and contentment. Yet he was not, by any means, parsimonious, and ever was ready, on fitting occasions, to prove his generosity by charitable and beneficent actions.

The year 1752 was an important one in Hume's life. He was then appointed Librarian to the Faculty of Advocates, after a severe and spirited contest, in which, besides the junior members of the bar, his chief allies were the ladies of "modern Athens," who made strenuous efforts and exerted their utmost fascinations in his behalf. When the triumph was achieved he found himself in a most advantageous position in regard to an excellent and well-stocked library, which fortunately suggested to his brain the scheme of furnishing the world with a classical history of England, then a serious desideratum in national literature. "Being frightened," he states in his autobiography, "with the notion of continuing a narrative through a period of seventeen hundred years, I commenced with the House of Stuart, an epoch where I thought the misrepresentation of faction began chiefly to take place."

When the first volume, recording the events in the reigns of James I. and Charles I., was issued, in 1754, the effects of the author's earlier training were sufficiently apparent to kindle the wrath of one party without flattering the prejudices of the other. Accordingly, it was assailed by one cry of reproach and disapprobation; the sale was quite inconsiderable, and almost the only token of encouragement worth having came from the Primates of England and Ireland, who advised him to take heart, and proceed in his undertaking. But, whatever may be thought of Hume's historic leanings and political sympathies, it must be admitted that he acted courageously, conscientiously, and without fishing for the favor of those who had in their hands all the patronage and disposal of such places and rewards as he could have aspired to. He followed what appeared to him the true and just course, notwithstanding the storms to which he felt he would on that account be exposed; and his genius, more potent than had been the swords of his insurgent kinsmen, threw a wall of defense around the memory of the exiled race which, with all its defects, succeeding writers, whatever their ability and energy, have never been skillful and vigorous enough to scale or break down. Nevertheless, the reception of his work inspired him with feelings of such dislike for the British public, that he resolved upon leaving the country, renouncing his name, and passing the remainder of his days on the Continent; but a French war luckily put an end to his scheme of self-expatriation, and he determined to persevere with his laborious and ungrateful task. In 1756 his second volume appeared, and proved not less obnoxious than the first; but by that he had, as he says, "grown callous against the impressions of public folly." It was fortunate, in any case, that he did not succumb till the tyranny was overpast. His victory was secure, slowly as it might approach.

He had already published the "Natural History of Religion," which was severely censured; and when the author had arrived at his fiftieth year, his matchless and magnificent "History of England" was completed in six volumes. His easy, elegant, and interesting style ere long rendered the work highly popular. Hume was by universal consent, placed on a lofty pedestal of fame; and, though its reception had originally been so disheartening, the sum obtained for the copyright, and for his former productions, together with his economical habits, had made him not only independent but, as he considered it, opulent. He, therefore, looked forward to passing the remainder of his days in peace, and in his native land, congratulating himself on having never, in his struggle for fortune, courted the smiles of any great man, or treated the humble with discourtesy. He was, though plain and careless in manner, eminently qualified, by his frank and social humor, to enjoy the company of his chosen friends, with whom, in spite of their wide differences of opinion on the most serious subjects, he was ever on terms of affectionate intercourse and uninterrupted friendship. Nevertheless, within two years, he consented to forego his cherished plans, at the earnest and repeated solicitations of Lord Hertford, who was going as Embassador to Paris. Thither Hume accompanied that nobleman, and was shortly after appointed Secretary of Embassy. In 1765, when Lord Hertford departed to undertake the government of Ireland, the historian remained in the French capital as Chargé d'Affaires, and performed the functions pertaining to the office in a manner highly creditable to his clearness of judgment, his talent for business, and capacity for state affairs. In the gay and fashionable circles of Paris his fame, station, and agreeable bearing, secured him so hearty a welcome that ladies and princes, wits and philosophers, vied in their attentions. It was there that, in an evil hour, he consented, in a spirit of excessive amiability, to take under his wing the frantic and erratic Rousseau, whose connection afterward involved him in much trouble, and caused him infinite annoyance.

Hume returned to this country in 1766, and was, the next year appointed Under-secretary of State for the department presided over by Marshal Conway, an office which he retained for more than twelve months. His annual income, the fruits of real industry, now amounted to a thousand pounds a year; and, taking a house in the new town of Edinburgh, he settled to spend his remaining days among his old and most attached friends. For some time his peaceful existence was uninterrupted, but in 1766 his health became so precarious that he was under the necessity of undertaking a journey to Bath, when he was attended by his friend and remote relative, John Home, the author of "Douglas," with whom he had many a jocular debate about the correct orthography of their name, and the comparative merits of port and claret. The illustrious historian was fond of relieving his sinking spirits by a playful jest at the expense of his clansman's warlike propensities, and did not omit so favorable an opportunity as that presented by the poet's pistols being handed, with much ceremony, into the traveling-carriage:

"You shall have your humor, John," he said, "and shoot as many highwaymen as you like; for," he added, with as much melancholy, perhaps, as a philosopher could well feel, "there's too little life left in me to be worth fighting about."

It appears that the martial predilections alluded to were shortly afterward gratified by a commission in the "Buccleuch Fencibles," though on this occasion they were not in requisition; unless, indeed, to inspire the young soul of Walter Scott, who was then exercising his precocious imagination at Bath, where he made the acquaintance of the bard, soldier, and divine, whose fame his pen, more than fifty years later, did something to extend and perpetuate. If the eye of the great historian, from which the world and all its vanities were fast vanishing, lighted on that lame boy, vigilantly guarded by a sarcastic and high-spirited female, how little could he have supposed that there was the being destined to invest with the charms of romance and the glow of chivalry that old royal cause, which he had employed all his wisdom and all his intellect to restore to public favor and render permanently attractive!

Meantime the veteran philosopher and historian, deriving little or no benefit from his visit to Bath, returned to die under his own roof. His decline was gradual; and, to the last, his most ultimate associates could not observe any diminution of gayety. He talked familiarly with them during their calls, and alluded to his approaching dissolution in a tone of whose levity even Dr. Smith, his most ardent admirer, could not approve. Whatever twinges of doubt or dread in regard to the future he might in his last hours experience, were encountered and borne with the semblance of indifference and tranquillity. He could not, indeed, feel the blessedness of those who have fought a good fight and kept the faith; nor could he, like Addison, exclaim with hopeful and serene resignation, "You see how a Christian can die:" but, five days before his last, he wrote, "I see death approaching gradually without anxiety or regret." On the 25th of August, 1776, he breathed his last; and was buried in a cemetery on the Calton Hill, where a monument to his memory has since been erected.

ROBERT SOUTHEY

Among "the laborers of literature" Southey was eminently distinguished by skill, regularity, perseverance, and other qualities hardly less essential to continuous and satisfactory success in his profession. Few men have practiced more resolute industry, or exhibited the literary character in a more estimable light; and his example, in this respect, is peculiarly worthy of being presented to the attention of aspiring and intellectual youths.

He was descended from a sturdy race of yeomen, who had been settled for a considerable period in the county of Somerset. He would, it seems, have liked well to believe that his ancestors had fought beneath the cross in Palestine; but was fain to content himself with ascertaining the less gratifying fact that one of them had risen in rebellion with the reputed son of "the merry monarch," and narrowly escaped the fangs of such law as was administered by the ruthless and unsparing chief-justice of the last popish sovereign of England. It happened that, during the last century, a kinsman of the family being engaged in trade as a grocer in the city of London, Southey's father was sent to try his fortune in the metropolis; his relations, in all likelihood, regaling their fancies with the agreeable delusion that he would in good time, and by some easy but mysterious process, attain the wealth and dignity of a Whittington. The young apprentice, however, was naturally, to a great extent, disqualified for pursuing his occupation with success, being by birth and training excessively fond of rural affairs and field sports. The sight of a dead hare carried along the street brought tears to his eyes, and the mention of a greyhound made his heart sick. Many a time, no doubt, did he sigh with heaviness for the green pastures, running streams, and shady orchards of his native shire, as he pensively took down his master's shutters, and prepared to drag himself through the care, toil, and uncongenial duties, which were brought by each successive day in endless round. While thus occupied, the Somersetshire lad, on the death of his employer, had an opportunity of transferring himself to Bristol; and there he was placed, with due form, in the establishment of a linen-draper, who kept the principal shop in the rich old town. While thus situated learning his business, and applying the yard-wand to crapes and muslins, it was his fortune to become acquainted with the son of a widow lady, whose relationship was miscellaneous, and who resided on a small estate that had belonged to her husband's forefathers for generations. The bold draper speedily formed an intimacy with the family—got into the habit of being a regular Sunday guest—became enamored of one of the daughters, and took her to wife, after embarking in business on his own account; though it does not appear that he ever enjoyed much prosperity. Nevertheless, it was ordered that his name should not sink into utter oblivion, even though his shop—which, true to hereditary tastes, he had called the "Sign of the Hare"—was not the most flourishing concern; for under its roof, on the 12th of August, 1774, Robert Southey was born; and he was so fat, large, and ugly an infant, that the nurse in attendance expressed no slight disappointment at his unprepossessing appearance. The space of two years, however, served to change him completely in this respect; and by that time he had manifested a peculiarly sensitive disposition. In childhood he was often affected to tears by the songs, ballads, and stories, which were sung, recited, or told by the affectionate inmates of his father's house to amuse and interest him; and in after life the author of "The Doctor" never could listen to a tale of woe without experiencing painful sensations and feelings of sadness.

Southey was still less than three years old when it was his fate to be removed to Bath, and soon after placed, though by no means willingly, at the school of a dame whose countenance seems almost to have frightened him out of his wits. Indeed, her aspect was so forbidding, that the little pupil was shocked at its excessive plainness, and loudly expressed the terror with which he was inspired, entreating, but vainly, to be sent home. His struggles and complaints proving of no avail he was compelled to submit to this petticoat government until his sixth year; and while under it conceived the idea of going, with two of his school-mates, to an island, and living by themselves. As it was to include mountains of sweetmeats and gingerbread, the place, as may be supposed, was sufficiently fascinating to their imaginations. Southey at this time lived with Miss Tyler, his mother's half-sister, a full-blown spinster of considerable personal attractions, but with an imperious will and a violent temper. The discipline to which she subjected the young poet, though irksome and despotic, was not altogether disadvantageous to the rise of his intellect. He was not permitted to play with any of his companions, and he was made aware that to soil his garments was deemed an inexpiable crime; but being much in the company of people older than himself, he mused and romanced at an unusually early age; and he was soon, like other boy-bards, inspired

> "By strong ambition to out-roll a lay,
> Whose melody would haunt the world."

His original aspirations, however, were of a martial cast; he longed, with all the enthusiasm of an incipient poet, to be a soldier, and to possess the various weapons used in battle. On one occasion he was lulled into a temporary feeling of full and complete happiness by being allowed to take the sword of a military visitor to bed with him; and sadly was he mortified, on awaking, to perceive by the morning light that it had in the mean time escaped from his grasp, and disappeared. On another, he incurred a sharp infliction of the horsewhip for strolling from home with a barber's assistant, who had promised to furnish him with a suitable blade, but proved faithless to his plighted word.

As soon as Southey had learned to read, one of his aunt's friends presented him with a number of children's books, which he much prized and eagerly perused; and thus, perhaps, was implanted in his glowing breast the germs of that extraordinary passion for literature which made him in later days regard the fame arising from it as the most worthy and desirable, as well as least evanescent of any. Moreover, his maiden guardian was extremely fond of frequenting the theatre, and had an extensive acquaintance among people connected with histrionic affairs. Thus, at the age of four, Southey was taken to witness a play, which so much delighted him, that he speedily, conceived a keen relish for the stage. He heard more of theatrical matters than of any other subject; and soon essayed to write dramas himself. His aunt was also much given to reading romances, and trained her little nephew to do likewise.

Notwithstanding this unquestionable fascination held out by her, the capricious sway which she exercised with incessant vigilance was so much felt by the boy, that he rejoiced exceedingly when allowed to return to his father's house, where he enjoyed comparative freedom, and could walk into the neighboring fields, which with him, at this period, was the greatest of all pleasures and the chief of all delights.

Miss Tyler had sternly prohibited her charge being breeched, like other juveniles of the day; and though he was six years old, and tall for his age, she had forced him to wear a childish, fantastic dress. It was now gladly exchanged for a garb befitting the dignity of ambitious boyhood; and the youthful dramatist was placed at a day-school, kept by a Baptist minister. There, though a docile boy, he received somewhat harsh treatment, and the only flogging on record that he ever underwent at the hands of a teacher; but he did not profit, to any extent, by the tuition. In twelve months the reverend pedagogue died; and Southey was sent to a boarding-school about nine miles from Bristol, at a house which, in other days, had been the seat of a provincial family of consequence. The broken and ruinous gateways about which the urchins sported, the walled garden transformed into a play-ground, the oaken staircase on which they aspiringly scrawled their names, and the tapestry which covered the old walls of the school-room, conveyed to the heart of the young rhymer mournful impressions and associations, and produced an impression on his memory not soon effaced. When in the pride of youthful and eccentric intellect, he visited the spot in company with a versifying friend, and described it in his early poem, the "Retrospect." He knew well how to appreciate the ideas suggested by such a scene.

Meantime, at this educational institution he managed, rather by assisting his comrades than any guidance he himself had the advantage of, to acquire some knowledge of Latin, which was only taught occasionally by a Frenchman who came from Bristol for the purpose. Southey and his fellow-imps were rather meanly fed; and their ablutions, performed chiefly in a stream that passed through the grounds, were conducted with much less precision and completeness than would have satisfied the scrupulous cleanliness of the fastidious Miss Tyler. Indeed, the carelessness habitually permitted and practiced in this respect would with some reason have driven her into one of her boiling passions, which such an event as the wedding of a servant-maid never failed to raise. The seminary was, besides, much too disorderly to be in any degree comfortable; yet the boys were not without days and seasons of juvenile enjoyment. In spring each was allowed to cultivate a small allotment of garden-ground, on which was grown salad, which served for a frugal supper; and in the autumn there was a plentiful and animating crop of apples and other fruit to gather from the adjoining orchards. On one occasion they unfortunately exceeded all discretion, and appropriated so liberally those set apart for the master's use, that grave suspicions were excited and acted on, their drawers and boxes searched, and the whole plunder recaptured. The youthful band knew well that a moderate extent of pocketing would not have been inquired into. As it was, every apple was taken from them, and *Inopem me copia fecit* might have been the exclamation of each votary of mischief, as he hung his head and reflected on the vexatious incident. They were dressed in their best, Southey, doubtless, wearing his cocked hat, when Rodney went from Bath to Bristol, to be entertained by the corporation of the great commercial emporium; and they were marched to a convenient spot on the wayside, to give him three cheers as he passed. They exerted their lungs with no small effect, and the gallant admiral returned the salute with right hearty good-will.

At this not very advantageous seminary Southey remained for twelve months, but at the end of that period a panic occurred, in consequence of some disease prevailing in the establishment; and the future Laureate was withdrawn from its precincts in tremulous haste, and given again into the safe custody of his irascible but affectionate aunt.

Miss Tyler had by this time deserted Bath and all its social and theatrical delights. On the death of her mother she had taken possession of the latter's house at Bedminster; and it was deemed expedient to deliver Southey over to her tender mercies, while his father looked out from his linens and broadcloth for a proper school at which to place the clever youth. In this old-fashioned retreat, the successful biographer of the greatest of English admirals confesses to having spent some of the happiest days of his boyhood. Even at that early age his pleasure seems to have been in retirement, and his satisfaction in secluded labor; he had little relish for boyish games, and he found so much amusement in the garden among flowers and insects, that, had his taste in this branch of study been encouraged and taken advantage of, he might, perhaps, have figured as a distinguished naturalist. But that was not his destiny. His pen, wielded by a willing hand and directed by a suggestive brain, was his weapon; and before thirteen he had indulged his young ambition by compositions of various kinds, and his imagination by perusing and devouring the pages of Tasso, Ariosto, and Spenser.

Meantime, as early as assorted with his worthy father's convenience, Southey was placed as a day-boarder at a school in his native city, where he appears to have been tolerably well taught. He had already, as has been intimated, aspiringly commenced composition in verse. Wordsworth dated his love of rhyme, and the tendency which colored his manhood, from his tenth year; but his future friend and eulogist seems to have received the "poetic impulse" at a much less mature time of life, and to have commenced gratifying his sensations and prepossessions by practicing the "art divine" at an age when he could hardly have learned to hold or handle his pen with any degree of facility. Owing to his aunt's histrionic predilections, Shakspeare, as the prince of dramatists, had been put into his little hands almost as soon as he could read; and he went through the historical plays with rapture. It then occurred to him that there would, in all probability, be civil wars in his day, similar to those of which he read; and he conceived the ambitious desire of rivaling the valorous feats and lofty fame of Richard Neville, earl of Warwick, the setter-up and puller-down of kings. So imbued did his mind and spirit become with this notion, that he began nightly to dream of tents, battle-fields, beating drums, clashing spears, and all the "pride, pomp, and circumstance of glorious war." Besides perusing with avidity the works of Shakspeare, he had read those of Beaumont and Fletcher before he was eight years old; and his fancy, thus stimulated, glowed with romantic thoughts and charming visions. Moreover, he had already been present at numerous plays, and listened with awakened and lively curiosity to interminable conversations about their writers and actors, whom he regarded as the greatest of men. In this way his first aspirations after authorship naturally took the dramatic form; and he did not hesitate to express his opinion on the subject with great confidence and complacency.

"It is the easiest thing in the world to write a play," observed he one day, at this period, to a female friend of his aunt, with whom he happened to be on a journey.

"Is it, indeed?" she said, not a little surprised.

"Yes," replied Southey; "for you have only to think what you would say if you were in the place of the characters, and make them say it."

Acting on this not very correct principle, he not only produced pieces himself, but endeavored to persuade his puerile associates to do likewise. In the latter attempt he, of course, found his zealous efforts altogether futile, but experienced much consolation from the pride derived by his gentle mother, when she discovered that her boy was so highly gifted. These were not the days of popular literature; and the worthy draper's dusty shelf did not present to his son's keen appetite for knowledge any very various or interesting collection of books; but Southey about this time had the good fortune to meet with Spenser's "Faëry Queen," which charmed him much with its sweetness. He was soon, however, removed once more from under the paternal roof into more congenial company.

His aunt, Miss Tyler, took a small house near Bristol; and he was once more handed over to her care. A brother of the restless spinster also went to live with her—a strange, half-witted man, whose enormous consumption of ale and tobacco astonished his young kinsman, and brought on himself a premature old age. He had a strong affection for Southey, and loved well to have a game at marbles with him when an opportunity presented itself; though apparently, he was better pleased to smoke a pipe and drink beer in the shady arbor during summer, or by the kitchen chimney in colder and less agreeable seasons. Some of his wise, old-world saws, his nephew did not soon forget.

During his twelfth and thirteenth years Southey, ever eager in his beloved pursuit, exercised his poetic powers with much industry and enthusiastic perseverance. When writing, he searched and labored diligently to make himself master of the necessary historic facts and information relating to the particular subject with which he happened, from inclination, to be occupied. Even at this date he was fitting and accomplishing himself, by solitary and unaided study, and by practice in the coining and structure of sentences, for the career which circumstances and a genuine love of such matters led and incited him to select; and which he afterward did follow with an ardor, patience, and resolution in the highest degree creditable to himself, though rarely if ever equaled, and never surpassed by others. It was perfectly natural that the members of his family and their relations should experience a very justifiable elation at talents which were thus, perhaps, a little too precociously displayed; and Miss Tyler, flushed with pride at the acquirements of her clever nursling, insisted on his being educated to one of the learned professions. In this proposal she was, luckily, supported by Southey's maternal uncle, a clergyman, who handsomely offered to defray the expenses which this otherwise satisfactory scheme would entail. Accordingly, in the spring of 1788, it was resolved that the young prodigy should be sent to Westminster School. His gayly-disposed aunt was rejoiced at so favorable an opportunity for going to London—then no such easy business as at present; and he was conveyed thither under her protecting wing.

After a short time spent in visiting some of the imperious lady's friends and acquaintances he was duly entered, and soon after had the task of writing some Latin verses from Thomson's "Seasons," which was a process quite new to him, and productive of some trouble and perplexity. However, he surmounted the difficulties, and even practiced himself so far as to produce about fifty verses on the "Death of Fair Rosamond" from choice. But that classical effort satisfied his ambition, and he never afterward strove to excel save in his native tongue. At this period the success of the "Microcosm," and the reputation it won for its institutors, the Eton boys, set the ambition of the Westminster scholars on fire, and a weekly paper, entitled the "Trifler," was speedily commenced among them. In this little periodical Southey requested the insertion of some verses of his on the death of a dear sister, but he was balked in his wish by a mortifying neglect. He next, in conjunction with several of his new associates, projected a paper bearing the title of the "Flagellant," which only reached nine numbers, when a fierce attack on corporal punishments annoyed and enraged the head-master of Westminster so highly that he commenced a prosecution for libel against the more responsible parties. Southey at once confessed himself to be the author of the obnoxious article, and he was, in consequence, compelled to leave the school. In the age of boy-periodicals this was certainly a most provoking consequence of his first effort at furnishing contributions, and misfortunes, according to the proverb, seldom come singly. His expulsion from Westminster was speedily followed by circumstances still more adverse and distressing. His father who, behind the counter, had languished, like an animal transplanted to an uncongenial climate, became bankrupt and died.

Southey was now sent to matriculate at Oxford. It had been intended that he should enter at Christ Church, and his name had accordingly been put down there. But the Westminster mishap having reached the dean's ears, that dignitary, alarmed at the idea of insubordination, refused him admittance, and he consequently entered at Balliol College in 1792. His views and opinions, in regard to the forms and discipline of the place, were not such as to favor his profiting much by his residence there; and, though destined by his well-meaning relations for the Church, he seems never to have cherished the prospect of clerical honors with any degree of mental satisfaction. Yet, with all his eccentric tenets and sentiments, he was staid and decorous in demeanor, and meritoriously refrained from the excesses which he too frequently witnessed.

Southey was, by this time, animated and deluded by all the too sanguine credulity and glowing enthusiasm which so often mark and cloud the morning of genius, and lead its possessor astray. While in a state of intellectual fever and political excitement he made the acquaintance of Coleridge, with whom he soon devised the fanciful and bubble-like scheme since known and ridiculed as "Pantisocracy." This consisted of fantastic plans for collecting a number of discontented youths, as brother-adventurers, and forming a colony in the New World, on a thoroughly social basis. Southey wasted much time and care on this chimerical idea; and it was decided that the aspirants to perfect earthly content and felicity should commence operations by purchasing, with their common contributions, a quantity of land, which they were all to spend their labor in cultivating. Each was to have a fair share of work assigned to him, while it was arranged that the female emigrants—for one important regulation provided that they were, without exception, to be married men—should manage all domestic matters. Southey luxuriated in golden dreams and visionary anticipations; his ardent spirit swelled and rose high. All obstacles disappeared before his enthusiastic gaze, and he engaged the hand and affections of a dowerless but captivating damsel in his native place, who rejoiced in the very romantic name of Edith, and had no insuperable objections to accompany him to the land of promise, which lay sweetly, as his fancy pictured it, ready to receive them on the banks of the Susquehannah River, flowing with milk and honey. So far all went as smoothly with Southey as a total inexperience of the real world, and full and entire confidence in his own untried powers of action, could render matters to a strong imagination. But there was yet a lioness of no ordinary ferocity in the way. Miss Tyler had still to be informed, and the startling intelligence that her hopeful nephew had, without consulting her wishes, selected a partner for life, was instantly productive of one most inconvenient result. It brought upon him the sudden and rebounding torrents of her wrath. The night was rainy, but she was cut to the heart; and, mercilessly turning him out of doors, she never condescended to see his face again. This was a sufficiently portentous commencement for the Pantisocratic form of society; and the scheme, as might have been foreseen, proving utterly impracticable, the day-dream vanished into thin air when the most distant effort was made to realize it.

Southey was now, for the first time, thrown entirely on his own resources, and that struggle for existence by exertion, which invigorates the mind and influences the understanding, began in earnest. Under no circumstances could his ambitious spirit have been still at this date. The stream was still near its rise, and fretted itself into foam against each opposing rock; but the time was approaching when its course was to be more smooth, and its waters not less clear. His first step was to arrange with Mr. Cottle, of Bristol, for the publication of "Joan of Arc," with which he had been for a considerable time occupied, and the next to deliver a course of historical lectures, which were numerously attended. Nevertheless, it appears that his pecuniary affairs were not by any means in a flourishing condition at this crisis.

In 1794 he had, in conjunction with his friend Mr. Lovell, under the names of Moschus and Bion, published a volume of poems; and about the same period Southey, then glowing with revolutionary zeal, composed his "Wat Tyler." It is spoken of as a production of no merit, and utterly harmless from its weakness. Long after the author had recanted his early heresies, it was published surreptitiously to annoy him, and he, in self-defense, applied for an injunction against the printers. But the Chancellor refused to interfere in the matter, on the ground of the peculiarly objectionable principles which the book contained. The writer of this hapless—and, as it turned out, perplexing—revolutionary *brochure,* in after life thus accounted for its unwelcome existence:

"In my youth, when my stock of knowledge consisted of such an acquaintance with Greek and Roman history as is acquired in the course of a scholastic education, when my heart was full of poetry and romance, and Lucan and Akenside were at my tongue's end, I fell into the political opinions which the French revolution was then scattering throughout Europe; and, following those opinions with ardor, wherever they led, I soon perceived that inequalities of rank were a light evil compared to the inequalities of property, and those more fearful distinctions which the want of moral and intellectual culture occasions between man and man. At that time, and with those opinions, or rather feelings (for the root was in the heart, and not in the understanding), I wrote 'Wat Tyler,' as one who was impatient of all the oppressions that are done under the sun. The subject was injudiciously chosen; and it was treated as might be expected by a youth of twenty, in such times, who regarded only one side of the question. Were I to dramatize the same story now, there would be much to add, but little to alter; I should write as a man, not as a stripling; with the same heart and the same desires, but with a ripened understanding, and competent stores of knowledge."

Next year, while "Joan of Arc" was still in the press, Southey was, with a view to his welfare, urged and persuaded to accompany his uncle, Mr. Hill, to Lisbon, where that gentleman was chaplain to the factory. Consequently, when the epic poem appeared, its author had left the country; but not until he had contracted a matrimonial alliance, under circumstances so romantic as to put to shame the inventive faculty of novelists, and furnish another instance of truth being often stranger than fiction. His reverend friend and patron was under the impression that a change of scene and society would effectually dissipate and banish all fine visions of love, emigration, and social perfection on the banks of a North American river: but Southey clung to the object of his affection with poetic indiscretion and disinterestedness, and took a very conclusive precaution that the first part of this anticipation should be falsified. On the eve of departure for the continental excursion, he took the bold and irretrievable course of privately leading the adored Edith to the altar, where he received her hand as his bride, and united their earthly fortunes forever. It is stated that they parted immediately after their marriage, at the portico of the church; and the bridegroom set off on his travels. Doubtless, in subsequent years he had no cause to repent of having thus baffled the well-meant designs of his relative, anxious as the latter unquestionably was to promote his interests; and many, as well as Southey, who have, after a similar fashion, defied the fears of the wise, and rushed desperately on matrimony, have found in the duties which attend it, the best incitements to exertion, and the elements of honorable success in life. Yet early marriages in circumstances like his are extremely unsafe to stand upon; and Southey's kinsman was quite justified in telling him to beware.

In the year 1796 Southey joyfully returned to England where his poem had in his absence been published; and he began to form the notes he had made while abroad into "Letters from Spain and Portugal." He found it necessary to accept the fulfillment of an old promise of pecuniary assistance from a very intimate college friend; and then he proceeded to London, with the grand intention of studying and accomplishing himself in the laws of the realm. He was duly entered as a student at Gray's Inn, and made an attempt to combine legal studies with poetical prepossessions; but this, as might have been expected, proved quite futile. Law and poetry—the perusal of Blackstone and the writing of "Madoc"—were not very harmonious conjunctions, as he soon discovered, to the neglect of the former.

Sometime afterward Southey took a small house at Westbury, a beautiful village, where, in the society of his beloved wife, he resided about twelve months, and spent some of his most satisfactory days. He then produced more poetry than he ever did in the same space of time before or after; and he enjoyed the particular intimacy of Sir Humphry Davy, whose ardent genius was then making itself felt at Bristol. The rising man of science took a deep interest in, and heard passages read from, "Madoc," as its composition was proceeded with by the aspiring and painstaking author.

Southey was likewise employed, at this time, in preparing a volume of minor poems, and a new edition of his "Letters from Spain and Portugal," to which he had paid a second visit; besides editing the "Annual Anthology," the first portion of which then appeared. His literary occupations were so decidedly and undeniably to his taste, and became so much "the life of his life," that the idea of being chained to the law, and harassed by the beckonings of conscience in the direction of dry and dusty volumes, was gradually found to be more irksome and intolerable. Thus his attention was wisely and deliberately withdrawn from the concerns of a profession for which he was not calculated, and wholly concentrated on literature. Indeed the law is, of all others, a jealous mistress, and will accept of no divided allegiance; and such a result as that at which the poet arrived might easily have been foretold, in the case of one who commenced the marvelous achievement of "eating terms," with indulging in the prospective pleasure of burning his law-books after he should, by their aid, have amassed a magnificent fortune, and retired to enjoy it in Christmas festivities among lakes and mountains.

Trusting now chiefly for support and distinction to his literary effusions, Southey speedily became one of the most industrious of living mortals. His devotion to his pursuits was intense and unparalleled, and indeed so great, that he considered the correcting of proof-sheets as a luxury of the highest kind. In fact, he seems to have regarded literature as the most agreeable of worldly concerns, and the fame arising from its successful cultivation as that kind of which a wise man should be principally ambitious, because the most permanent. This principle regulated his conduct and stimulated his exertions in his chosen field. He guided himself by it with singular resolution; his actions became extremely uniform; and the eccentric workings of his youthful spirit having ceased, his life was as calm and cheerful as could have been desired.

In 1801 Southey had the good fortune to obtain the appointment of private secretary to the Irish Chancellor of the Exchequer, whom he accompanied to Dublin; and in the same year published "Thalaba the Destroyer," an Arabian fiction of considerable power, beauty, and magnificence. Soon after this, a pension was bestowed upon him by Government.

Southey now deemed it advisable to settle on the banks of the Greta, near Keswick, and pursued his avocations with keen and constant diligence. He wrote perpetually. Each day, and each hour of the day, had their appropriate tasks. He secluded himself much from society, but found consolation in the company of his pretty numerous household, and the well-stocked library which it was his fortune to collect and possess. He now sent into the world, from his agreeable retreat, a volume of "Metrical Tales," and "Madoc." After them appeared "The Curse of Kehama," considered as the most meritorious of his poetic works, but founded on the Hindoo mythology, and therefore not peculiarly interesting to general readers. Some years later he published "Roderick, the last of the Goths," a noble and pathetic poem.

In the mean time, Southey had not disdained the less pretending species of composition. His "Life of Nelson" is considered the best of his admirable prose works. When published, in 1813, it instantly rose into popular favor, and was recognized by the public as a standard biography. It was originally issued in two small volumes, since compressed into one. He subsequently contributed to "Lardner's Cyclopædia" a series of lives of British admirals. Besides, he again testified his biographic skill by a "Life of Wesley," the celebrated founder of Methodism. He evinced therein a minute acquaintance with the religious controversies of the day, and presented curious and interesting sketches of field-preachers and their performances. There were successively other works, less generally admired, relating to history, politics, morals, and philosophy. His numerous writings are characterized by an easy and flowing style, yet they did not secure him much real popularity; but this must, in a great measure, be attributed to the nature of the subjects. His prose was described as perfect by Lord Byron, who styled him "the only existing entire man of letters."

Southey had, long ere this, relinquished the opinions which prompted him to produce "Wat Tyler;" and when the "Quarterly Review" was established in 1809, he became connected with the enterprise which was then entered upon, and furnished several of the prominent articles to that distinguished periodical in the earlier stage of its career.

Though not enjoying that measure of popular favor to which, as an author of merit and a man of worth and prudence, he was justly entitled, Southey ranked high among the writers of his day; and he was fully appreciated by those most capable of judging critically.

In 1821, the degree of LL.D. was conferred on him by the University of Oxford; and other marks of distinction were within his grasp, if he had chosen to accept them. He was unambitious of public celebrity, and cared little for going into the world. In fact, he is pronounced to have mixed too little with his fellow men, and was therefore wanting in that particular kind of intelligence and information which can only be obtained by a free and familiar intercourse with the world. That "the proper study of mankind is man," is a doctrine with which he appears to have had little or no sympathy, so long as he had it in his power to say with truth:

"Around me I behold,
Where'er these casual eyes are cast,
The mighty minds of old;
My never-failing friends are they,
With whom I converse night and day."

One of Southey's latest prose compositions consisted of his "Colloquies on the Progress and Prospects of Society," in which Montesinos is made to converse with the ghost of Sir Thomas More.

On the death of Mr. Pye, the poet-laureate, the vacant dignity had been offered to Sir Walter Scott; but the great Border Minstrel declining to accept of it, used his influence in favor of Southey, who was accordingly appointed. In this capacity he composed his "Carmen Triumphale" and "The Vision of Judgment," which, like the productions of other laureates, encountered much ridicule. His latest poetical emanations were, "All for Love," and "The Pilgrim of Compostella."

Southey's repute as an author and political writer rose so high, that he was offered a baronetcy, and election to the representation in Parliament of a ministerial borough. However, his knowledge was rather of books than human affairs; he was by no means qualified to "make himself formidable" as a senator; he was ever in extremes, and had no experience of that middle path which can alone be permanently maintained in dealing with public affairs, and which is ever chosen by those not incapacitated by nature to learn from the past, and meet the shadowy future with prescience. Under these circumstances he acted with wisdom and prudence: he considered that his fame and prosperity could only be preserved by a resolute adherence to his studious occupations; and he declined both distinctions, continuing his habits of ceaseless reading and composition. It seems that, in his entranced devotion to his literary projects, he had neglected that exercise which he had declared so essential to health, and during his three last years he became the victim of disease. The early partner of his joys and sorrows had already sunk into the grave; and Southey had contracted a second union with a lady known for her poetic accomplishments. He is said to have left a considerable fortune—the result of his industry—at his death, which took place on the 21st of March, 1843. He was buried in the church-yard at Crosthwaite, in the neighborhood of his residence by lake and mountain; and an inscription for the tablet to his memory was furnished by the venerable Bard of Rydal Mount, who succeeded him in the laureateship, and was, ere long, laid at rest at no great distance from his former compeer.

THOMAS MOORE

The original genius, exquisite sensibility, independent spirit, and incorruptible integrity, which the greatest scholar of his age ascribed in his will to this bright and fanciful bard from the "Emerald Isle," have been generally admired and acknowledged. Indeed, notwithstanding his multitudinous and peculiar temptations to love patrician personages not wisely, but too well, few men of genius have ever excelled or equaled Moore in these important and laudable qualities for which Dr. Parr gave him credit, any more than in the brilliancy of his intellect or the strength of his domestic affections. That he passed through a severe ordeal, and was exposed to many trials, can hardly be doubted. The early recognition of rare talent is too frequently fatal to its possessor; and the celerity of Moore's transit from the humble parlors in the Irish capital to fashionable saloons and the banquets of princes was quite amazing, and well-nigh unprecedented. Yet he appears, without ostentatiously and perpetually proving the fact by bellowing it into the public ear, to have maintained his freedom of thought and action almost unimpaired to the end of his life. The career of such a man is necessarily fraught with interest and instruction; and the boyhood of a poet is always a subject especially worthy of being dwelt upon, as being replete with profit to the young and information to all. Who, indeed, can read without emotion of the gentle Cowper, being maltreated by his school-fellows at Westminster, and not daring to lift his eyes above the shoe-buckles of the elder boys; or of Scott, seated by some ruined edifice devouring ancient ballads, and gazing with rapture on the landscape in view; or of Byron, stretched on the old tombstone of Harrow, with the strong ambition in his mind and the bitter disappointment in his heart that were destined to unite and bring forth glorious but melancholy fruits; or of Wordsworth, the Bard of Contemplation, receiving the poetic impulse while led to and fro on the romantic banks of the Derwent? In a different and less attractive scene must we look for the earliest aspirations and exploits of the gifted youth whose songs, so gay, rich, and choice in their language, afterward held the fair and courtly in mute attention—whose sparkling wit proved so effective a weapon in political controversy; and whose spirit qualified him so perfectly to unite his national music to immortal verse.

Thomas Moore was born on the 28th of May, 1779, in the city of Dublin, where his father, a decent and respectable tradesman, at that time carried on a limited business as a wine-merchant. His mother appears to have been a rollicking Irish woman, with much honest humor, and no particular indisposition to indulge occasionally in an expletive, indicating any thing rather than Asiatic repose or excessive respect for the third commandment. This worthy dame, joyous and dashing, was fond of all such festivities as came in her way, and of all such society as she could obtain access to. She could, doubtless, sing delightfully at the supper-parties she frequented, enjoy herself without stint, when "the mirth and fun grew fast and furious," and let care and all its horrid concomitants wait for her attention till the morning. In fact, she was blessed with no small portion of Hibernian indifference as to the future. Moreover, she had the advantage of being a strict and sincere Roman Catholic; and her husband also "held the ancient faith," though with a philosophical moderation which his decorous spouse by no means approved of. Though a genuine Irishman by parentage and nativity, Moore, strangely, advanced no imaginary claim to estates confiscated for centuries, to wealth dissipated before he entered the vale of tears, or to ancestral honors. He even declined the distinction of having aristocratic kindred; and it must be admitted, that without these aids to inspiration he contrived to do "excellently well," and leave a brilliant name. In one quality he assuredly was not deficient, that of fervid nationality and warm love of his country.

Almost in the earliest stage of his existence the prophetic eye of Mrs. Moore discerned signs of her little Tom being a marvelous child, and he was nursed and reared with a view to his attaining due and enviable eminence ere his sun set. The happy days of the boy have, perhaps, too often no certain existence save in the imagination of the same being when grown into a man, and looking on past scenes with that enchantment which distance lends to the view. Gibbon remarks, that while the poet gaily describes the short hours of juvenile recreation he forgets the tedious daily labors of the school, which is approached each morning with anxious and reluctant step. He declares that he never knew the boasted happiness of boyhood, against the existence of which, as a general luxury, he therefore enters a feeling protest; but in this respect the experience of the fanciful Irish poet was quite the opposite of that confessed to by the skeptical historian of the Roman Empire. Moore was sent, with all convenient haste, to a day-school, kept by a person who "quaffed his noggin of poteen" with much less than proper consideration for his tutorial avocations. He was afterward placed under Mr. Samuel White, who had been the preceptor of Sheridan, and proved his want of prophetic skill by pronouncing the future wit and orator an incorrigible dunce. At this seminary Moore displayed a remarkable taste for music, poetry and recitation. This was much strengthened by the master of the school, who encouraged a habit of acting which was not in any degree relished by the majority of his pupils. However, Moore speedily became a favorite "show scholar," and in that capacity had the gratification of seeing his name in print at the age of ten, as one of the juvenile performers who were to contribute to an evening's entertainment at the private theatre of a lady of rank. He began forthwith to compose in numbers, and became more and more the delight of his mother's eye. She watched with tender anxiety and sanguine hope his extraordinary ascent, step by step, of the social ladder; and he repaid her solicitude by a filial devotion which no poetic triumphs were ever in subsequent life allowed to interfere with. Being extremely ambitious in regard to his worldly prospects, she early, despite the disabilities then attaching to those of her religious faith, destined him for the bar, and afforded him every opportunity of cultivating his mind and extending his knowledge which her means and position permitted. He soon gave cheering indications of being not unworthy of such anxious care, and was highly applauded by his teacher, who, while doing so, did not neglect so opportune an occasion of saying a good word for himself; and he signalized his precocious powers at the age of fourteen by contributing verses to the pages of a Dublin Magazine. "Master Moore" was already a sort of celebrity on the banks of the Liffey.

The friends and relatives among whom the melodist was brought up were, without exception, ardent in their Irish patriotism; and in 1792 he was carried by his father to one of the demonstrative gatherings held in welcome of the French Revolution, and was perched on the chairman's knee. The excitement of the festive scene, and the hallucination of those who took part in it, may be judged from such toasts as that recorded by him as having been enthusiastically sent round: "May the breezes from France fan our Irish oak into verdure." Surely, Donnybrook Fair must ever afterward have seemed tame to those who were present at such assemblies.

The young poet espoused these principles with warmth and sympathy; and having been entered at Trinity College in 1795, supported his opinions with a lively eloquence, which, as matters stood, might have caused danger. He passed through the academic course with much credit, was distinguished for his classical acquirements, took part in the debates of the Historical Society, and was much admired for the wit and playfulness he exhibited among his associates. Having brought his collegiate studies to a termination, taken the degree of bachelor of arts, and won the character of a most pleasant companion, he proceeded to London in 1799, and had the happiness of being enrolled as a student of law at the Middle Temple.

Meantime he had been prompt to seize every means of improvement, and his innate talent for music had been cultivated with assiduity and effect; he had gained no inconsiderable amount of classical learning; and he had acquired some knowledge of the French and Italian languages. In the middle of the year following his arrival in England, the translation of Anacreon's Odes, with which he had been engaged for some time, was published by subscription. This work had been contemplated by the eager and aspiring boy even in his school days, and it now appeared, with a dedication to the Prince of Wales, to whom the poet had already been presented. Its reception was most flattering; public favor was bestowed in abundance, and it elicited this complimentary impromptu—

"Ah, mourn not for Anacreon dead!
Ah, mourn not for Anacreon fled!
The lyre still breathes he touched before,
For we have one Anacreon Moore!"

The rhyming adventurer from the "Green Isle"—small in form but sprightly in mind—was introduced to fashionable circles, excited the curiosity and interest of royal personages, and charmed patrician assemblies with his vocal powers. He had, moreover, the distinction of dining twice at Carlton House with the Prince of Wales, and of being admitted to a grand *fête* given by his royal highness on becoming regent. At a subsequent period he was one of the same exalted individual's keenest assailants and sharpest satirists.

In 1803, Moore, through the influence of his friend Lord Moira, to whom he had been introduced by a Dublin Mæcenas, obtained an official appointment at Bermuda, and went thither to undertake the duties attached to it. The novelty of the situation might, for a brief season, lend it some slight charm and attraction; but after a year's trial of the island he considered it intolerable, as might have been anticipated in the case of one who had revelled in all the joys of poetic celebrity, and whose delightful singing had been rewarded in glittering halls with the dazzling and fascinating smiles of aristocratic beauty. He therefore resolved on fulfilling its functions, in future, by deputy; and after a flying visit to America, returned to England.

Moore, soon after this brief absence from the world of wit and fashion, published his "Odes and Epistles," suggested by this rambling excursion. In these poems, as in the volume given to the world under the assumed name of "Thomas Little," the glowing and irresistible imagination of the bard led him to commit what were very generally regarded as nothing less than most objectional offenses against delicacy and decorum. Accordingly he was attacked in the "Edinburgh Review," with, as he conceived, so much and undeserved severity, that he thought himself called on to challenge Jeffrey, as the responsible editor, to mortal combat. In consequence, the poet and critic met at Chalk Farm to enjoy the doubtful luxury of being fired at by each other; but, fortunately, the interference of lurking police-officers stopped the matter in time to prevent mischief, otherwise it is not improbable—so great was their awkwardness—that it might have resulted in involuntary suicide; at all events, the seconds seem to have been in a position of no slight peril. If any thing could have added to the absurdity of the affair, it would have been the report, which asserted that the pistols, on examination, were found to contain paper pellets, substituted in place of leaden bullets. This proved to have been erroneous; but the whole transaction exposed the actors to much tantalizing but well-merited ridicule. "A fellow-feeling makes us wondrous kind," and the parties principally implicated formed a close and lasting friendship.

Having already essayed dramatic composition, in a piece entitled the "Gipsy Prince," Moore, in 1811, made a second attempt in an opera, "M.P., or the Blue Stocking," which was produced at the Lyceum theatre with partial success. He was infinitely more fortunate in a matrimonial adventure, made about the same period; after which he removed from the metropolis, and chose a residence in Dorsetshire. Then appeared the "Twopenny Post-bag," a political effusion, in which several eminent persons, holding opinions at variance with those of the author's patrons, were lashed with sparkling wit, sharp sarcasm, and humorous pleasantry: but he was not unoccupied with projects more worthy of his fine taste and beaming fancy. He now came forth with his "Irish Melodies," which are replete with real feeling and true delicacy, and fully entitle him to be rewarded, as he desired, with the proud title of "the Poet of the Irish people." They are the happiest emanations of his gay and fanciful muse. Among song-writers he is almost unrivaled. No matter what may be the theme—playful or pathetic, light or impassioned, his verse flows onward like a "shining river" with graceful fluency; and his cadences tell how exquisitely the ear was tuned to the expression of the sentiment, which had its origin in the mind. It is as the producer of lyrics for the ancient music of his country that he gave proof of his peculiar and felicitous combination of power, and achieved so wide a reputation. He poured out these verses with unexampled readiness and fertility. In some he appeared not only as poet, but musical composer also; and his delicious words and graceful music thrilled and captivated the public ear and heart. His popularity had now risen high, but it soon appeared that his name had not yet gathered all the fame which was to enrich it, when, in 1817, "Lalla Rookh" made its appearance. This Oriental romance, rich, brilliant, and gorgeous, was his most elaborate poem. It had been produced in frost and snow, yet his potent imagination had conjured before him the sunniest of Eastern scenes, with all their splendor and magnificence; and, what was a most important part of the business, the manuscript is said to have brought him three thousand guineas. When presented to the public, it was found to unite the purest and softest tenderness with poetic fervor and lofty dignity. Its effect was immediate and extensive; it was received with eager enthusiasm; and the readers showed their appreciation by committing large portions to memory. No doubt the English public were, at the time, athirst for verse; but even under such circumstances nothing but high merit, taste, fancy, feeling, and delicacy, could have ensured such rapturous approval, and wrought such enchantment as Moore's poem, rich with imagery and ornament, now did, though on a subject by no means calculated to interest the bulk of the community.

His next work, "The Fudge Family in Paris," saw the light in 1818, and was one of those brilliant trifles in which its author was considered to be altogether unrivaled in his day and generation. It arose from a passing visit made by the poet to the Continent, and ran through successive editions. He afterward reproduced the actors in "The Fudge Family in England;" but with a felicity and success utterly unequal to the original effort.

Moore had now, as a poet, achieved splendid triumphs, and excited immense admiration.

> "Crowned with perennial flowers,
> By wit and genius wove,
> He wandered through the bowers
> Of fancy and of love;"

while, in social points of view, few men, similarly situated, were more courted by persons of rank and distinction. He had made comparatively few enemies, for his satirical shafts, sparkling with wit, were discharged with so much sportiveness, that they rarely created much venomous feeling. The kindness of the heart from which they emanated was naturally too great to admit of that being very frequently the case. He continued, though tried by vicissitudes of fortune, to retain all his amiable and domestic feelings in full vigor; his rural dwelling seems to have had greater attraction than the gay and glittering drawing-rooms, which he still now and then enlivened with the flashes of his graceful wit and refined genius. He was a man of the world as well as a poet and scholar, and he relished the taste of sparkling glasses of "liquid ruby," as well as the sight of bright eyes and brilliant glances. He seems to have generally enjoyed himself with little restraint;

and ministered to the amusement of others without compromising his personal dignity, or in any degree violating the independence of his spirit. His wit and cheerfulness, when exerted, were fascinating in the extreme, and he could at pleasure "set the table in a roar." One day, at a dinner-party where he was, the absence of game having been lamented, one of the guests, struck with his fine display, remarked—

"Why, gentlemen, what better game could you wish than 'Moore-game?' Surely you have that in abundance."

In the circles he frequented it was his lot to become intimate with Lord Byron, to whom he had introduced himself by something resembling a challenge; and when, in 1819, he made that journey to the Continent which furnished him with matter for his "Rhymes on the Road," Moore visited the great, but erring and unhappy, author of "Childe Harold," then residing near Venice. It was then that the noble and long-descended bard confided to his charge the autobiography, which was ultimately consigned to the flames, after it had entailed on the Irish melodist infinite trouble, anxiety, and annoyance, and that shortly after the time when the conduct of the individual who acted as his deputy at Bermuda had driven him from England, and involved him in serious pecuniary difficulties and embarrassments. On leaving Italy, Moore betook himself to Paris, where he was treated with high honor and distinguished by a public dinner, which, as a mark of esteem and admiration, was particularly grateful to the heart and feelings of the accomplished exile. While there, he wrote the "Loves of the Angels," containing passages of great beauty, passion, and tenderness, but considered inferior to the former effusions of his versatile muse. This may be accounted for by its publication having been hastened by the announcement of Lord Byron's "Heaven and Earth," understood to be founded on the same passage of Scripture—a very sufficient explanation of its holding a secondary place among its author's productions. His latest work of imagination was the "Epicurean," an Eastern tale in prose, and in a spirit of pure romance.

In 1825, Moore visited Sir Walter Scott at Abbotsford, and was entertained with wonted hospitality by the mighty novelist, who did not fail to conduct his charming and interesting visitor to the Rhymer's Glen, and all the spots renowned in Border history and tradition, which he was accustomed daily to haunt and draw inspiration from. Yet it may fairly be questioned whether the sunny heart and voluptuous imagination of the sentimental love-singer, which had luxuriated in all the gorgeousness of Oriental scenery, and in the meeting of "bright waters" in sweet and happy valleys, would be very deeply impressed while viewing the purple peaks of Eildon, or crossing the "Leader's silver tide," which were the pride and consolation of the "last minstrel's" checkered existence.

In 1825, Moore appeared before the public in the character of a biographer, with the "Life of Sheridan," which, though valuable and amusing, was not considered fully to establish his reputation in his new literary field. Indeed, it was the fashion of the day to say that Moore had murdered the marvelous and witty orator, whose skillfully-prepared and dexterously-delivered jokes had so often made the walls of St. Stephen shake and resound with laughter and merriment. "No!" exclaimed George IV., on hearing this grave charge; "but he has certainly attempted his life." Lord Brougham says, that the frankness with which Moore gave the secret note-books of the famous wit to the world, must almost have made their author shake in his grave.

Four years later, Moore was again an aspirant to public favor, with "Notices of the Life of Lord Byron." From the large space which the poetic peer had during life filled in the eye of the world, and the extraordinary reputation he had left behind him, this work was, and could hardly fail to be, extremely interesting. Much had been expected, however, on account of the close friendship that had existed, and the frank intercourse that had taken place, between the distinguished writer and the hero whose sayings and doings his pen aspired to immortalize. Moreover, the mystery attached to the autobiography that had been destroyed was not forgotten. The literary enterprise, when executed, was not deemed quite satisfactory; it was encompassed with perplexing and insuperable difficulties, and the book was necessarily the reverse of faultless. In fact, even if he had the inclination, it was almost impossible for him to comment with any degree of freedom or severity on the failings and follies of a man with whom he had been long on terms so intimate; even if the danger and delicacy of the arduous task had not been indefinitely increased by respect and consideration for the feelings of many persons then still living.

The notices of Byron's life were followed by "Memoirs of Lord Edward Fitzgerald," whose career had attracted Moore's ardent and most consecrated sympathies. The life of this ill-fated nobleman was written throughout with heart and feeling; and, perhaps, may be taken as the most favorable specimen of its author's prose style. Besides, he had shown his prowess in political and religious controversy, in the "Life of Captain Rock," as also in the "Travels of an Irish Gentleman;" and he contributed a history of Ireland to "Lardner's Cyclopædia." These emanations are characterized by much of the beauty of language, liveliness of remark, and tenderness of sentiment, displayed in his metrical writings, but without being received with similar tokens of approbation. The surpassing charms of his happy and exuberant verse, ever displaying a fancy rich, spirited, elegant, and impassioned, though not sublime, or always immortal, have been universally felt and confessed; the enchantment they produced for a time on the public mind and imagination, was beyond all dispute or question: but with his prose works it was widely different. Whatever their intrinsic merits, they have failed to rank in public interest or estimation with his poetic compositions.

Nevertheless, the nature of some of them, the subjects to which they related, and the principles they sought to maintain, support, and vindicate, were such, that the Irish patriots of the period conceived their author fairly entitled to share in the glories they were acquiring, and the laurels they were reaping in the British Parliament. This conclusion being arrived at, Moore was graciously requested to leave his quiet and peaceful abode in Wiltshire, and appear as a candidate for the representation of Limerick, in order that he might "pursue the triumph and partake the gale." He was not, however, so ambitious of senatorial rank as to accept of an honor, which the peculiar circumstances under which it could have been conferred, and the conditions on which it would have been held, rendered, to say the least, equivocal in character.

Moore, by the favor of his political friends, enjoyed a pension from the crown during the latter years of his life; but they were darkened, and his beaming intellect clouded, by the domestic losses and calamities, which, at this period, he had to endure.

The once gay, vivacious, and captivating poet, died at his residence, Slopperton Cottage, near Devizes, on the 26th of February, 1852, and he was laid at rest in the green church-yard at Bonham.

SIR JOSHUA REYNOLDS

Three months previous to the date when the ashes of Sir Godfrey Kneller mingled with kindred dust, the first Englishman who, according to the eloquent eulogium of Burke, added the praise of the elegant arts to the other glories of his country, was cradled, with time-honored formalities, in a borough town of Devonshire.

Joshua Reynolds was the tenth of the numerous family with which his parents—a worthy and old-fashioned couple—were blessed. His father was a scholar and divine, known and valued in the province for the respectability of his learning, the innocence of his heart, and the simplicity of his mind. Besides, he is stated to have been of so singularly absent a tendency, that once, while performing a journey on horseback, he dropped one of his top-boots by the way, without perceiving the unusual and inconvenient loss he had met with. Doubtless when he arrived at home, this laughable and disastrous incident would furnish his fruitful dame, Theophila, with the text of a diffuse and impassioned curtain-lecture, and, perhaps, make the reverend personage considerably more careful when in future he escaped for a while from his toils and fatigues as head-master of the grammar-school of Plympton. There his distinguished son was born on the 16th of July, 1723; and there he was ere long inspired with the ambition of linking his name indestructibly with that glorious art of which he became so successful a cultivator.

The occasion of the high-fated infant's presentation at the baptismal font was rendered memorable by a mistake so awkward and peculiar, as to furnish reasonable grounds for believing the mental characteristics of the elder Reynolds to have been then at work. In any case, the officiating clergyman was led by some process to pronounce the Christian name of Joseph instead of that by which the child then presented has since been known to the world, as well as registered in the records of fortune and the rolls of fame. On the education of young Reynolds much less attention was bestowed than might have been expected from the circumstances of his birth; and he did not profit to any large extent by such instruction as he received. He did not obtain any great stock of classical knowledge; but his deficiency in this important respect, though never supplied, was, in after days, countervailed and thrown into the background by the information which he had acquired in untiring study of Nature and perseverance in Art, in that commerce with the most refined portion of the British public, of which, for many long years, he had the advantage, and in the constant and familiar intercourse which, during prosperous manhood, he maintained with men of genius, intellect, and erudition. But, however little inclined to pore over Latin and Greek books, his heart was, without loss of time, turned toward an accomplishment which he afterward found of infinitely greater value. Almost in infancy he began to show signs of his vocation for the pursuit which made him one of the most remarkable men, and the greatest painter, of his age; and his first effort was the copying of some drawings made by his sisters. He was then in early boyhood, and he next applied the artistic skill he possessed to the imitation of such prints as illustrated the volumes in his father's library; particularly those in an old Book of Emblems, which was inherited, along with her Dutch blood, from a grandmother, who had come from Holland. The clerical pedagogue did not smile on these juvenile attempts, nor did he look with a propitious eye on the direction his son's talents were taking. However absent scholars may be in regard to other matters, especially those which chiefly concern themselves, they are usually observant enough when the welfare and interests of their children are at stake. Even Adam Warner awoke from day-dreams about the Eureka when he saw the lordly chamberlain whispering soft tales in the ear of his beauteous daughter; and Parson Reynolds, though so much occupied with sage reflections that he could only find time to indicate to his wife by monosyllables whether he would have tea or coffee on an afternoon, opened his eyes to the fact, that Joshua's industry in drawing and coloring, with the rude materials within his reach, contrasted disagreeably with his remissness in attending to the lessons of the school over which he presided. Thus he denounced the boyish essays as the offspring of pure idleness, and the author of them was destined for the medical profession. Though, perhaps, this was decided on with little consideration for his own wishes, Reynolds stated in after life, that if such had been his fortune, he would have exerted himself as strenuously to become an eminent physician as he strove with success to be a great painter. However, the paternal views were suddenly and fortunately changed.

Having, about his eighth year, met with the "Jesuit's Perspective," young Reynolds read and digested its contents with so much earnestness, that he was enabled to execute a drawing of the school-house on the principles asserted in the treatise. This, when exhibited in the family circle, quite astonished the anxious father, who, with gratified pride, pronounced the execution wonderful; and he began to regard the juvenile artist's predilections with comparative complacency. Upon this, Reynolds devoted himself more arduously to his chosen studies, took likenesses of the inmates of the house, improved perceptibly in execution, and quite neglected his school exercises. He was confirmed in his love of art by reading Richardson's "Treatise on Painting," which so captivated and inspired his mind and imagination, that Raphael seemed to him the most marvelous name in ancient or modern annals. Thus charmed and stimulated, he continued to make numerous sketches and portraits, which were recognized by his friends as evidencing progressive improvement. Nothing was now wanting but a field in which to practice and bring to perfection the talents with which he had been bountifully endowed, to confer pleasure on his fellow men, and to refine their tastes.

While Reynolds was in his nineteenth year, a neighbor and acquaintance of the family, observing that a provincial place was too limited a sphere for the proper cultivation of such powers, recommended that the aspiring lad should be placed under proper tuition in London. Accordingly, in the autumn, the future knightly President of the Royal Academy was on his way to the metropolis, and consigned to the care and superintendence of Hudson, who, though at the period much employed in the manufacture of portraits, was not possessed of any surpassing skill or taste in art. A contract was entered into, that if the veteran approved of his pupil's conduct, he was to retain the latter's services for a term of four years; but he reserved the power of discharging the assistant at pleasure. Perhaps, in this position Reynolds was merry enough; for there were other youths in Hudson's studio, and on warm summer days they had opportunities of making agreeable excursions, rambling about the country and admiring the scenery.

While thus situated, Reynolds had the gratification of exchanging courtesies with a famous poet, who had aspired, without any particular success, to excellence in the kindred art of painting. He was attending a public sale of pictures; and just before the hero of the hour raised his voice and brandished his hammer, the name of Pope was passed round, and all respectfully made way for the friend of Bolingbroke. Those who were near held out their hands; and Reynolds being among the number, had the distinction of a gentle shake from those bony fingers which had so often been made the instruments of bitter and brilliant sarcasm. The wheel of time rolled round; the painter, seated among the literary magnates of another generation, still felt pride in relating this interesting little incident; his admiration of the crooked bard was unabated; he was at great pains to procure a fan on which was one of Pope's efforts in painting; and the recollection of their meeting filled him with satisfaction, even when youths, as in the case of Northcote, were pressing forward, through crowds, to indulge in the luxury of touching his own skirt.

Reynolds continued to pursue his artistic career under Hudson's inspection for two years, during which he drew many heads with so unquestionable a success, that he thereby excited and inflamed the jealousy of his instructor, who foretold, with a pang, that his pupil would yet arrive at rare celebrity. At length he executed the portrait of an elderly domestic, who acted as cook in the establishment, which, on being exhibited in the gallery, was immensely applauded for its superiority of style. The praise was by no means grateful to Hudson's ear. Perhaps it was more than flesh and blood could reasonably be expected to bear with patience. In any case, he seized upon the first decent pretext to pick a quarrel with the ambitious juvenile.

The latter had been one day requested to convey a picture to a certain drapery-painter; but as the weather happened to be rainy, he concluded that there would be no harm in delaying its delivery till next morning. At breakfast, Hudson querulously inquired why it had not been taken the evening before, and was informed that the rain had been the cause of the delay.

"Well," he exclaimed, "since you have not obeyed my orders, you must leave my house."

Reynolds pleaded for a brief reprieve, but in vain. He asked to be allowed to write an explanation of the matter, and obtain his father's advice. But Hudson was inexorable; he adhered sternly to his harsh mandate, and Reynolds, going to an uncle who resided at the Temple, thence wrote to his father that he had been dismissed. The latter took the affair into grave consideration, held a sage consultation with his neighbor, Lord Edgecumbe, and directed the young artist to return home. Retirement to the obscurity of Devonshire might delay the progress, but could not altogether conceal the reality, of the talents which were to establish for their possessor so splendid a reputation. His father's limited means rendered some effort for independence imperative; and during the next three years he executed several portraits of much merit, particularly one of a boy reading by a reflected light. When viewing these pieces thirty years afterward, he is said to have lamented that he had made so little progress in art; just as Canova did a few months before his death, when gazing mournfully on his marble statue of Esculapius in a villa near Venice.

Somewhere about 1745, Reynolds took up his quarters for a while at Plymouth Dock, and employed his time in taking portraits of naval officers and other persons in the vicinity. Most of the likenesses then produced were good; but the example of Hudson had placed him at a disadvantage. His sitters were generally represented with one hand inserted in a waistcoat pocket, and the other stiffly holding a hat. One gentleman did, indeed, request to be drawn with his headpiece on, and his desire was complied with; but—alas for the vanity of human wishes!—when the portrait was sent home, and scrutinized by the capricious individual's dame, she discovered, with inexpressible horror, that the artist, true to habit, had placed a hat under the arm in addition to that on the head!

Among those whose features he now transferred to canvas was Miss Chudleigh, afterward the celebrated Duchess of Kingston, a young lady of surpassing beauty, then on a visit in the neighborhood, and a Captain Hamilton, of the Abercorn family, whose portrait was considered admirable. Besides, he made the acquaintance of the future Lord Keppel, and when that gallant personage was appointed Commodore on the Mediterranean Station, the artist was invited to accompany him in the "Centurion."

Reynolds had, some time before, lost his venerable father; and he had now to act entirely on his own judgment and discretion. But having been long and enthusiastically eager to visit Italy, and being in possession of funds sufficient to defray the expense, he availed himself of the friendly proposal, and sailed in May, 1749. Having visited various places of interest, and been introduced, at Algiers, to the Dey, he landed at Port Mahon, in Minorca, where he was treated with much courtesy, and entertained with great hospitality, by the governor. There he added to his skill and means by painting portraits of many officers on the station; but at the same time encountered, and suffered from, an accident of considerable severity. One day as he was refreshing himself with a ride, his horse suddenly took fright, ran off, and rushed wildly over a precipice. The rider was not unhurt by the fall; and indeed his upper lip was so sadly bruised that part of it had to be cut away; so that a scar, which remained visible to the close of his life, was the consequence. Meantime he proceeded to Rome, where he had been advised to place himself under the tuition of Battoni; but on examining the works of that master he deemed it most judicious to trust to his own perception, and concentrate his study on the paintings that had stood the test of time and criticism. In this resolution he persevered, with so little reference to the inclemency of seasons that he was attacked, while pursuing his investigations, with a serious cold. The effect of this mishap was permanent. It brought on the deafness which reduced him to the necessity of using an ear-trumpet while engaged in conversation, and furnished his acquaintance (Goldsmith) with the well-known and oft-quoted lines in the "Retaliation,"—

"When they talked of their Raphaels, Corregios, and stuff,

He shifted his trumpet and only took snuff."

While at Rome, Reynolds was less employed by English travelers than might have been anticipated; and he seems to have considered the time so occupied as being almost lost. Before leaving, however, he executed an approved likeness of himself, and an interesting parody on Raphael's "School of Athens." He remained as long as the state of his finances rendered prudent, and afterward gave it as his mature opinion, that any artist, with large views, should rather live on bread and water than forego advantages never enjoyed a second time, and not to be found but in the Vatican. Michael Angelo he regarded as "the Homer of Painting." On his way home, at the foot of Mont Cenis, he encountered his old master, Hudson, in company with Roubiliac the sculptor. The former hurried on, with hot speed, to gratify his eyes with a sight of the "Eternal City;" and accomplished his purpose so hastily that he arrived at Calais in time to cross in the same packet with the pupil, whose excellence had excited his apprehensions and kindled his ire.

Reynolds had been absent for about three years from England when, in the autumn of 1752, he had the gratification of setting foot on her sacred soil. He immediately went to Devonshire, to recruit his health and inspire vigor from fresh breezes and his native air. Early in the next year he returned to London, and, quartering himself in St. Martin's Lane, commenced his professional career with earnestness and resolution. His talents were such as, if properly exerted, could hardly fail to meet with encouragement and lead on to fortune; and their possessor not only recognized the great fact that unflinching perseverance was essential to success, but maintained the opinion that any one aspiring to excel in art must make it the subject of his thoughts from the time he rises till he goes to bed. Nay, more; he said that those aiming at distinction must work, whether willingly or with reluctance, morning, noon, and night, and expect to find their occupation no pastime, but hard labor. Undoubtedly during youth he carried this wholesome doctrine too far, in asserting that the man would never make a great painter who looked for the Sunday with pleasure, as a day of rest. But it is satisfactory, and ought to be instructive, to understand—thanks, perhaps, to the dying precept of Johnson—that he did not act on the pernicious doctrine to the end of his career.

With all his taste, ease, felicity of invention, and power of rich, harmonious coloring, Reynolds did not acquire his legitimate position without a salutary struggle. His boldness, freedom, and brilliancy were regarded as strange and objectionable novelties. The old dogs began to bark. The portrait of a pupil whom he had brought from Rome, in a Turkish dress, and known as "a boy with a turban," gained notice and excited observation. Hudson, perhaps nourishing the old wound in his breast, declared that the youth's painting was not so good as when he left England; an eminent disciple of Kneller denounced it, as not the least like Sir Godfrey's—it would never answer; and others were by no means sparing in sharp and invidious strictures. The artist was as little guided by such remarks as was the disinherited knight by the well-meant hints of the crowd around the lists at Ashby; but, moving onward undismayed, he soon convinced the public that he would pursue his chosen course and win high renown in doing so. He painted the second Duke of Devonshire with a success which extended his reputation in patrician circles; and universal attention was attracted by the noble picture which he executed of his friend and patron, Lord Keppel. But still his celebrity was too recent to be secure against the winds and tides of capricious fashion, and a rival artist entered the field. This was a Genevan, named Liotard, described as having little skill and no genius, but who, by the patronage of persons of rank, was elevated to an ephemeral and unmerited position. His works were wanting in vigor—in fact, such as ladies paint for amusement; and they might have passed with credit in an amateur exhibition. Such was the man before whom the star of Reynolds, for a moment, paled, ere it shone fully and inextinguishably forth. This unequal competitor had his little day; and then, deserted by those who had mistakenly supported his pretensions, he sank into the obscurity for which nature had intended him, and retreated to the Continent.

Reynolds was a thorough Englishman. In other lands he had, with all his outward coldness, shed tears on hearing the ancient ballad tunes of his country played in the theatre; and his heart must now have swelled with no small pride at the reflection that it was the first time a native of England had been victorious in such a contest. The aspirations which, for years, he had fondly cherished, were now to be gratified; and he could rejoice in the thought that future generations would gaze with wonder on his paintings, and hold his name in veneration. To pursue his career with befitting dignity, he took an advantageous house in Great Newport Street, where he lived for eight years. The grace and felicity of his former efforts brought him abundant employment; his rooms were filled with noble ladies and famous men; and his popularity rapidly grew and increased. He was a diligent observer and student of life and manners, had amassed a large store of general information, and could appreciate the taste and capacity of his sitters sufficiently to speak the appropriate word to each. He ever seized on the happiest attitude, and thus transferred to his canvas the most fascinating glance of the beauty, the liveliest expression of the wit, and the most thoughtful look of the judge or statesman. His confidence in his own powers strengthened with experience; and every new effort was hailed with encouraging applause.

On the occasion of a visit to his native county, Reynolds accidentally laid his hand on Johnson's "Life of Savage;" and standing by the fire, he leant his arm against the mantle-piece, opened the book, and began to look through it. Gradually he became so completely absorbed with the contents, that he continued in this position till he had perused the volume; and then found his arm quite benumbed, his heart almost enchanted, and his curiosity raised to be acquainted with the author. This satisfaction was not long denied him. They met at the house of the daughters of Admiral Cotterell, and Reynolds was as much delighted with the conversation of his great contemporary as he had formerly been interested in his pages. Moreover, he had the good fortune to make a remark which won, with irresistible effect, on the heart of the sage. The ladies were mournfully deploring the death of a friend to whom they were under many obligations; "You have, however, the comfort," suggested Reynolds, with grave politeness, "of being relieved from the burden of gratitude."

"Oh, how shocking and selfish!" exclaimed the sisterhood; but the man who had lived on a groat a day, and stood behind greasy screens to conceal his worn-out clothes, appreciated this remark as being that of a person who thought and decided for himself. He therefore defended its justice in a clear and forcible manner, though, perhaps, without conveying conviction to the minds of the decorous spinsters. At all events, he was so pleased with his new friend that they left the party together. Johnson went and supped at Reynold's house; and thus was commenced an intimacy which was only terminated by death. Johnson became a frequent visitor, and went without ceremony to enjoy the great painter's society, who, on his part, declared that no one had, like his illustrious friend, the faculty of teaching inferior minds the art of thinking.

There is not, perhaps, in the wide world, so full of guile and selfishness, a fairer field for the cultivation of friendship than that which lies between the studio of the painter and the desk of the man of letters. There is little ground for envy, but many incitements to a generous rivalry; and the intercourse must be peculiarly advantageous if the artist is endowed with poetic perception, and the author gifted with an artistic eye. Reynolds and Johnson no doubt experienced, in their respective pursuits, the benefit of their familiar meetings, altogether independently of the pleasure derived from those hours of social enjoyment which were irradiated by the matchless discourse of Burke, and enlivened by the ludicrous displays of Goldsmith. His friendship with Johnson led to Reynolds furnishing three papers for the "Idler"—his first essay in literary composition, and in which may be traced the ideas which grew into his lectures. The effort cost him much thought and trouble: he sat up writing them all night, and had a sharp illness in consequence. Besides this contribution to the "Idler," he supplied some notes to Johnson's "Shakspeare," published in 1705.

The year 1758 was, in a pecuniary point of view, one of the most fortunate that Reynolds ever experienced; and he soon gave signs of his prosperity by purchasing a mansion in Leicester Square, which he inhabited ever after. It was a maxim with him, that an artist who marries is ruined for life; and he seems to have guarded the passes to his heart with singular vigilance, as we do not read of any fair damsel making havoc in its chambers, though it is quite possible that some early disappointment may have created this rare aversion to matrimony. But whatever the origin of his prejudice on this point, there is no question that a sensible woman who, without being ambitious of prematurely dissipating her natural roses at midnight parties, can take a becoming part in the innocent gayeties which brighten the human heart, is a pearl of price; and why the artist should be the worse of such an enviable companion any more than a poet or orator, is a question which does stagger plain men, as it would, perhaps, have puzzled the most philosophic of British painters. He acted on his principle by living and dying a bachelor; but, in accordance with the custom at that period pursued by men of the middle class, he placed one of his sisters at the end of his board and in charge of his domestic concerns: thus attempting to secure the comforts of a home without being subject to connubial responsibility. Miss Reynolds, it appears, scarcely realized or sustained the character of a perfect spinster. She was possessed of great wit and talent; and though remarkable for her good sense, she was too much given to essays of her skill in poetry and painting to make a model housekeeper. Thus the internal affairs were not conducted with any excessive taste or regularity; and the table was distinguished chiefly by a rough plenty; little regard being paid to order or arrangement. The dinner was generally a scramble, in which the host took little or no concern; and the guests looked sharply after their own interests. There was no splendor but great abundance. Ease was more valued than comfort or elegance. Nevertheless, Reynolds had furnished his new residence with much propriety, besides adding a handsome gallery for the exhibition of his paintings, and an elegant dining-room, often the scene of "the feast of reason and the flow of soul." There the literary giant of the day rolled his unwieldy body, bit his dirty nails, and poured out his copious talk; though often a little cowed by being face to face with that profound political sage and prophet who alone could encounter the huge author of "Rasselas" with advantage. Side by side were the greatest actor of the day, and the restorer of that English ballad-poetry which fascinated the young genius of the mightiest of dead and the most accomplished of living novelists. In an uneasy posture, "staring right on," was that extraordinary being "who could write like an angel, but talk like poor Poll." With eyes reverentially fixed on men whom he could admire without comprehending, stood Boswell, the minute chronicler of their sayings and doings; while the master of the house—mild, gentle, and unassuming, round in feature, florid in complexion, and of middle stature—listened with lively, but calm and refined intelligence, to the colloquial conflict of the wonderful specimens of the human race whose features his easel has, in immortal colors, transmitted to posterity.

It is doubtless a proud day with most persons who have struggled into affluence, when they can set up an equipage of their own. Pepys, in his gossiping diary, relates the mighty pleasure he felt when that joyous day arrived for him; when he could disdain the humble shelter of a hackney-coach, and drive about the park in his own chariot, even at the disadvantage of having his pretty wife eyed with menacing admiration by a royal duke. Reynolds conceived that the time had now arrived when he might decorously indulge in a carriage, which he had magnificently carved and gilded, the four seasons being emblazoned on its panels. The pride and propriety of Miss Reynolds were shocked at this display. "It is far too showy," she complained with good reason. "What!" exclaimed the owner, as he regarded his purchase with calm complacency—"would you have a carriage like an apothecary's?"

In 1762, the health of Reynolds rendering relaxation and a rural excursion necessary, he repaired to Devonshire, accompanied by Dr. Johnson, who thus had a favorable opportunity of seeing Plymouth, in which he expressed particular interest. Falstaff regaling himself with cheese and carraway pippins in Justice Shallow's orchard, or the Spectator enjoying the ancient hospitality of Coverley Hall, are hardly more than equal in interest to the sage of Bolt Court, who knew human nature only as exhibited in the streets and suburbs of London, being refreshed with an adventure in the country. The two friends were received with no small respect by men of rank, learning, and distinction; and entertained at the seats of several noblemen in the west of England. One of their hosts indulged Johnson with a feast on new honey and clouted cream, of which the moralist partook in such quantities, that the hospitable individual grew exceedingly alarmed for the consequences. Reynolds bore off a prize of another kind—a large jar of old nut-oil, which was carried home in his coach as a valuable trophy. The change of air had a most beneficial effect on his health, and he returned to town in a condition to pursue his labors without interruption.

Reynolds was an ardent lover of his profession; his pride in art was high, and he was ever ready, when there was occasion, to stand forward in its defense. But his character was cold and stately; he deemed it impossible for two artists in the same line to associate in friendship: he thought Poetry the twin-sister of Painting, and found his companions chiefly among literary men. It was natural, therefore, that when the Literary Club was established in 1764, he should have been one of its members. A man, however, is known by the company he keeps; and Reynolds was disagreeably surprised to hear himself spoken of as "one of the wits." Perhaps the term did not convey the most pleasing sensation to a person with a coach of his own and six thousand a year; and he exclaimed, in alarm, "Why do they call me a wit? I never was a wit in my life!"

His commissions had gradually become so numerous, that he found it necessary to have several assistants to work out the minor details: he had arrived on an enviable eminence; and though artists of ability made their appearance, he still maintained his supremacy, and constantly struck out wonders to vindicate his claim to the favor of the public. In 1766 he painted the Queen of Denmark, before she sailed on her ill-fated voyage. Coming events cast their shadows before; and he never went without finding the hapless princess in tears. Reynolds increased in wealth and reputation; his enthusiasm for art never cooled into indifference, and he was never so happy as when putting life into canvas. He rose betimes, and commenced operations; he spoke little when occupied, but painted rapidly for six hours, and devoted the remainder to society. He was animated by warm affections, and had a strong love for children.

Reynolds was not one of the originators of the Royal Academy; but in 1768, when it was instituted, he was waited on by West, and requested to give his aid in promoting the objects which the undertaking was intended to serve. He was rather doubtful whether the scheme was likely to be favored by Fortune; and he was one of those who had no relish for engaging in an enterprise,

> "Save when her humorous ladyship was by
>
> To teach him safety."

It was, therefore, after considerable hesitation, and a conference of two hours, that he was persuaded to accompany the American artist. Then ordering his carriage, he drove to the place where the promoters were assembled. On entering the room he was saluted by all present as "President;" but being still convinced that the scheme would prove a delusion, he declined to accept the honor thus voted to him by acclamation, till he had consulted Burke and Johnson, who advised him to consent. The king, whose aid had at first been regarded as doubtful, came forward to offer the Academy his royal patronage; and that it might have the semblance of greater dignity, its president was forthwith invested with the rank of knighthood. The latter was, by no means, backward in fulfilling the functions with which he had been so cautious in burdening himself. Of his own accord he undertook the duty of preparing and reading discourses on the principles and practice of art, for the instruction and guidance of the students. Of these he wrote fifteen; the delivery of which extended over several years. They were pronounced by Sir Thomas Lawrence to be "golden precepts, which are now acknowledged as canons of universal taste."

In 1773 Reynolds paid visits to Paris and Oxford. At the latter place he received, amidst much applause, the honorary degree of Doctor of Laws, in company with Dr. Beattie, of whom he produced a celebrated picture on returning to London. About the same date he went to his native district, and was elected mayor of Plympton. This mark of esteem from his townsmen seems to have given him particular pleasure. Accidentally meeting with the king shortly after, at Hampton Court, he stated that it had afforded him more satisfaction than any distinction he had met with: "Always," he added, with the skill of a courtier, "excepting that which your majesty graciously conferred on me—the honor of knighthood."

Sir Joshua was chosen a member of the Academy of Florence, and, in accordance with its rules, required to furnish a portrait of himself. This he accomplished with his wonted success; and it was added with pride to their interesting collection.

In 1780 he commenced a series of allegorical figures for the window of the New College chapel at Oxford. These were followed by the "Nativity," which being sold to the Duke of Rutland, perished in a fire at Belvoir Castle. About this time he made a tour to inspect the Continental galleries. On returning, he sustained a paralytic attack, which much alarmed his friends, but his recovery was speedy; and he quickly proved that his powers had suffered no decay, by the production of his "Fortune-teller," his portrait of Miss Kemble, and that of Mrs. Siddons, in the full might of her beauty and power, as the Tragic Muse. While engaged with the latter, he wrote his name on the border of her robe; and on the great actress looking at the words, and smiling, he remarked, with one of his most courtly bows, that he could not lose such an opportunity of sending his name down to posterity on the hem of her garment. When at work, he is said to have been in the habit of using enormous quantities of snuff. Thus, while occupied with the large picture of the Marlborough family at Blenheim, a servant was ordered by the duchess to sweep up the snuff that he had let fall on the carpet. However, when the man entered with a broom, Sir Joshua quietly requested him to let it remain till he had finished; observing, that the dust would do more harm to his painting, than the snuff could possibly do to the carpet.

On the death of Allan Ramsay, the king's painter, Reynolds was, at the request of his majesty, induced to accept the vacant office. He soon after produced "Love unloosing the Zone of Beauty," and a portrait of the notorious Duke of Orleans. Then he gave his time and attention to painting the "Infant Hercules Strangling the Serpents," for the Empress of Russia; who acknowledged his attention by a note of thanks from her own imperial hand, a gold snuff-box, on which was her likeness, and a purse of fifteen hundred guineas.

SIR JOSHUA REYNOLDS AT BLENHEIM.

Sir Joshua had now reached his sixty-sixth year; his fame was high; his influence on the taste and refinement of the country was not disputed; and his artistic powers remained unimpaired. His career had indeed been characterized by the strictness and temperance essential to the possession of "a healthy body and a vigorous mind;" he had realized a fortune; he had associated with the noble and beautiful of the land; and his wealth, his heavy purse, and hospitable table, gave him dignity in the eyes not only of many who were incapable of appreciating his merits, but of others to whom his fine abilities were no mystery. But his days were numbered. In the month of July, 1789, while finishing a portrait of Lady Hertford, he was aware of a sudden loss of sight in his left eye; and, laying down his pencil for the last time, he sat for a while in sad and pensive reflection. Goldsmith had already been laid at rest in the Temple Church; the eyes of Burke had overflowed with tears, and his voice faltered by the death-bed of Johnson; and the immortal painter was ere long to follow. He in a short time altogether lost the sight of his left eye, and determined to paint no more; yet under this affliction he strove to appear happy, cheerful, and resigned. His illness was borne with much fortitude, and whatever he had to suffer was endured without complaint or irritability. He amused and diverted himself in his drawing-room by changing the position of his pictures, and exhibiting them to his friends. Besides, like some imprisoned knight of old, he took a fanciful liking for a little bird, which became so tame and docile that it perched on his hand, while he fed and talked to it almost as he would have done to a human being. At length, one bright summer morning, the feathered warbler made its escape by an open window; and Sir Joshua was so inconsolable for the loss, that he roamed for hours about Leicester Square in the hope of seeing and recovering so harmless and cheerful a companion.

On the occasion of the gold medals being bestowed on the students of the Academy in 1790, Sir Joshua went thither for the last time, with all due pomp and circumstance, to deliver an address. With unabated admiration, he recalled to their memory the triumphs achieved by the genius of his great idol, and concluded by earnestly desiring that the last words he should pronounce from the presidential chair might be the name of Michael Angelo. The crowd being unusually large, a beam in the floor gave way with a loud crash. All rushed to the door, stumbling over each other, except the venerable president, who remained silent, composed, and dignified. Fortunately no damage was done, and the proceedings were resumed.

Sir Joshua offered to the Royal Academy his collection of paintings by the great masters at a low price. But, much to his mortification and amazement, his proposal was declined; and he exhibited them publicly in the Haymarket for the benefit of his servant Ralph. This transaction gave rise to the suspicion that Reynolds shared in the profits; and two lines of Butler—

> "A squire he had whose name was Ralph,
> Who in the adventure went one-half,"—

were applied with audacious and merciless malevolence. He was soon beyond the reach of such assailants and their weapons of offense. After a visit to Beaconsfield, the residence of his mighty friend Burke, his health and spirits sunk with the rapidity which frequently heralds a speedy dissolution; and on the 23d of February, 1792, he expired, with little apparent pain, in the sixty-ninth year of his prosperous life. His body was laid in St. Paul's Cathedral, by the side of Sir Christopher Wren; and a monument, graven by Flaxman, has since been erected to his memory.

SIR FRANCIS CHANTREY

The artistic genius of England, however potent and exuberant it may be, has never been so freely or prominently displayed in sculpture as in poetry or painting; nor has it had equal encouragement. The creations of the sculptor's fancy and the emanations of his skill, unquestionable as may be their merits and real their beauties, have never ranked very high in the favor of the multitude. Many, whose sympathy might otherwise be followed by more substantial tokens, understand full well that a portrait costs less, and is more readily appreciated by their neighbors, than a marble bust; and even with those few who pride themselves in rivaling the Medici in their patronage of art, and lay the flattering unction to their souls that they know something about it, the popularity of sculpture is by no means excessive. But the name of Chantrey is one which his countrymen have reason to regard with patriotic pride and satisfaction. He formed his style on the beauty and manliness of his native land; he was thoroughly her own. His taste in this respect was created when the inhabitant—while a boy—of a quiet and secluded village; and it was adhered to with splendid results when he was depicting statesmen, warriors, orators, and poets—our Pitts, Wellingtons, Grattans, and Scotts. Instead of struggling in vain to recall cold shapes and uncongenial visions from remote antiquity and distant realms, he embodied in simple but fascinating works, for the instruction and gratification of native talent and taste, the life, manners, and costume which came around him in his daily existence. Thus his works are not only more popular than those of the sculptors who had preceded him, but they are fitted to excite no small portion of that sympathy which one feels when gazing on the canvas, whereon the features of some distinguished man or beautiful woman have been gloriously portrayed by the pencil of Reynolds or Raeburn. His success in this line first secured him general notice; and they are not inferior to any that ever were produced; while his statues executed for public places, with those singularly plain and unadorned pedestals, wisely calculated not to detract from the effect of the more important part of the composition, exhibit surpassing grace and vigor of outline. The story of a great sculptor's life can, with rare exceptions, be soon told; his existence being unmarked except by the works which he sends into the busy world from his solitary, secluded, and laborious studio.

Francis Chantrey was born on the 7th of April, 1782, at Norton, a little village in the county of Derby. His father, a stout and sagacious yeoman, cultivated with frugal industry the small estate he was fortunate enough to possess; and the future sculptor doubtless delighted, when a sportive child, to lend a helping hand in the operations of the season. The worthy farmer died when his son was in boyhood, little anticipating that the latter was destined to touch the hearts of men by a process and after a fashion which were hardly dreamt of in the philosophy of the tillers of Derbyshire soil. Indeed, hardly any thing could have been more improbable; for unless it were the statues in the quaint, curious, and terraced old garden of some "large-acred" aristocrat, he had no opportunity of gazing on any specimens of art likely to excite his imagination or guide his aspirations. Nevertheless, at an almost infantine period of existence he gave indications of his natural bent; and ere long, in communion with nature and all its beauties, he was inspired by the fine feelings and ambitious desires which afterward animated his spirit to splendid efforts, and nerved his hand to resolute toil in completing the conceptions of his ardent brain. The contemplation of natural objects in all their simplicity filled his young heart and memory with lovely and charming images, which in other days contributed to his success, established his reputation, and laid the foundation of his lasting fame.

Chantrey was about eight years old when he lost his father, and was thus early deprived of the paternal influence and direction. His mother soon after yielded herself, and such charms as she could boast of, for a second time, into matrimonial bonds; and though she reared her fanciful boy with great care and tenderness, and survived to witness his artistic achievements, perhaps his exhibitions of talent and inclination were less attended to than they might otherwise have been. However, he was educated with the ordinary solicitude, though to what precise extent does not appear.

On leaving school, he was occupied with agricultural operations. Like the Scottish poet, Burns, he could hold the plow to some purpose, as in after life he used to relate. Besides, he accomplished feats in mowing; in the barn wielded his flail with signal prowess, and, doubtless, found favor in the eyes of those laughing rustic beauties, who look so enchanting and leap joyously at hay-makings and harvest-homes. But whether his friends and acquaintances regarded him as one *gaudentem patrios findere sarculo agros*, or the reverse, he had long since began to develop a turn for art, by making various models in clay for amusement, though without any idea that it would ever create for him a splendid reputation, and conduct him to a position of dignity and honor. At this period, no doubt, he caught among those steep Derby Hills, celebrated in verse, that love of field-sports which ever actuated him. He liked the exercise and delighted in the recreation. He became a keen fisher, an excellent shot, and had a fancy for dogs. In after life, and on fitting occasions, he was almost as indefatigable in rural sports as in his professional exertions; and in the indulgence of his humor in this respect he was not daunted or deterred by unpropitious weather.

When Chantrey had arrived in his seventeenth year, his relations deemed it proper to take his prospects into their serious consideration; and they came to the conclusion of placing him in an attorney's office at Sheffield. Thither, therefore, he was conducted with that object; and had it been realized, his artistic predilections might speedily have altogether vanished; but

> "There's a divinity that shapes our ends,
> Rough-hew them as we may."

CHANTREY'S EARLY STUDIES.

The intention of Chantrey's guardians and his apparent destination were changed by an accident, which, though seemingly trifling in itself, was of the utmost importance in his career. He was passing along the street, and staring about with all the wonder of a youthful peasant, when suddenly some figures in the window of a shop arrested his eye, and filled his heart with an irrepressible longing to be a carver of wood. This wish he repeated with so much ardor and earnestness, that his friends saw reason to accede to a desire, which was evidently the result of no mere ephemeral sentiment. They had, of course, as little idea of sculpture as they had of the moon, or the north pole, or the Chinese empire. A picture, indeed, they could have admired. A lady shining on the painter's canvas, in all the pride of gems and rich attire, would have raised their wonder: but the severity of marble catches not the popular fancy; and had the boy's tendency been explained, they would still have been in the dark as to what he would be at. Luckily, common sense taught them that it would be downright stupidity to place at the dreary desk a lad whose heart was set upon a very different occupation from that of copying deeds. They, therefore, consented to his being apprenticed to a wood-carver in the town; and he entered on that course which led him on, from small beginnings, to affluence and celebrity. It happened that at his new master's house he had the good fortune to make the acquaintance of a distinguished draughtsman in crayon, and immediately exhibited a lively interest in that individual's occupations. He took infinite pleasure in seeing him paint, and was careful to make himself as useful and agreeable as was in his power. In this way he soon felt ambitious of following art as a profession, in some higher field than that to which his labors were then confined. He had already made all the progress in carving which, under the circumstances, could be achieved by skill, perseverance, and enthusiasm. During the intervals of business he did not waste or dissipate an hour of his precious time, but was constantly at study; and even at the midnight hour he might have been found in his lodgings, with a light burning, engaged with groups and figures, and working with the utmost spirit and the rarest diligence.

This system did not exactly quadrate with the views of his employer, who, naturally enough, wished his pupil to be a workman and not an artist. Moreover, Chantrey, finding his tastes in this respect perpetually thwarted, and his desire becoming uncontrollable, grew much too enthusiastic in his aspirations to be longer limited or restrained by ordinary circumstances. Therefore, though only six months of his term of servitude remained unexpired, with the impatience of genius he gave his master all the wealth he possessed to cancel the indentures, gained a little money by taking portraits, repaired to London, and, thus thrown into the mighty vortex, determined to triumph. But with the hereditary caution and common sense, which were finely exhibited by him throughout life, he made "the hardest circumstance a helper and a slave," and at first sought employment as assistant to a wood-carver, that he might live by the craft he had resolved to leave, while pursuing those studies that were so nobly rewarded, rather than make any premature attempt to win that fame which he instinctively felt must one day be his in no small measure.

He reached the metropolis in his twenty-second year, and shortly after his arrival was induced to pay a visit to Ireland, with the intention of making a tour through that country; but while in Dublin he suffered so severely from a fever, that his life was for some time despaired of. Fortunately, he was restored to health, and returned to London, having during the illness lost his hair, which he never recovered. His appearance was fine and prepossessing; his mouth was beautifully formed; and he was complimented on bearing a remarkable resemblance to the greatest of English dramatists. In disposition he was frank, fearless, and communicative; and his affability and familiarity in company were acknowledged: but, at the same time, he was a man of the world, and would never, for a momentary triumph, commit himself by a conversational indiscretion.

On returning from the "Green Isle," and having about the same period made an excursion to the Continent, he devoted himself with zeal, anxiety, and earnestness, to his professional studies and pursuits. He still continued the occupation of a certain portion of his time as a carver, and executed several figures in wood, which are still in existence as interesting memorials of the great sculptor's earlier career. Doubtless he had his struggles, and did not forget them when better times came. On the contrary, he was ever prompt to encourage rising artists; he excused their shortcomings, and recommended their works; and when unable otherwise to serve them, though not in any respect negligent of his pecuniary concerns, he was not slow to use his purse for that purpose. Neglecting no means which might aid him in ascending the steep and slippery pathways of fame, he turned his attention to portrait-painting, and obtained some notice on account of the success of his efforts. But, like Pope, he found an insuperable barrier to excellence in the defectiveness of his sight.

Meantime he had continued his exertions and improved his powers in that department of art with which his name is now associated, by modeling the human form in clay, and arraying it with pieces of drapery, studying attentively the best and most picturesque attitudes in which it could be represented. One of his first works was a bust of Mr. Raphael Smith the artist, whose paintings had exercised so much influence on his early career; but it was that of the celebrated Horne Took which gained him fame in the metropolis. Then appeared his colossal head of Satan, which, by its gaze of dark and malignant despair, attracted notice; and the artist had reason to look to the future with hope.

When Flaxman ventured on marrying a very accomplished woman, Sir Joshua Reynolds shook his head at the perpetration of such a piece of eccentricity, and frankly told the struggling sculptor that he had thereby ruined himself for life. The spirit of prophecy did not, however, rest on

Leicester Square, for to the inspiration of his wife Flaxman attributed his subsequent successes. Example is more powerful than precept; and Chantrey profiting, perhaps, by that so spiritedly set by his more classical contemporary, resolved on taking a similar step.

In 1811 he married his cousin, who brought him so considerable a fortune, that he was enabled to pursue the success he had achieved with a feeling of greater security; and he was soon intrusted by the city of London to execute the statue of George the Third, to be placed in the council-chamber at Guildhall, as well as with many private commissions, which added to his reputation.

He now undertook a professional tour in Scotland, and executed, besides other works, statues of the famous Lord Melville and Lord President Blair, as also an admirable bust of Professor Playfair, for Edinburgh; and on returning, he was commissioned by Government to execute some monuments for St. Paul's Cathedral.

About this date, Chantrey had the penetration to perceive and the fortune to secure in Allan Cunningham, the popular biographer of British artists, an assistant who united literary capacity and a fertile pen to the shrewdness and indefatigability usually supposed to appertain to the natives of North Britain. That Scottish adventurer, the son of a gardener to the person from whom Burns rented his farm, after having been apprenticed to a builder, composed a volume of songs, and came to push his fortune in London. He was now engaged by Chantrey, who had a sharp eye to his own interest, as clerk in his studio, and superintendent of his works.

At the conclusion of the war, Chantrey made a journey to Paris, which he had previously visited at the peace of Amiens, and inspected the various artistic works in the Louvre with much interest. From this point his progress in public esteem was steady and gratifying. On returning from the Continent he commenced the monument of the Two Sisters for Lichfield Cathedral; and when this exquisite specimen of his skillful fancy was exhibited at the Royal Academy in 1817, it was regarded as marvelous for its grace, pathos, and beauty. The press to see it was unprecedented; mothers wept over the representation; children lovingly kissed the figures; and the effect it produced on the minds of beholders was deep, impressive, and enduring. Soon after he produced the statue of Lady Louisa Russell, daughter of the Duke of Bedford, fondling a dove in her bosom. She stands on tiptoe; and the attitude of the figure is said to be so singularly natural, that a little child of three years old coming into the sculptor's studio held up its little hands to the figure, and addressed it under the impression that the form was a living one.

In 1818, Chantrey was worthily elected a member of the Royal Academy, and as his presentation work executed a bust of West, its venerable president. Becoming about the same time a member of the Royal Society, he presented a bust of the celebrated Sir Joseph Banks, then president. Next year he went to Italy, and while at Rome he had much friendly and familiar intercourse with Canova and Thorwaldsen. With the former he enacted the amicable ceremony of exchanging cloaks on parting.

In 1820, Chantrey's admiration of Sir Walter Scott induced him to request the northern poet to sit for his bust. This being agreed to, it was finished in 1822, and presented to the illustrious bard six years later, on condition of his sitting for another, which was accordingly executed. It ultimately passed into the possession of Sir Robert Peel. These are by many considered not only the most felicitous of Chantrey's busts, but the most striking portraits of the great Borderer's variable countenance. The original has been viewed by multitudes at Abbotsford, always with the highest admiration by those most qualified to judge of its merits. The ample forehead, so full of thought and sagacity; the penetrating eye, which had looked with rapture on many a frowning fortress and fair landscape, and the mouth, grave but humorous, are portrayed with rare and fascinating skill. The whole face is represented with fine effect, and has altogether the expression likely to be produced when Chantrey was chiseling, and laughing merrily at some happy remark which had just escaped from the "Great Unknown."

The few years following that on which this memorable sitting occurred, were the busiest of the eminent sculptor's life. Between 1823 and 1826 he is stated to have received the largest number of commissions, and to have labored in their execution with intense devotion and exemplary industry. Nor was he without another kind of encouragement, which, whatever may be said to the contrary by the very persons who would most loudly rejoice in having it, has always proved strangely fascinating to the imaginations of men of talent. Royal and patrician favor was freely bestowed upon him throughout his career; and he knew how to use without abusing it. He enjoyed the countenance of successive sovereigns, was distinguished by the honor of knighthood, and had the comfort of believing that George the Fourth, who, with all his faults, understood something of such matters, appreciated his artistic genius. When this statue was erected on the grand staircase of Windsor Castle, his Majesty, patting Chantrey familiarly on the back, said, "I have reason to be obliged to you; for you have immortalized me."

Among the numerous and admirable statues which attest Chantrey's power and success in this branch of his art, a few may be mentioned: as that of William Pitt, in Hanover Square; George the Fourth, in Trafalgar Square;

James Watt, in Westminster Abbey; and the Duke of Wellington, in front of the Royal Exchange. Watt's statue at Glasgow, Roscoe's at Liverpool, and that of Canning in the hall of the latter town, have, as draped figures, rarely been surpassed. Dalton's statue at Manchester, exhibited in 1837, is likewise thought to be of great merit; and one of his early, though great, monumental efforts was that of Perceval, in All Saints' Church, Northampton. But there are seen, elsewhere than in his own country, monuments from his hand to commemorate the deeds, the virtues, and achievements of the departed great. He furnished an equestrian statue of Sir Thomas Munro to adorn Madras; and for the State-house of Boston he executed a statue of Washington, which is ever mentioned with praise and honor. The hero of the War of Independence stands erect, and wrapped up in thought. The costume, which the sculptor knew well how to deal with, is a military cloak, which displays the historical figure to advantage; and the effect is altogether good and imposing.

Chantrey's genius was most prolific and successful in busts. It is stated, that such was his art, that he could generally seize on the likeness of a head in an hour; but, both in his conceptions and in working them out, he was particularly fastidious. He was singularly quick and skillful in seizing the very best expressions which the countenances of his sitters were capable of presenting.

In 1839 a perceptible and melancholy change came over the famous sculptor; and at length, on the 25th of November, 1841, he expired. He left a large fortune, the result of his industry; and munificently destined it to the service and promotion of the fine arts in his native land. With a view to its responsible application to the intended purpose, he constituted the President and Council of the Royal Academy his trustees forever.

In his works, Chantrey trusted entirely to form and effect; and his dislike to ornament appears to have been almost excessive. His successful efforts were the result of deep reflection, a fine taste, and a noble imagination. He strove to exhibit the perfections of nature, and to impart an air of grandeur to all his productions. He commenced art where Art itself began. Nature was, from first to last, his chief study, the safe school in which he learned his art, and the exhaustless fountain from which he drew the inspiration that carried him onward to lasting fame as a truly English and really great sculptor. He thought that an artist should daily ponder what to avoid, as well as what to imitate; and unlike his predecessors, who were perpetually striving to rival the productions of by-gone ages, he wisely aspired rather to guide the future than follow the past. He had imbibed in youth a fondness for landscape scenery, which he could represent with success; and he made many interesting drawings when traveling to view the marbles and pictures in Italy.

He was plain and unpretending in manner; and, as became so great a man, above all little affectations in society, which, however, he liked and relished. Under his own roof he was distinguished by hospitality and kindliness of spirit; and his house was frequently the resort of men who had won renown in art, science, or literature.

SIR CHRISTOPHER WREN

The architectural skill and superiority of this illustrious man were most conspicuously displayed in the age which his rich genius adorned. A multitude of buildings bore honorable testimony to the fertility of his brain, and the success of his undertakings, at a time when a terrible devastation had rendered such services as he rendered to his country peculiarly necessary; and later generations have confessed with high pride and admiration, that the inscription, *"Si quæris monumentum circumspice,"* has lost none of its point.

The pious architect of so many churches was closely connected by birth with the ecclesiastical establishment, whose edifices he did so much to improve and beautify. The family to which he belonged was of Danish extraction, but had been settled on English ground long ere it produced the most famous representative of the name. From a branch planted in Warwickshire came Sir Christopher's grandfather, who traded and flourished as a mercer in the city of London, and left two sons. The elder obtained the bishopric of Ely, suffered and survived persecution, and went down to the grave in peace, after many trials and vicissitudes. The ambition of the other was seemingly less lofty in degree, and his existence less checkered. However, he became a royal chaplain, dean of Windsor, and rector of Knoyle, in Wiltshire, and had the good fortune to marry one of those young ladies known and sighed for as heiresses. In due time, on the 20th of October, 1632, Christopher Wren was born at East Knoyle.

Like many destined to eminence, the future architect was an exceedingly weak, small, and delicate child; and more than ordinary care was required in rearing him. From this cause he was for several years educated by a domestic tutor in his father's house, which at this period received in its oak hall the Elector Palatine. Wren took care to recall to memory the pretty long visit, when he afterward addressed to that prince a rather high-flown epistle, calling attention to some of his youthful inventions, among which were the instrument for writing with two pens and the machine for sowing corn. The boy showed much fondness for classical learning, and was sent to Westminster School to pursue his studies for a while, under the auspices of Dr. Busby. There he exhibited his remarkable powers of mind, as well as a strong liking for the pursuits of mathematics and astronomy, rather than the useful art with which his name was afterward associated. But his father was a man of talent and ingenuity, and of such architectural taste as to have attracted the notice of Charles the First, to whom he was chaplain in ordinary. This circumstance, in all probability, gave Wren's mind a bias toward the profession in which he achieved the triumphs on which his fame chiefly rests, and led to his raising up, in the face of the world, visible and enduring monuments of his greatness. Every step of his juvenile career, however, was marked by the vigor, prudence, and intelligence befitting one destined for European celebrity.

At the age of fourteen Wren was removed to Oxford and entered at Wadham College, where he was speedily recognized as "a rare and early prodigy of universal science," and distinguished by much attention. He proved his mathematical knowledge by writing on spherical trigonometry; he invented several instruments; he translated Oughtred's "Geometrical Dialling" into Latin; and at the instance of Sir Charles Scarborough, a celebrated physician and mathematician, he formed some admirable architectural models from pasteboard. In his eighteenth year he took the degree of Bachelor of Arts, and soon after published an algebraical tract relating to the Julian period. While he was thus achieving academic distinction, Wren's pillow was visited by a dream, which Aubrey deemed not unworthy of being chronicled and recorded. He was staying at his father's residence in Wiltshire, in the year 1651; and one night, among the visions which his brain conjured up in sleep, he saw a great battle in a market-place unknown to him. He marked the bloody strife for victory, the rapid flight for safety, and the keen pursuit for vengeance; and among those who sought to escape the cruel carnage he perceived a young cousin of his own, who had formerly gone with the king into Scotland. Probably, on waking, he thought little more of the matter; but next evening, the kinsman, whose retreating form had been so strangely presented to his sleeping fancy, appeared unexpectedly, after dusk, at the rectory-house, and surprised its inmates with the startling news of the king's forces having sustained a defeat at Worcester, where he had been. Surprise was, of course, depicted on the fair and intelligent countenance of the Oxford scholar, at an occurrence which seemed so natural a sequel to his dream of the previous night.

But Wren wasted not much time in musing over dreams. He was so busy and enthusiastic in the pursuit of knowledge, and so dexterous in turning it to account, that he was spoken of as a "miracle of a youth." He soon took the degree of Master of Arts, and was elected a Fellow of All Souls. He was exemplary in his conduct, and regular and temperate in his habits.

The great abilities and scientific acquirements of the Wiltshire miracle becoming widely known, he was, about his twenty-fifth year, appointed Professor of Astronomy in the Gresham College. About the time of his entrance upon its duties, this blushing youth, as he frankly described himself in one of his lectures, had a memorable interview with Cromwell, whose son-in-law, being fond of mathematics, had sought the learned professor's acquaintance, and cultivated it by frequent invitations to his house. While dining there one day, he suddenly found himself face to face with the mighty Protector, who stalked in without ceremony, and took his place at table. After a while he fixed his eyes on the future architect to the kings of the house of Stuart.

"Your uncle has long been confined to the Tower," he remarked after a pause, during which he keenly surveyed the short but dignified person of the youth.

"He has," replied Wren, with some stateliness; "but he bears his affliction with patience and resignation."

"He may come out, if he will," said Cromwell.

"Will your highness permit me to tell him so?" asked Wren, with eagerness.

"Yes, you may," said the Lord Protector.

Wren seized an early opportunity of retiring, and, with something of boyish delight, hurried to his venerable relative with the glad tidings; but the imprisoned prelate disdained the thought of obtaining liberty from the great usurper, and, after denouncing the proposal with ardent indignation, declared that he was determined to tarry the Lord's leisure, and owe deliverance to Him only. The Restoration soon after set him free.

Wren resigned his chair at Gresham College when promoted to the Savilian Professorship of Astronomy at Oxford, where had for years existed the club out of which arose the Royal Society, of which he became a member, and afterward president. His reputation as a successful cultivator of the sciences had already extended his reputation to foreign lands, when he gloriously proved his possession of a very different and more popular kind of accomplishment. He had previously attracted the attention of the king, who must have been aware that the youth had been unostentatiously storing his mind with that minute knowledge of architecture which proved his source of power; and at the age of twenty-eight he was summoned to Whitehall, and informed that the time had arrived for putting his powers to the proof. He was appointed to assist at the public works then contemplated: namely, the building of a new palace at Greenwich, the embellishment of

Windsor Castle, and the completion of old St. Paul's, whose interior had been used as a stable by Cromwell's troopers, and its beautiful pillars defaced and applied to the most sordid purposes. The Government were in no haste to commence operations. Perhaps

> "The delay was wrought by want of thought,
> As well as want of heart."

At all events, Wren remained unemployed for two long years; and at the end of that period, delay having done its work, and there appearing no prospect of his talents being in requisition, he manifested symptoms of impatience. Under such circumstances ambitious spirits are not seldom troublesome, and Wren, no doubt, bore himself like other people; but his complaints were cut short by the offer of an office at Tangier, whither he was requested to go and direct the defenses of the harbor and citadel. The young architect did not pause long to consider the course he should pursue: an ample salary was indeed rather tempting; but, with characteristic decision, he declined the appointment, and returned to Oxford.

The condition of St. Paul's, however, was such as could not be altogether disregarded. Soldiers had converted the body of the ancient church into quarters for their horses; the beautiful pillars of Inigo Jones's portico had been hewed and broken down, and large portions of the roof had fallen in. The spectacle it presented was woeful in the extreme, and could no longer be overlooked; and, accordingly, Wren was commissioned to survey the building and furnish plans for its complete restoration.

While preparing designs with that view, he made a tour to France for the purpose of widening and improving his conception of architecture, and visited the most admired works of the greatest professors of his art in that country. In Paris he viewed, and made drawings of, the various edifices, and took due notice of every thing likely to elevate his ideas and improve his taste. He had, moreover, the distinction of being introduced to Bernini, the celebrated sculptor.

"I would have given my skin for Bernini's design of the Louvre," said Wren, with becoming ardor; "but the old reserved Italian gave me but a few minutes' view. It was five little designs in paper, for which he had received as many thousand pistoles. I had only time to copy it in my fancy and memory."

He strove to make himself acquainted with the most esteemed buildings in the city and its vicinity. With a mind refreshed by travel, and an eye impressed with the fabrics it had gazed on, Wren gladly enough returned to England, having, as he stated, surveyed and brought with him "almost all France on paper." He was now enthusiastically intent on proceeding with the restoration of St. Paul's; but there had arisen among the commissioners disputes, which effectually checked his eagerness. Public works are, in their progress, too frequently victims of private whims; and Wren now found so, to his dismay. Those who had been intrusted with the management of the business formed themselves into two parties. One of these obstinately contended that the church should be merely "patched up" to the best advantage; while the other were zealous for the full and complete restoration proposed by Wren. The architect, whose fortitude and patience were ever remarkable, reasoned with them in that calm tone which he ever adhered to under all annoyances; but he argued in vain. Suddenly the Great Fire not only put a period to the strife, but opened up a large stage for the genius and energy of this truly great Englishman, whose schemes speedily became the talk of Europe.

The dreadful conflagration had destroyed the principal part of St. Paul's, while helplessly damaging the remainder; and Wren, perceiving that any efficient repair was now utterly impracticable, conceived the idea of associating his name with a grand ecclesiastical structure worthy of the capital of royal England. His path, however, was not yet quite clear; for the hearts of the commissioners, "untraveled, still returned" to the old building, and another effort was made to reconstruct it. The rubbish was removed, and the enterprise entered on; but the fall of a pillar soon indicated how vain and futile such an attempt really was.

Wren was on a visit at Oxford, when he received the intelligence of this disaster; and perhaps he felt that his day of triumph had at length arrived. He forthwith wrote and recommended a total removal of the ruins of the former church, and the erection, from the foundation, of a cathedral that should exhibit the taste and dignity of the country. Nevertheless, so perverse is human nature, when a change of opinion involves a confession of error, that the system of "patching up any how" was persisted in till the middle of 1668, when it was resolved that a new cathedral should be built. Wren now applied himself to the production of several designs and models for the contemplated structure, and, in due time, they were laid before the proper authorities. It appears that, whatever credit pertains to the rejection of the best and adoption of the worst plans, must be assigned to that royal duke whose insane bigotry and superstition afterward cost him the proudest crown in Christendom. The architect's temper did not give way; but he shed tears at the injudicious selection.

Operations were forthwith commenced in earnest, but though there was practiced none of the tardiness which had characterized the preliminary arrangements, the gigantic magnitude of the work occasioned a delay of years; and it was not till the third quarter of the eventful century had passed that the scorched ruins were altogether removed, and the first stone laid by the great architect, under whose superintendence it was completed in the comparatively brief space of thirty-five years. Previously to the work being entered on, Wren had the honor of knighthood conferred on him; and about the same period he married a lady of Oxfordshire; though he had reached his forty-second year—an age at which men are generally rather disinclined to relinquish their freedom. He was speedily blessed with a son, who, in 1700, laid the last and highest stone of the cathedral, in presence of the principal persons employed in the building. Wren subsequently planned no fewer than fifty new ecclesiastical edifices for the metropolis; and no man, however high in that art, which is half a science, and therefore requires mathematical knowledge in its votaries, ever imitated with so much success the churches of Italy. His mind was vigorous, his judgment accurate, and he excelled in unity and elegance.

In July, 1669, he had experienced the satisfaction of seeing the first of his architectural designs realized. This was the theatre at Oxford, founded by Archbishop Sheldon. It was opened with great and imposing solemnity; and the munificent founder marked his appreciation of the skill displayed in the building by presenting Wren with a golden cup, and appointing him one of the curators for life.

Meantime the plague of London had drawn public attention to the defective state of its architecture, and the great conflagration had afforded an opportunity of introducing extensive improvements. Wren then stood forth as an architect capable of making a new and extensive city arise, phœnix-like, from the ashes. He earnestly desired to give beauty and dignity to a capital of whose greatness, in other respects, he spoke in language of enthusiasm. His proposal was to run a spacious street, in a direct line, from St. Paul's to the Exchange, another to the Tower, and a third westward to Piccadilly. The bank of the river was to be adorned with a terrace, and there he proposed to place the halls of the twelve great city companies. This scheme, which had the warm support of the king and his ministers, was all but frustrated by the citizens, who found that it unfortunately interfered too much with the rights and property of private individuals to be realized to any satisfactory extent.

About this period he was sauntering with Charles the Second through the hunting-lodge at Newmarket, in reference to which his majesty remarked—

"These rooms are too low."

"An' please your majesty, I think them high enough," said Wren, as he walked up, carrying his figure, which was the reverse of tall, with much of the stateliness of those cavaliers whom, in boyish days, he had seen at his father's deanery. Charles, with a merry twinkle of his eye, squatted down to Wren's height, saying, as he did so—

"Ay, Sir Christopher, on second thoughts I think they are high enough, too."

Sir Stephen Fox, progenitor of that family which has since produced so many celebrated persons—a man who had risen from obscurity to high honors in the state—persuaded the king that a military hospital should be founded. Wren furnished designs for, and superintended, the building at Chelsea, which was not completed till the reign of William and Mary. He also prepared designs for the palace of Winchester. In 1784 he was appointed Comptroller and Principal Officer of the Works at Windsor Castle.

Wren had been born and bred among men who, from their position, took a lively interest in political affairs; and, in spite of his multifarious duties, he was far from declining such distinction in that sphere as was not likely to interfere with his professional pursuits. He was indebted to the people of Plympton—the native place of Sir Joshua Reynolds—for his first election to the House of Commons, in 1685. After the Revolution he was returned for New Windsor, and became a great favorite with that daughter of the banished king who then shared the English throne with her Dutch consort. She admired his genius, and perhaps appreciated the affection which he entertained for the kingly race whose errors had been her husband's opportunity. Being pleased with the situation and scenery of Hampton Court, she commissioned the architect, who had done honor to the patronage of her merry uncle and her gloomy sire, to furnish designs for a splendid palace, to be connected with the pile which Cardinal Wolsey had reared and made over to the bluff Killer of Wives and Defender of the Faith. The queen was presented with several designs, and selected one which did credit to her character for taste and elegance, but the sanction of the royal Dutchman was required before she could finally decide. That great prince and soldier was a hero, though, unfortunately for his fame, one of no very scrupulous nature; and heroes are generally men of one design. If the question had been how to raise in England funds to carry on the war against France, his judgment would hardly have erred; but the construction of a palace was a different matter; and he chose and stuck by the very plan which had been prepared as a foil to the others. The queen was forced to yield, and the architect sighed at being thus obliged to erect a palace of which he disliked the plan; but regret could produce no remedy for the evil, and the work was proceeded with. He next designed Greenwich Hospital, and during the reign of Queen Anne he continued to enjoy from that royal lady a favor and protection not unworthy of a grand-daughter of Charles the First.

The distinguished architect, however, had not pursued his prosperous course without making enemies; and the time at length arrived when they could gratify their hoarded malice. When the first representative of the House of Brunswick left his delightful Electorate to ascend the throne of Great Britain, Wren was in his eighty-second year; and though so often thwarted in his designs during three reigns by citizens, and kings, and commissioners, he had done wonders, and on every side there were traces of his rare and fertile genius. The new sovereign, however, was almost as devoid of taste or capacity as he was destitute of virtue or popularity; and, from the beginning, he regarded the venerable architect with an inimical eye. After a lapse of four years the public learned, with astonishment and indignation, that Sir Christopher was dismissed from his office, and replaced by a wretched pretender, to whose undistinguished name Pope has given a somewhat unenviable notoriety.

The old knight had lived too long, and seen too much of the world, in a most eventful age, to be very deeply affected by this circumstance; though the insult touched his friends to the heart. He removed from his official residence in Scotland Yard, and betook himself to rural retirement. He had long survived his first wife; and not relishing a prolonged widowerhood, he sought and found a second bride in the daughter of a peer of Ireland. He now took a house at Hampton Court, where he passed the greater part of his remaining years in study and contemplation of the Holy Scriptures, which cheered his solitude and consoled him in his preparation for a higher state of existence. He indulged in a sleep in his easy chair after dinner, maintained the utmost serenity, and exhibited all his wonted vivacity. Gradually his limbs, which had been active, failed; and his movements thus became dependent on the assistance of others. Now and then he rejoiced in a visit to the metropolis, to inspect the repairs of Westminster Abbey, and look once more on the dome of St. Paul's. His intellect remained unimpaired long after his bodily vigor had ceased. A journey between London and Hampton Court, then a more formidable affair to a person of advanced age than it has since become, proved more than his frame could endure, and, after a short illness, he died on the 27th of February, 1723. His corpse was consigned to the vaults of the magnificent cathedral, which stands alike the monument and the master-piece of his architectural genius, as his most appropriate epitaph is the brief inscription which has been alluded to at the commencement of this sketch. Sixty-nine years later the surrounding earth was disturbed on the death of Sir Joshua Reynolds; and the mortal remains of the illustrious painter, whose magic pencil had redeemed Englishmen from the reproach of being indebted to foreign nations for artistic skill, were, with much pomp and circumstance, laid by the side of the great architect, in the consecrated cemetery.

DR. WILLIAM HUNTER

The name of Hunter is still of high account in the profession, which was raised and adorned by the talents and virtues of the two brothers. Indeed it is as inseparably connected with the progress of medical science in Great Britain, as is that of Wren with architecture, or that of Erskine with trial by jury. The career of the elder of the distinguished brothers is well worthy of attention, and eminently calculated to stimulate industry.

Dr. Hunter was not only a Scotchman, but to some extent a patriot; and an adventurer of mark or likelihood from that country, without a genealogy, would be like the year without the spring, or like the spring without the flowers. It serves to support his pride, and to sustain him in his poverty. In this respect the great physician was not deficient, his grandfather having been a younger son of Hunter of Hunterstone, chief of the name. Moreover, the parentage of this eminent man was respectable; for about the beginning of last century his father resided, in all the pride of territorial dignity, on the small hereditary estate of Long Calderwood, in the county of Lanark. The laird was, no doubt, a frugal-enough swain, with ideas as old-fashioned as the language in which they were expressed; but who lacked not sagacity, nor a stout heart and a strong hand. He had need of such qualities; for, however barren or the reverse might have been his acres, it appears that "the leddy," though doubtless exemplary and diligent in "doubling his joys and all his cares dividing," was, if any thing, inconveniently prolific; for with alarming rapidity, as years glided on, he was presented with no less than half a score of children—a progeny surely large enough, in all conscience, to daunt the bravest speculator on the probabilities of the future.

In the rustic abode, most likely one of those "thatched mansions" at that period commonly the residence of the lesser proprietors of the soil of North Britain, on the 23d of the merry month of May, 1718—if, indeed, all seasons were not then alike in that impoverished country, where, in the words of the clever but clumsy satirist,

> "No flowers embalmed the air but one white rose,
> Which on the tenth of June by instinct blows,"—

William Hunter, destined to be one of the most famous of medical practitioners, anatomists, and lecturers, was born and swaddled, with the usual form and ceremony. He was the seventh child of his parents; and ten years later, in the same place, appeared his brother, who is styled "the Prophet of the Healing Art," and whose wise countenance, as portrayed by the potent pencil of Reynolds, made Lavater exclaim—"That man thinks for himself!"

Young Willie was, no doubt, a shrewd, grave, talented boy, whose time was divided between learning that quantity of Latin prescribed by statute to the son of every owner of a portion of Caledonian soil, however stern and wild, poor or paltry, it might be. Indeed, in his case there was another reason for attention to classical learning, it being originally intended that the Church of Scotland should have the benefit of the talents and abilities with which Nature had blessed him. Sir Robert Walpole boasted over his cups that, if the intention of his taking orders had been carried into effect, he would have one day been Archbishop of Canterbury; and had Hunter applied his intellect as vigorously to the study of divinity and Scottish ecclesiastical affairs as he did to those of the profession of which he became so eminent a member, he might possibly have climbed to the position, earned the fame, and exercised the influence, of an Erskine, a Blair, or a Chalmers. It was otherwise appointed:

> "Scire potestates herbarum, usumque medendi
> Maluit, et mutas agitare inglorias artes."

At the distance of a mile and a half from his paternal mansion stood the village of Kilbride; and there, in the school-room belonging to the parish, some "Dominie Sampson," whose sayings and doings have been consigned to oblivion, imparted instruction with a stentorian voice, and flourished the odious leathern scourge, before which many an erring urchin has shrunk, and winked, and howled. To this establishment, in all probability, would Hunter travel daily, on the back of a donkey or shaggy pony, with a wallet on his shoulder; save when, to his heart's delight, a fall of rain or a snow-storm afforded a decent pretext for remaining at home, and making his escape at noon to the weekly market, or to one of the four parochial fairs held during the year.

At the customary age he was sent to the University of Glasgow; and no doubt, as it would likely be his first visit, gazed with wonder on such buildings as were there to be seen. The place was then very different from what it has since become. But to a boy, who hitherto had witnessed no scene more striking than a rural fair, who had only dreamt of greater things while reposing on a summer's day by the margin of some haunted and murmuring streamlet, or while driving the cows in the gloaming to the modest grange, the venerable precincts of the college and of the ancient cathedral, described with so much felicity in the pages of "Rob Roy;" the battlemented mansion, that had lately been the residence of an archbishop; the tall masts of the vessels that had brought colonial produce to an extending market; and last, though not least, the Exchange, whose covered pavement was traversed by those proud "Virginians"—the aristocracy of tobacco—who wrapped themselves closer in their red cloaks, shook their flowing wigs, grasped more firmly their long gold-headed canes, and raised their eyes with haughty stare, when any inquisitive stranger approached the scene of their operations, must have seemed grand indeed.

Hunter now commenced his theological studies; and the sagacious sire rejoiced in the prospect of seeing his son "wagging his head in a pulpit." But after a term of five years an obstacle to pursuing his course occurred, which could not be overcome without outraging his conscientious convictions. In fact, he entertained an insuperable repugnance to some of the articles of faith to which he was required to assent; and, sacrificing whatever prospects of preferment he had on the shrine of duty, he resolved to venture upon a new field, and make medicine and the art of healing the study and occupation of his life. He was still a boy, "showing a maiden chin," without that wisdom which is commonly, but not seldom erroneously, supposed to lurk about the beard; and it can not be questioned but that hope would extravagantly gild any future that his fancy might conjure up. Yet, strongly as he might have felt within him the spirit and the faculty to ascend the hill of life, and wave his cocked hat in triumph from its summit, he could hardly contemplate such enviable success as it was his good fortune to seek and find. Little, it may be well conceived, could he foresee how rapidly he was to emerge from obscurity, and be recognized as one of the most celebrated votaries to a profession at once delicate and laborious in that illimitable city of which, at his father's hearth, he had heard wondrous tales and accounts exciting curiosity.

Meantime, returning to his native district in 1737, he formed an intimacy with Dr. Cullen. This afterward celebrated man was a native of Hamilton. He had received an ordinary Scotch education, served an apprenticeship to an apothecary, and made several voyages in a vessel trading to the East Indies in the capacity of surgeon. He had commenced practice in a Lanarkshire parish, the clergyman of which had married Hunter's sister; and at the manse of his brother-in-law doubtless our hero made Cullen's acquaintance. The conversation of the latter exercised a mighty influence on the mind of his new friend; and when he had settled as a practitioner at Hamilton, a small town situated on the Clyde, Hunter entered into a sort of partnership with him. They even meditated it being of a permanent nature; but subsequent events rendered such a scheme altogether inexpedient, and it was abandoned with advantage to both. Nevertheless, it was pursued for years with mutual profit. Being equally and earnestly desirous of improvement, they agreed that each should pass a winter at one of the colleges, while the other should remain and attend to the patients who relied on the establishment for medical aid. Cullen's seniority gave him the privilege of taking the first session; and so signal was his progress, that he was enabled to impart valuable information to his young associate. After a season, they parted in friendship, to divide the world between them; and while his former companion in arms was winning metropolitan honors and achieving innocent, though not bloodless victories, Cullen was by no means shrinking from the exertions which establish a reputation. Hunter seems to have disdained the company of a fair being to comfort and console him in his way through this troublesome world; but his northern friend and contemporary was not so remiss or self-denying. He forthwith strengthened his position by taking to wife the daughter of some neighboring worthy; but his abilities were not to be confined within narrow limits. He attracted the notice of men of pride and nobility—was patronized by the ducal houses of Hamilton and Argyle—filled professorial chairs in Glasgow and Edinburgh—influenced, in no inconsiderable degree, the opinion of medical men as to the science of physic—exhibited delightful amiability in private life; and, leaving behind several works to vindicate the high estimation in which he was held, he breathed his last in peace and prosperity. Having thus briefly sketched Cullen's career, let us return to mark the footsteps of his redoubted countryman in pursuit of wealth and eminence.

Hunter went, in his turn, to the romantic capital of Scotland, and attended the lectures of several professors of distinction. In the year 1711 he set off to gratify his eyes with a sight of London, having obtained an introduction from a printer in Glasgow to James Douglas, who, as a surgeon and teacher of anatomy, had fattened in the rich South. This individual had early emigrated, but had not altogether lost his sentiments of nationality; and he had, perhaps, a keen eye to his own interests. Besides, he was a man of mark, and the author of several works of merit. He is spoken of by Pope and Harwood as an enthusiastic collector of the various editions of Horace, and eulogized by Haller for the art and ingenuity of his anatomical preparations. Doubtless at that date there were presented fewer letters recommending raw Scottish lads to the notice of their enriched countrymen, than when Wilkie charmingly depicted a similar ceremony. In any case, Douglas gave the young aspirant a gracious reception, and asked him to repeat his visit. Being engaged at the time with an elaborate treatise on the bones, he was anxious to enlist the services of some trustworthy youth as a dissector, and perceived that Hunter had the sense and acuteness requisite to qualify him for the situation. He therefore courteously invited our hero to live in his house, assist in his dissections, and superintend the education of his son.

When the curious and adulating Boswell had his cherished hopes crowned by an introduction, in the parlor of Tom Davies, to the great man whom he had long worshiped at a distance, and nervously blurted out, "I do indeed come from Scotland, but I can not help it," Johnson said with truth. "That, sir, is what a great many of your countrymen can not help." Such, however, was not the case with Hunter, who had sufficient influence to achieve a respectable position at home if he had wished. The offer of Douglas was, nevertheless, tempting. He requested time to consider it; and going to the house of a practitioner with whom he was staying in Pall Mall, he wrote to his partner and to his father on the subject. Cullen immediately approved of his accepting the post; but the laird, who was in his seventy-eighth year, and looked upon a journey to London as a most formidable affair, was already impatient for his son's return, and was with no small difficulty prevailed on to give his consent. Matters were at length accommodated; and Hunter took up his quarters under the roof of Douglas as pupil and assistant, and entered vigorously upon his new duties.

This was, unquestionably, an auspicious commencement of his career; for his patron was high in his profession, a Fellow of the Royal Society, and Reader of Anatomy to the Company of Surgeons. Besides, public opinion was not yet violently excited against the inhabitants of the sterile north. The "silver-tongued Mansfield" had, it is true, ridden from Perthshire to Middlesex, "drunk champagne with the wits," and distinguished himself at the bar; but he was not yet lord chief justice nor an English peer. Wedderburn had not yet crossed the Tweed to grasp successfully at the great seal. Lord Bute had still to be pulled out of the apothecary's chariot at a cricket-match to play at whist with, and become the favorite of, Frederick Prince of Wales. On the other hand, Wilkes had not indulged in what Lord Chatham called "the expensive delights" of contested elections, nor in the profanity and licentiousness of Medenham Abbey. His services as embassador to Constantinople had to be declined, and "The North Briton" to be called into existence to avenge the slight. Poor, deluded Churchill, was sitting on the forms at Westminster with Lloyd, Cowper, and Warren Hastings. The time had to come when he could "blaze the comet of a season," by applying such terms as "the poor, proud children of leprosy and hunger," to the natives of an ancient and noble land, whose powers he did not comprehend, and whose achievements in art, science, law, letters, and commerce, he possessed not the prescience to divine. The events of 1745 had yet to fill the citizens of London with anger and apprehension; national animosity had still to be excited to madness by public appointments being almost exclusively bestowed on bare-legged Highlanders. Hunter was, in some respects, an adventurer, and one of whom his country had reason to be proud; but it was well that he arrived and struck his root in public favor before the frenzied cry had gone forth.

Douglas was not disappointed in the expectations he had formed of his assistant's worth and ability, which he stimulated in various ways. He enabled him to enter as a dissecting pupil at St. George's Hospital, and to attend a class for anatomy, besides a course of lectures on experimental philosophy, given by Dr. Desaguliers; and Hunter availed himself so earnestly of such advantages, and became so expert in dissection, that his excellent instructor was at the expense of having several of his preparations engraved. This aid, so well calculated to afford encouragement, was rendered just in time; for within twelve months after Hunter's spirited expedition southward his employer died; and having apparently married past middle age, he left a widow and two children, with whom his talented *protégé* continued to reside for the next eight years.

In 1743, Hunter, ever aspiring and energetic, contributed a paper on the structure and diseases of the cartilages to the "Philosophical Transactions;" and, three years later, was appointed Lecturer to the Society of Naval Surgeons. For the first course he received seventy guineas, which was the largest sum ever in his possession up to that date, as he declared when carrying it to his lodgings, in a bag, under his cloak. But he had not yet learned prudence; and the amount was soon reduced to such dimensions, that he was reluctantly compelled to postpone the second course for a fortnight, from want of the money to pay for advertising them. This circumstance taught him, after a somewhat stern fashion, that in worldly affairs caution and economy are essential elements of success. In 1747 he became a Member of the College of Surgeons; and, next year, went to Leyden. There the anatomical preparations of Albinus inspired him with enthusiastic admiration, and he was fired with the worthy ambition of emulating their excellence. On returning to this country he commenced practice as a surgeon.

As a medical practitioner, with anxious and laborious duties in the widest of all fields—the metropolis of England—Hunter was conspicuously successful; and, in truth, there are few more responsible occupations. The person to whom is raised the vail which conceals the privacy of domestic life from the public eye, exercises no small influence on multitudes of his fellow-creatures. His aid is invoked to relieve bodily and mental suffering in seasons of distress and perplexity. Lives are confided to his skill, and the peace of families to his honor. To society, therefore, his character and conduct are matters of no inconsiderable interest. Hunter showed himself eminently, and in all respects, worthy of his position. He displayed remarkable tact in winning the confidence of his patients; and, even when he gave signs of being more than ordinarily doubtful of success in his efforts on their behalf, anxious friends and relatives placed implicit reliance on his tried skill and sagacious judgment. His merit and ability were speedily recognized by election to important offices in two hospitals, being recommended thereto by the most eminent surgeons of the day. His manner and personal appearance contributed much to his success, and he began to distance all competitors in the field which he gradually chose for the exercise of his skill and experience. In 1750 the degree of Doctor of Medicine was bestowed on him by the University of Glasgow; and in the summer of the next year he visited his native district, where time had wrought considerable changes among his relations.

His father had died shortly after consenting to his remaining in London; and his eldest brother had since followed. But his mother yet lived at Long Calderwood, of which he had become proprietor on his brother's decease. Nor had romance altogether disdained to alight on the unpretending mansion and its homely grounds. A cabinet-maker, fresh from the regions of Cockaigne, had settled at Glasgow, and ventured to pay his addresses to one of the sisters. He was the reverse of disagreeable, and "Miss Jenny" was quite content to be his. Her relatives, indeed, conceived that a match would compromise their gentility, and protested against its being consummated; but this "penniless lass wi' a lang pedigree" resolved, at all risks, to secure herself against the possibility of becoming an old maid, took the bit between her teeth, and insisted on having her own way. Then, questionless, preparations would be made for a gay wedding, and numerous guests would be bidden. Smugglers would supply foreign wine and brandy. The gun, the farmyard, and the pigeon-house, would furnish the table; friends and kinsfolk would congregate from all directions; damsels, with the prospect of a bridal ceremony and a dance, would willingly submit to the inconvenience of passing the preceding night six in a room; while men combining something of the haughty spirit of the Master of Ravenswood with a moiety of the pedantry displayed by the Baron of Bradwardine, would in hay-lofts luxuriate in such sleep as is not always vouchsafed to kings reclining under gilded canopies. Another event of greater importance had occurred. Hunter's brother John, the youngest of the brood, after attempting to work for some time at his brother-in-law's trade, despaired of success in that path of life, and returned home. He soon became tired of remaining idle, and joining Dr. Hunter in London, threw all the ardor and energy of his great mind into surgery, and ultimately arrived at the highest honors of his profession. He had been three years in the English metropolis, and won considerable reputation at the time of Dr. Hunter's visit to Scotland. As for the latter, he was now full of hope and courage; and his engagements were such that he could only stay for a few weeks. But he gave instructions for repairing and improving the house of Long Calderwood, and for purchasing any adjoining lands that might happen to be offered for sale. One day, while riding in a flat part of the country with his old comrade, Cullen, the young Glasgow professor, pointing out to his former colleague his birth-place, said, "How conspicuous Long Calderwood appears to-day!"

"By St. Andrew!" exclaimed Hunter with unwonted energy, emphasis, and enthusiasm, "if I live I shall make it still more conspicuous!"

There was, in this frank utterance, something of that glowing romance which generally animates and stimulates great men; and the future fully proved that this confidence in his own power and determination, however high, was not in any degree misplaced. When he was held in esteem by his sovereign, when his name and talents were known and respected in every part of Europe, when the scientific societies of foreign capitals were proudly conferring honors upon him, and when he was in possession of wealth and enviable reputation, he could reflect on this frank expression of sentiment without any of the regret experienced by those who indulge in such aspirations without having calculated the toil and labor necessary for their realization.

In 1756 Hunter became one of the physicians to the British Lying-in Hospital; in the two succeeding years, a Licentiate of the Royal College of Physicians, and a Member of the Medical Society. In 1762 he published his "Medical Commentaries," written in a correct and spirited style. Having been consulted by Queen Charlotte in the latter year, he was subsequently nominated Physician Extraordinary to her Majesty. He now found it necessary to admit his pupil, Mr. Hewson, who had for some time assisted at his lectures, as his associate. On the institution of the Royal Academy, the king appointed Hunter to the Professorship of Anatomy. In fulfilling the duties thus devolving upon him, he exhibited boundless zeal and singular mental vigor, as also ingenious resource in adapting his science to purposes of painting and sculpture.

When Goldsmith was, on the same occasion, graciously honored with the Professorship of Ancient History, he complained to his familiar friends, with some show of reason, that honors bestowed upon one in his circumstances were too like ruffles given to a man who had not a shirt to his back. With Hunter the case was widely different. By this time he was a rich man; and—what was of more consequence—actuated by the laudable ambition of making his wealth minister to the progress of the profession, in whose ranks the greater part of it had been earned. Accordingly, having set apart a sum sufficient to insure independence to his declining years, he proposed to expend a large amount of his hoarded treasure in the erection of an anatomical theatre, and to found a perpetual professorship; provided the Government would grant a proper site for a building. His request in this respect, being made to George Grenville, then prime minister, was not, of course, complied with. He was not, however, to be baffled in his purpose; and on failing to obtain the co-operation of Government, though Lord Shelburne handsomely offered to head a subscription list with a thousand pounds, he purchased a piece of ground in Great Windmill Street, where, at his own expense, he built an amphitheatre and museum, as well as a large and commodious mansion, to which he removed in 1770. The museum was at first furnished with the numerous specimens of human and comparative anatomy collected by him during previous years; but his efforts and expenditure did not cease at this point. He gradually added to the stores by purchasing various collections of note, particularly that of Dr. Fothergill, who directed in his will that it should be offered to Hunter considerably below its estimated value. Besides, he procured a number of fossils, a splendid cabinet of rare coins and medals, and a magnificent library, well stocked with Greek and Latin volumes. By and by his medical friends felt honored in contributing presents; and the institution became known and valued throughout Europe.

In 1775 Dr. Hunter published his most famous work, "The History of the Human Gravid Uterus," illustrated by large and splendid plates, and dedicated to his majesty. Several additions in matters of detail were made to the book from his papers, after the author had gone to his long rest. In 1780 he was elected an Associate of the Royal Medical Society of Paris. On the death of Dr. Fothergill he was chosen President of the Society of Physicians, and soon after a Foreign Associate of the French Academy of Sciences, as well as of the Royal Medical Society of Paris.

As a lecturer his powers remained unimpaired; and though in stature rather under the middle size, he was well formed, and engaging enough in person and deportment to set off to advantage discourses composed with clearness and illustrated to admiration. He continued to deliver them till within a few months of his death. In his last years he was attended by his nephew. This was Mr. Baillie, son of a Scotch clergyman, brother of the celebrated poetess of that name, and afterward a distinguished physician. The youth had studied at Glasgow and Oxford, and he now came to be drilled into excellence by his experienced kinsman. He was to this end employed in arranging preparations for the lectures, conducting the demonstrations, and superintending the operations of the pupils. He subsequently undertook the continuance of his uncle's lectures, in conjunction with Mr. Cruickshank; but, ere long, his extensive practice compelled him to relinquish the duty. Dr. Hunter having, contrary to the advice and solicitation of his friends, risen from bed during an attack of the gout to give a lecture, was seized with paralysis, and felt that his end was approaching; nor did he shrink from the presence of the great despoiler, whose ravages he had so often checked. His resignation was singular. "If I had strength to hold a pen, I would write how easy and pleasant a thing it is to die," he said, turning to Dr. Combe, shortly before breathing his last, which he did on the 30th of March, 1783. Within a week he was interred in the vault of St. James's Church, Westminster.

The museum, on which he had expended so large an amount, was bequeathed to the University of Glasgow, its use for thirty years being reserved in favor of Dr. Baillie.

To his young and rising relative he left by will his patrimonial estate; but as it was evident that, in this settlement, he had been actuated by the annoyance consequent on an irritating dispute between himself and his illustrious brother, in regard to the merit of a discovery which both claimed, Baillie declined availing himself of the circumstance. He therefore, with a touching and becoming generosity, abandoned the property to his uncle, in whose mind it was associated with a hundred endearing recollections—kith, and kin, and home—the freaks of boyhood, and the vague aspirations of a clouded and cheerless youth, destined to be so nobly redeemed by the exertion and industry of a useful manhood.

BLACK

On the afternoon of an autumnal day in the last quarter of the eighteenth century, two gentlemen, who had considerably passed the prime of life, and looked like confirmed, but highly-respectable bachelors, as indeed they were, might have been observed to leave the vicinity of the South Bridge of Edinburgh at a leisurely pace. They had just succeeded in negotiating the hire of a room, where, with several of their literary friends, they proposed to hold a convivial meeting once during every week of the winter that was coming on. In pretty light spirits, from having proved themselves men of the world by bringing this important matter to a satisfactory conclusion, they were—it might be—discussing and denouncing the ridiculous prejudice, as they believed it to be, which prevented their countrymen making use of snails as an ordinary article of food, and vowing that they would, ere long set an example in this respect which should have the effect of divesting the public mind of such an absurd delusion; though it must be confessed, that when they did attempt to execute this bold intention they suddenly discovered that their appetites had taken an unceremonious flight. Each of these personages was distinguished by amiability of character, and utter unconsciousness of the guile and wickedness that prevailed around him. Their studies and pursuits were somewhat similar; and though frequently taking opposite views of debated questions, they were ever bosom friends. But in dress and manner they presented a striking contrast. One wore on his slender but active person garments plain to affectation, and might have easily passed for a member of the Society of Friends but for his cocked hat. He conversed with force and animation, always displaying much original information; but the accents that came from his lips, which parted while listening, were undiluted Scotch; and his bearing was so remarkably simple, that it was necessary to mark the thin, intellectual face, the high, thoughtful forehead, and the keen, penetrating eye, before being aware that he had "stuff" in him, or was more than an ordinary citizen. The other was of a different stamp. He wore a sort of academic dress; but it had received such careful and harmonious additions, as proved that he was by no means indifferent to external decorations and the propriety of costume. His aspect was comely and prepossessing; his manner was correct and graceful; he was evidently a person of elegant tastes and no inconsiderable refinement; and he used a musical voice to speak good English, with a punctilious accuracy of expression not often heard so far north at that time.

The former—the plain, unvarnished Scot—was Dr. Hutton, the ingenious philosopher, who thought out and published the "Theory of the Earth" that goes by his name, having previously shown his public spirit, and rendered essential services to the agriculture of his native country, by bringing, at much exertion to himself, an improved system of husbandry from the rich and fruitful shire of Norfolk, and introducing it into the district where he possessed a small estate. His companion, whose countenance looked that of a being inwardly satisfied with himself and all who came around him, was Dr. Black, the eminent Professor of Chemistry in the northern capital; he whose experiments tended to open up that path of scientific discovery which others have since so successfully pursued.

Joseph Black, than whom few men have ever lived and died more truly respected by his daily associates, was a native of France. He was born in the year 1728, on the banks of the Garonne, hard by the place where that river visits the city of Bordeaux. There his father, who belonged to Belfast, had settled as a wine-merchant, and married the daughter of an individual engaged in the same trade. But with all these temptations and advantages in one of the largest and most opulent of French towns to embark the boy in the commercial pursuits which formed the business of his nearest relatives, young Black was very early destined to a medical career. Arrangements were made with that view; and at the age of twelve the future chemist left his home and native soil, to be fittingly educated at the grammar-school of the flourishing Irish sea-port town from which his worthy sire had emigrated to the fair land of vines. For several years he pursued his preparatory studies in Belfast; and his maternal grandfather being, though resident in Bordeaux, connected by birth and some territorial possession with Scotland, Black was, most likely from that cause, transported in his eighteenth year to Glasgow, and entered as a student at the University. He was immediately introduced to, and patronized by, the Professor of Natural Philosophy, with whose son he formed a juvenile intimacy, which was cemented by the similarity of their tastes.

About the date of Black's arrival at this college, it happened that the celebrated Cullen—he who influenced the career of Dr. Hunter—made his first public appearance at that seat of learning, in the capacity of Lecturer on Chemistry; his reputation speedily crept abroad, and the attendance at his class became large. The clever and acute French student was brought under the notice of Cullen, who, being frank and generous to his pupils, almost to a fault, made himself perfectly accessible at all hours, and treated them with much respect. He immediately perceived the bent of Black's genius; and not only recommended, but strongly urged, him to apply himself with determination to cultivate the science of chemistry, and gave him every assistance in doing so. Cullen was not, perhaps, a first-rate chemist himself, but he had an admirable method of imparting instruction; and his gifted pupil's preference for the study became so apparent, that he was ere long employed to assist his friend and teacher in the experiments of the classroom; and, when thus occupied, exhibited so much address and dexterity as contributed in no small degree to the success and fame of the lectures.

Black was still engaged in medical studies, and in order to complete them under advantageous circumstances he repaired, in 1751, to Edinburgh, where he stayed in the house of a cousin, who held one of the professorships. Having, during three sessions, attended all the requisite classes, he duly took the degree of Doctor of Medicine. On that occasion he chose for his theme a chemical topic—the acid arising from food and magnesia alba. Next year he, "still achieving, still pursuing," communicated his further ideas on the subject to a scientific society, in a paper which was then read by him, and afterward published in the second volume of "Essays, Physical and Literary," and gave an account of a most important chemical discovery. This was the existence of an aërial fluid, which he called fixed air, the presence of which gives mildness, as its absence gives causticity, to alkalies and calcareous earths.

In 1756, on Cullen's removal to Edinburgh, Black was appointed Professor of Chemistry and Anatomy at Glasgow in his stead; but not relishing, nor feeling particularly qualified for, the anatomical part of the business, he requested and obtained the assent of the heads of the university to an exchange, which he effected with the Professor of Medicine. While in this position he matured and made public his theory of latent heat, and explained to a society in Glasgow his experiments on the subject, in the clearest and most satisfactory manner; and this proved a principal leading step to the discoveries of Laplace, Lavoisier, and others: though they niggardly and enviously abstained in their dissertations from giving him that credit in the matter to which he was so justly entitled. In 1764 he had as one of his pupils the celebrated Watt; and it proved most fortunate for the interests of science and for the fame of both, that these great men were thus brought together.

Dr. Black was, in 1766, recalled to Edinburgh to fill the professorial chair of Chemistry, which was rendered vacant by the appointment of his old friend and adviser, Cullen, to that of Medicine. During the remainder of his career he was regarded as one of the chief ornaments of the university, as well as a most distinguished member of the literary circle which then adorned the Scottish metropolis, where his private character was highly esteemed. He continued his researches with perseverance and success; and his lectures were so remarkable for ease and elegance of style, novelty of information, and originality of reasoning, that few students ever left college without having attended a course or two. His devotion to the duties of his professorship was so complete, that it interfered materially with the spread of his fame, as others were thus allowed to pass him in that very path of discovery which his genius had illumined and opened up. A paper which he furnished, on the "Effects of boiling upon water in disposing it to freeze more readily," was published in the "Philosophical Transactions" for 1774; and an "Analysis of the water of some hot springs in Iceland," appeared in the Scottish "Philosophical Transactions for 1791." In due time he became a member of the societies of London and of the city where he resided, and, moreover, had the distinction of being selected as one of the eight Foreign Associates of the Academy of Sciences at Paris. His lectures on the "Elements of Chemistry," delivered in the University of Edinburgh, were, as late as 1803, published in two volumes, by Professor Robison.

While thus achieving scientific triumphs, the pecuniary affairs of Dr. Black had flourished better than even the most inquisitive of his neighbors had supposed; and the manner in which he disposed of his money by his will was peculiar and characteristic. When he felt the approaches of age, and found it necessary to employ an assistant, about his sixtieth year he had a list drawn up of persons who had a claim on his bounty, and whom he wished to inherit his treasure; and he destined it in such proportions as seemed consistent with the extent of care and solicitude to which they were entitled at his hand.

His health had long been in a delicate state, insomuch that he was under the hard necessity of refraining from writing an account of his brilliant discoveries, as the exertion of doing so for any continuous period invariably brought on a spitting of blood; and he felt himself in no condition to encounter the criticism or engage in the controversy likely to follow such a publication. Moreover, he is said to have been apprehensive of a long sickness, which for many reasons he anxiously wished to avoid. This fate was averted by the sudden nature of the summons he received to another world. On the 26th of November, 1799, while he was seated at table partaking of such abstemious fare as he had lately restricted himself to, the messenger of death was upon him, and struck the fatal blow. His servitor went into the room according to custom, but observing the cup of the venerable philosopher in his hand, as if about to be raised to his lips, and naturally supposing him to be in deep thought, he noiselessly withdrew. Entering soon after, he perceived his master still in the same posture, but on going up to the chair, was beyond measure surprised to find that the lamp of life had gently expired.

BRINDLEY

Few more remarkable men than Brindley have appeared in these latter times. He was not only the architect of his own fortune, but added enormously to the wealth of others, and to the public resources. In the acquirement of that knowledge which gave him the power of accomplishing great schemes, he had none of the appliances and facilities which competence furnishes and wealth commands; but he possessed advantages which were of more value to a man like him—a mind not to be startled at the prospect of its faculties being exerted—a resolution which, in the true spirit of industry, held difficulties at defiance—and a determination whose intellectual efforts circumstances could not baffle or subdue.

James Brindley was born in the year 1716, at Tunsted, within the county of Derby. His father had reduced himself to extreme poverty by habits of dissipation and extravagance. Accordingly, any education that Brindley received at school was, no doubt, of the very slightest and most limited description. It appears, however, that the statement of his inability to read and write is quite incorrect; several specimens of his penmanship having been produced. He is said never to have been instructed even in the first principles of mechanics, but was able by a peculiar process of his own invention, to make most accurate calculations. Besides, his memory adhered with amazing tenacity to any facts or information committed to its keeping: and by such means did this unquestioned benefactor of his kind countervail his deficiency of early training and scientific knowledge.

Having passed a few years in agricultural operations—plying with the flail or whistling at the plow—he was, at the age of seventeen, apprenticed to a millwright at Macclesfield, in Cheshire. In this situation his ideas were rapidly enlarged, and his faculties sharpened by experience in the trade which he had selected, probably from feeling that it would accord better with his tastes than the labors of the husbandman had done. His mechanical genius now began to develop itself, and to become perceptible; and so apparent was his progress in obtaining a knowledge of the business, that his employer frequently when absent from the mills, left him to execute pieces of work without finding it necessary to give any instruction in regard to them. Moreover, the different millers by whom they were employed soon discovered his superiority, and infinitely preferred his services to those of the master or any of the workmen belonging to the establishment. On approaching manhood, Brindley himself felt that he was destined for higher matters; and vague presentiments of better days in store occupied and agitated his powerful mind as he resolutely pursued his daily labors. Little could he imagine that he, the poor journeyman of a rural millwright, should, ere long, be the instrument of contributing materially to the national wealth; but it was ordered that it should be so.

Meantime his employer became so advanced in years, that he was incapable of working with effect. Brindley wisely seized the opportunity of applying his skill and ingenuity to the business, proved quite equal to the occasion, and exerted himself with so much success, that he not only kept it up against all competitors, but rendered it so flourishing a concern, that the old man and his family were enabled to live in comfortable circumstances. Indeed the apprentice was now the more skillful mechanic of the two, and he about this time gave proof of such being the case.

The aged worthy happened to be engaged in the construction of a paper-mill at some distance from his own workshop, and had proceeded to a considerable extent with the operation, when some one skilled in such matters observed that he was merely throwing his employer's money away. This remark reached the ears of Brindley, who, though perhaps by no means so zealous for his master's fame as the last minstrel was for that of the jovial harper who had taught him when a youth, resolved that it should be redeemed from such a reproach. He therefore determined to go and inspect the work in question; though that was not in any respect convenient, his time being otherwise occupied. But "where there's a will there's a way;" and one Saturday evening he set off on foot, without apprizing any one of his intended excursion, and, having obtained a sight of the object of his journey, returned on Monday morning in time for his work, after having walked a distance of fifty miles. He was altogether without the advantage of having seen a mill of the same kind before; but, nevertheless, was by this brief and cursory survey enabled to comprehend every thing necessary to its being properly completed. Taking the work under his superintendence, he brought it to a termination that gave the proprietor perfect satisfaction.

Brindley's reputation after the success of this undertaking rose high in the neighborhood, and he was induced to commence business on his own account. His abilities soon became widely known and appreciated, and he was extensively employed. He reaped much credit from the erection of an engine intended to drain a coal-mine at Clifton, in that bustling Lancashire where the cries are ever "Onward!" and "Haste!" which was afterward the sphere of his scientific triumphs, and with the history of which his name is so honorably linked. Under his auspices this piece of work proceeded with unexpected and amazing rapidity, notwithstanding the difficulties by which it was encompassed.

About this period a silk mill was being erected at Congleton, in Cheshire. The more intricate machinery was intrusted to a more experienced person, and Brindley was engaged merely to furnish the larger wheels and coarser apparatus. It soon appeared, that in this division of labor the Derbyshire aspirant had been treated with less than justice. He was constantly compelled to point out and rectify the errors and blunders; and at length, tiring of the irksome and invidious task, he resolutely refused to remain in a subordinate capacity to a person whose inferiority, in all that related to the matter in hand, was proved incontestably by the experience of each succeeding day. Then his employers, seeing how the case really stood, and prudently considering that their own interests were concerned in Brindley's services being retained, appointed him sole manager of the work; which he not only brought to a satisfactory conclusion, but added several improvements of no inconsiderable value or importance.

While his name was rising and his reputation increasing, he had the good fortune of becoming known to the Duke of Bridgewater. The latter was no ordinary man. The youngest of five children, who successively died off, he was, in boyhood, regarded as so sickly that his life was despaired of and his intellect doubted. On this account his education was for a time neglected. However, he was sent on a Continental tour, under the guidance of a traveling tutor, and no doubt used his eyes to better purpose than had been anticipated by his guardians, or than his immediate pursuits would have led them to suppose. On returning to England, he set about enjoying himself after the fashion of the day. He appeared as the owner of race-horses, as a gentleman-rider, as the frequenter of aristocratic assemblies, and as the successful suitor of a celebrated beauty. It was on the last point that his fate turned. Circumstances of a peculiar nature interfered with the matrimonial project, and prevented the union. The young duke vowed perpetual celibacy, declared he would never address another female in accents of gallantry, and abandoning fashionable society, with all its pains, and pleasures, and excitements, retired, with honor, to his estates in the county of Lancaster.

Fortunately this representative of Lord Chancellor Ellesmere was gifted with an ardent diligence which his illustrious progenitor might have envied, and he forthwith began to develop the resources which lay dormant in his hereditary possessions. Mr. Gilbert, a person who had been much engaged in mining operations, became his assistant, and exhibited a spirit of energy and perseverance kindred with that of his employer. Brindley's provincial fame was now not inconsiderable, and he soon became acquainted with the young patrician, who had fled from the wiles of noble matrons, and the fascinations of their fairer daughters, to bleak coal-fields and barren moors.

The man who was now introduced to the then thin and slender duke, who had escaped from race-courses, ball-rooms, and gaming-tables, to earn for himself the proud and honorable title of the "Father of British Inland Navigation," was plain in appearance and boorish in manners. But whenever he spoke bystanders listened with pleased surprise at the enterprising courage which his words betokened; and his conversation was in no small degree indicative of one of the strong, rough, resolute, master minds, whose workings—stern and independent—frequently benefit largely the human species, and minister to the civilization of the wide world. He was just such a man as the duke stood in need of for the carrying out of his plans of improvement, and he readily consented to take service with that view.

The first undertaking on which Brindley entered in his new position was the Bridgewater Canal. Having surveyed the ground, and reported that it presented no insuperable difficulties, an Act of Parliament was obtained, and the enterprise proceeded with under his superintendence. The self-taught engineer was branded by turns as an enthusiast, a madman, and a person unworthy of trust; but his intellectual courage and unshrinking confidence in the expedients of his own bold, powerful, and original mind defied all such assaults; and he remained unmoved by the sneers, scorn, and ridicule directed against his projects. His heart and soul were in the enterprise, and obstacles disappeared before his determined will. Strangers came from afar to view the gigantic operations, and marveled at the facility with which the plain, hard-headed, illiterate man, found means to handle huge rocks, and remove them at his pleasure. This pursuit completely monopolized his thoughts and occupied his attention; he cared not for recreation or amusement. Unceasing industry seemed the law of his being. When in London he was once persuaded to go to the theatre, but declared that the whole scene so confused his ideas, and unfitted him for business, that he would, on no consideration, repeat his visit.

He appears to have had no idea of the beauties of nature, nor any perception of the objects which make up fine scenery. When under examination by a committee of the House of Commons, he was asked for what purpose he conceived rivers to have been created? and, after a slight pause, replied,

"Undoubtedly to feed canals."

To the end of his extraordinary career, this wonderful man was occupied in his favorite pursuits, and his application to the subject was intense throughout. While the Grand Trunk Navigation Canal, to which he devoted so much thought and energy, was progressing toward completion under his auspices, and he was feeding his mind with visions of the great things it was to accomplish, his death, hastened by mental exertion, took place at Turnhurst, in Staffordshire, on the 27th of September, 1772.

WATT

Among "famous men," Watt occupies a most distinguished position as a real benefactor of the world. Though he stated that he knew only two pleasures—idleness and sleep, study and business might not improperly have been added. His industry and perseverance eminently qualified him for a career of invention and enterprise, and he pursued it with almost unparalleled success. His intellectual faculties were exercised without ceasing to the end of his long and momentous life; he practiced constant meditation; and he was thus enabled to minister more than any of his contemporaries to the progress of material civilization.

James Watt was born on the 19th of January, 1736, at Greenock, where his father was a merchant. He was first instructed in reading by his mother, and then placed at a day-school; but being exceedingly delicate, his attendance was somewhat irregular. When absent from school, he was far from suspending the exercise of those faculties which afterward accomplished so much; for his mind was of so inquiring a nature, that he began almost in childhood to manifest a strong and ardent taste for geometry and mechanics. This was probably, in some measure, inspired by the example of his grandfather and uncle, both of whom had excelled as teachers of mathematics.

It is related that a person one day calling on his father, and observing the little boy busily occupied in drawing numerous lines on the hearthstone with a piece of chalk, remarked that the child ought to be sent to school, and not allowed to idle away his time in such a manner.

"But," said his father, "look what he is about before you condemn him."

The gentleman then looked, and in no small degree was he surprised to see that he was studiously attempting to solve a geometrical problem. His natural bent thus becoming evident, his father encouraged it by providing him with a set of tools; and he showed his comprehension of the uses to which they might be put by forming several childish toys, and among others, an electrical machine.

His mother's relations resided in Glasgow, and there he frequently went on a visit, when his ardent love of knowledge and his faculty of learning were matters of considerable astonishment. Doubtless, his rich and enthusiastic conversation enlivened some of the extraordinary supper-parties, where the guests of the wealthy but frugal traders, who altogether eschewed the idea of earlier or more extensive entertainments, partook of the evening fare, and indulged in the cold punch, just in such measure as the means or inclination of the host permitted or prompted. At all events, it appears that he had no objection to steal a few hours from the night when he could find listeners to his various and interesting stories and enlivening discourse.

On one occasion he was chidden by his aunt for continuing to take off and put on the lid of a tea-kettle, holding by turns a cup and a silver spoon over the steam, watching its rise from the spout, and catching and counting the drops of water formed by condensation. So early was his active mind engaged in investigating the "condensation of steam."

Though he had given considerable attention to several other subjects, mechanics was his favorite study; and in conformity with his own wish he was, at the age of eighteen, indentured to an instrument-maker in Cornhill, London, who employed him chiefly in preparing and adjusting sextants, and other nautical instruments. His apprenticeship was brought to a premature termination by a relapse of bad health, which obliged him to return to the banks of the Clyde.

Some time after this a visit to Glasgow suggested to his mind the scheme of commencing business there, with the little instruction he had received. But not being qualified by the requisite freedom of craft or guild, he had the mortification of finding that his plan was incapable of being carried into execution. It was vain to plead or remonstrate. The members of the corporate body, principally concerned, were deaf to entreaty. They strenuously adhered to

> "The good old rule, the simple plan,
> That they should take who have the power,
> And they should keep who can;"

and sternly refused him permission to open even the very humblest workshop.

From this rather tantalizing difficulty, the University rescued the man destined to increase the resources of his country, and add immeasurably to the power of his species, by granting him a room within the building, and appointing him mathematical instrument-maker to the college. While in this position he executed some small instruments, which still exist, and exhibit most skillful and dexterous workmanship. His earliest drawings of steam-engines are likewise preserved, and are described as being distinguished by neatness, strength, and accuracy of outline. He enjoyed the favor and intimacy of several celebrated men, who were then professors in the University; among whom were Adam Smith, Professor Simson, and Dr. Black, whose discoveries in heat aided him much in his inventions. Moreover, his workshop was the resort of all such students as interested themselves in scientific matters. Indeed, they are said to have consulted him as an authority almost conclusive, when any difficulty presented itself which baffled their knowledge; and Watt never allowed his course to be barred by any obstacle that could possibly be overcome by resolute efforts of intellect, and a determined application of industry. He studied anatomy, chemistry, and natural philosophy, and occupied many a leisure hour with inquiries into the nature of steam. Though unacquainted with the mysteries of music, he undertook the construction of an organ, and, by dint of perseverance, furnished an instrument exhibiting many improvements, and capable of delighting the most fastidious performers. And all this time his daily devotion to his business was most exemplary, and quite uninterrupted by his reading or speculations, which were pursued in hours not taken up with the labors of his craft. The principle upon which he then acted in this respect guided him throughout life.

Before he reached the age of twenty-four, Watt's attention had been attracted to the employment of steam as a mechanical agent. His friend, Mr. Robison—afterward Professor at Glasgow and Edinburgh—had suggested its application to wheeled carriages, and they made experiments together. Watt doubtless thought much, and submitted the question to close, earnest, and vigilant study. But it was not till 1763 that his abilities were practically applied to the discovery, which has associated his name inseparably with the progress of the world. At that period the model of an engine was sent to him to be repaired by the Professor of the Natural Philosophy class; and on his examining it with care and attention, all the impressions which he had conceived as to the imperfections of the atmospheric machine were at once renewed in his mind. He therefore devoted himself to its improvement with diligence and determination. He soon perceived that the rapidity with which water evaporates depends simply on the degree of heat that is imbibed, and that the latter circumstance is in proportion to the vessel's surface containing the water. He likewise arrived by experiment at a knowledge as to the coals requisite for the evaporation of any given quantity of water, the heat at which it boils under various pressures, and several other points never before ascertained with accuracy. Bringing his genius to bear on the matter, he proceeded to attempt remedies for the two chief defects of Newcomen's engine—the necessity of cooling the cylinder before each stroke of the piston by the injection of water, and the non-employment of the engine as a moving power of the expansive force of the steam.

Having overcome the first defects by a process which saved three fourths of the fuel required to feed the engine, and at the same time added considerably to its power, Watt was gradually conducted to an improvement which effectually removed the second imperfection; and thus he effected the fundamental amendments in the engine, that, as has been remarked, it appears a thing almost endowed with intelligence.

Having progressed thus far in his object, Watt had a difficulty of a very formidable character to surmount; namely, that of bringing his discoveries into public notice, without any considerable means of his own at command. Moreover, he had to contend with the opposition of such persons as conceived their interests to be at stake. However, he had just provided himself with a witty, cheerful, and accomplished wife, and thus furnished an additional spur to exertion. In this emergency he applied to an early friend, Dr. Roebuck, who had just founded the Carron Iron Works, to advance the requisite capital, which was agreed to on condition of the profits being shared. A patent was accordingly obtained, and an engine erected; but Roebuck soon after meeting with reverses in his daring speculations, the sagacious inventor was under the necessity of establishing himself in Glasgow as a civil engineer, and as such obtained high reputation in furnishing surveys and estimates for canals, and other public operations, of which Scotland was then the scene.

At length, in the year 1774, he accepted the proposal of Mr. Boulton, a celebrated hardware manufacturer in Birmingham, that he should remove thither, and enter into partnership on equitable terms. An extension of the patent was forthwith obtained for twenty-five years from that date; and Watt's genius having now a field, entered on its career of public triumph. Though he shared the fate of most inventors in being perpetually involved in lawsuits, he succeeded in realizing an ample fortune. His scientific achievements were duly appreciated by those who were qualified to judge of their merits; and in 1785 he was elected a Fellow of the Royal Society, being subsequently chosen one of the eight Foreign Associates of the French Institute. The University of Glasgow, which had first befriended him, conferred the honorary degree of LL.D. in 1806.

Near the end of his life he engaged in the construction of a machine for copying pieces of statuary and sculpture. His friends claim for him the distinction of having discovered the composition of water.

This illustrious mechanist passed the last years of his long and memorable life in the society of his family and friends. He died August 25,

1819, in his eighty-fourth year, and was buried in the church of Handsworth, near Heathfield, his residence in Staffordshire.

A monument to his memory, graven by the hand of Chantrey, was erected in Westminster Abbey, and on it was placed this inscription by Lord Brougham:

Not to perpetuate a name
Which must endure while the peaceful arts flourish,
But to show
That mankind have learned to honor those
Who best deserved their gratitude,
The King,
His Ministers, and many of the Nobles
And Commoners of the Realm,
Raised this Monument to
James Watt,
Who, directing the force of an original genius, early exercised in philosophical research, to the improvement of the
Steam-engine.
Enlarged the resources of his country,
Increased the power of man,
And rose to an eminent place among the illustrious followers of Science,
And the real benefactors of the world.

ADAM SMITH

If there are "suppressed characters" in literary and scientific, as well as in parliamentary history, the great apostle of political economy is certainly not of the number. Indeed, the posthumous glory he has derived from his most celebrated work, goes far to justify Southey's enthusiastic preference of the fame arising from authorship over all others. After the lapse of a century, his name is still familiar in the mouths of men, and still continues to gather fresh fame as it flies along the stream of time. The maxims of policy which he taught are now inseparably associated with the recollection of a long controversy, a memorable struggle, and a triumph under extraordinary circumstances. But without venturing to expatiate on the latter somewhat exciting topics, it may be possible to furnish a sketch of the learned Doctor's earthly career, not altogether uninteresting to youths accustomed to "mark, learn, and inwardly digest."

The father of this famous professor of political science had originally practiced in Edinburgh as a writer to the signet; for so an attorney is there styled. He had afterward become private secretary to the Earl of Loudon, who held the now abolished office of Secretary of State for Scotland; and when his lordship's career in that capacity terminated, the elder Smith was appointed Comptroller of the Customs at Kirkaldy, a small Fifeshire town, situated on the Firth of Forth. Removing thither to fulfill the duties of the office, and perhaps finding himself more solitary in his new sphere than he had been in the capital, he married a very amiable and affectionate woman, bearing the "conquering name" of Douglas. He was not, however, spared to see the son whose achievements have saved his memory from oblivion, for, somewhere about the beginning of 1723, he departed this life; and a few months later, on the 5th of June, the birth of Adam Smith took place.

The future economist had not, in infancy, the advantage of such strong health as enables children to frisk, and riot, and tumble about without danger. It required all the care and attention which a widowed and disconsolate mother generally bestows upon an only son, to sustain his weakly and delicate constitution against the perils which beset beings in that immature season of earthly existence; and she executed her task with so much real tenderness and solicitude, as to have been charged with the venial fault of too readily gratifying his whims and humors. Unbounded indulgence toward a child is certainly highly imprudent; but it does not appear that it either spoiled Smith, or produced in his case any other evil consequences.

Another, and a more substantial kind of danger, he is related to have been on one occasion exposed to. The tribes of gipsies, who then infested the country, carried on a most indiscriminate system of plunder. Nothing came amiss to them that was not too hot or too heavy; and they not only anticipated the doctrine of buying in the cheapest and selling in the dearest markets, but acted on it to an extent which would make teachers of economy "stare and gasp" with surprise and horror. They seem to have loved the trade of pillage, "not wisely, but too well;" for, though it is not difficult to understand their motive in appropriating the pigs, poultry, and game of the district, periodically favored with their portentous presence, it is certainly not so easy to imagine what advantage they found in carrying off, and burdening themselves with, their neighbors' children. But, whatever their views in this predatory system, the little boy destined to become the author of the "Wealth of Nations," narrowly escaped their clutches. When he was three years old, his fond mother carried him on a visit to the family of her brother, who resided at Strathenry; and one day, while there, he was playing noiselessly about the door of the house, when up came a gang of gipsies. The sight of a child, thus alone and helpless, was a temptation not to be resisted; and the scene may readily be fancied. Some tall prophetess, whom Sir Roger de Coverley would have called "a baggage," dressed in a long, faded, red cloak, would separate herself from the troop, and, after turning and carefully glancing round on all sides to ascertain that she was safe from the eyes of fair-haired Christians, insure the fatal silence of her tiny victim, by placing in his hand a rosy-cheeked apple. Then, stealthily lifting him up, she would with cunning caresses deposit his slight form beneath her cloak, and hastily rejoin her comrades. And now there was every probability of Smith being brought up to a life of theft and vagrancy, passing his nights in plundering hen-roosts and breaking game preserves, or seated by some watch-fire blazing within a circle of stones, and uttering "uncouth gibberish" to damsels, whose dusky brows seemed to tell of their Eastern origin, and whose "white teeth and black eyes" might well, indeed, excite the admiration of that susceptible old knight so finely portrayed by the pen of Addison. Fortunately, however, he was soon missed; and the alarm that he had been kidnapped was sounded in time to give his uncle the opportunity of being, according to Dugald Stewart, the happy instrument of preserving to the world a genius which was destined not only to extend the boundaries of science, but to enlighten and reform the commercial policy of Europe. The stout kinsman would, doubtless, run quickly to the stable, saddle his mettled steed, and throw himself on its back. Then, setting out in pursuit, he speedily came up to the migratory band, who, feeling quite secure, had encamped in Leslie Wood. He joyfully rescued the terrified child from their keeping, and hurrying back, restored him in safety to his weeping and agitated parent.

At a proper age after this adventure, Master Adam, still the pride and delight of his mother's eye, was placed in the parish school of Kirkaldy, which at the time was, luckily for him, taught by a man of considerable ability and repute. The youth took kindly to his book. His delicate health rendered him unfit, or, at all events, averse to playing any active part in the games and pastimes of his class-fellows. He avoided the field or the market-place, where his rough and hardy compeers, caring not a jot for sun or dust, exercised their limbs at golf, or urged the flying ball, sometimes to the destruction of windows; and he engaged not in those puerile displays of strength and skill, out of which the pugnacious and aspiring imps, not seldom, came with livid faces and bloody snouts. Instead of boisterous mirth, he loved quiet retirement; and while the others were taking part in mischievous freaks and diversions he was reading, and laying the foundation of the peculiar habits of self-communion which distinguished his subsequent career. His memory was tenacious, and he rapidly stored up information to be used when the proper time arrived. When in company, he, even at this date, displayed those peculiarities which afterward characterized him. He was generally absent and inattentive to the conversation going on; the motion of his lips could be observed as he muttered to himself; and his manners were artless and simple in the extreme.

At the age of fifteen, Adam climbed to the top of a coach, and was sent to be entered at the University of Glasgow. While there, he manifested great partiality for mathematics, the chair of which was then filled by the celebrated Professor Simson, the restorer of Euclid; his other bias being toward natural philosophy. He remained in the city on the Clyde for three years, and subsequently acknowledged infinite obligations to the institution. Luckily for Smith, and several other eminent men who have since flourished, a person of the name of Snell had, in the year of the Revolution, bequeathed an estate in the county of Warwick for the support, at Balliol College, Oxford, of Scottish youths, who have, for a certain period, been students at Glasgow, in whose professorial body the patronage is vested. Smith was selected as one of the exhibitioners on this foundation, and repaired to Oxford, with the prospect, as his relatives believed, of appearing ere long as a divine of note and reputation. He did not in after life confess to having owed much to the seat of learning to which—thanks to old Snell's laudable liberality—he had thus been admitted; but it must be taken into account that Scotchmen of his generation, however reflecting, were violently, and perhaps excusably, prejudiced in regard to much of what they witnessed in a country so much wealthier than their own. In any case, the philosophic Fifeshire lad luxuriated in his favorite subjects and speculations in private; and was equally assiduous and successful in his study of languages, both ancient and modern. He became intimately acquainted with the poetry, and gained a knowledge of and mastery over the language, of England, which more than counteracted the effects of his Northern education. In his efforts to acquire the art of composing with ease, freedom, and elegance, he translated much from foreign models, particularly from the French; and this method he ever recommended to those who aspired to accomplish themselves, or to improve their style in the structure and formation of sentences. During his residence at Oxford his secret studies unfortunately provoked the suspicion of his academic superiors, who thought fit to pay an inquisitorial visit to his chamber. They found him engaged in an intellectual banquet on Hume's "Treatise of Human Nature," then recently published, and considered somewhat dangerous fare. This they seized, proving at the same time their respect for the principle of "reciprocity" by bestowing upon him a severe reprimand in exchange. Whatever his chances of ecclesiastical preferment, and however great the anxiety of his friends that he should take orders, they were wrecked and defeated by his opposition to the long-cherished scheme. He, contrary to the wishes of his relatives, totally abandoned the idea of a clerical career, left the classic precincts of Oxford University, and resided with his mother for the next two years, without doing any thing in particular or fixing upon any plan of life.

The intellectual faculties of Smith were at this season in almost as great peril of being lost to the world as when he had been carried by gipsies into the recesses of Leslie Wood. The crisis of his fate had arrived, and while pondering in his solitary chamber, or subjected to embarrassing questions at Kirkaldy tea-parties, he must often have mused, with concern, over the magnitude of the sacrifice he had made in relinquishing the course which had been chalked out for him. It was really one of no trifling character, for the circumstances of his native land, never very favorable, were then such as to render it in the last degree difficult for youths, even of the most respectable parentage, to discover a career worthy of being followed. A chivalrous writer of this generation, in his zealous defense of a new school of artists, apparently flushed with triumph, and under the impression, not only that things are sadly out of joint, but that he was born to set them right, travels out of his way to suggest a new school of philanthropists, and recommends some half-dozen thorough-bred gentlemen to take to the green-grocery trade or some other of the kind, just to show that there is nothing dishonorable in such occupations, and thus regenerate society. The sagacious Scots of another day seem to have, to a considerable extent, anticipated that counsel, though without pretending that they were thereby entitling themselves to the credit of any very sublime or beneficent self-sacrifice. Smith's friend, the romantic author of "Douglas," whom Nature seems to have designed for a knight-errant, was somewhat unreasonable in his complaint—

> "Sprung from the haughty nobles of the land,
> Upon the ladder's lowest round I stand;"

for hundreds of the younger sons of ancient and honorable families were glad if they could, without having their gentility openly impeached, gain a livelihood as merchants in the provinces, or even as tradesmen in the Canongate. Nor was it on younger sons only that Fortune bestowed such merciless kicks. Caledonian noblemen of long pedigrees, high names, and sounding titles, were found in situations aught but dignified. One peer kept a glove shop in Cornhill. Another, still less fortunate, employed each day in contriving how he was to fall in with a dinner. A third, on being arrested, was so dirty in his person, and so shabby in his dress, that the officer of justice stubbornly refused to credit the possibility of his being a man of rank. Even "females of quality" were not exempt from the miseries of the period; for one Scottish baroness was hostess of a tavern whose character was not the highest, and pleaded the privilege of her order when sued for keeping a disorderly house. What prospect was there in a state of society thus overcast for a youth, whom his plebeian name would all but disqualify for the position of a traveling tutor, and whom absorption in intellectual contemplation rendered utterly unfit to figure as a man of business? We shall soon see.

Among the cadets of patrician houses who in the Scottish capital had sought a way of escape from the horrors which attend the union of pride and poverty, none had struggled with greater perseverance and success than that very distant kinsman, but close friend, of the great philosophic historian of England, since known to fame as Lord Kames. Having been educated by a tutor under the roof of his father, a Border gentleman of Jacobite leanings, and studied law at the University of Edinburgh, he was placed as apprentice in the office of a writer. But feeling, like Lord Mansfield, a real calling for the bar, he deserted the attorney's desk before completing the term agreed on, and not only distinguished himself in his professional exhibitions, but by his deep learning and acute genius won a very extensive reputation as an author on various subjects. Smith had the advantage of being appreciated by this eminent jurist, philosopher, and agriculturist; and he prudently availed himself of the circumstance. In 1748, the Economist came forth under his patronage to lecture, in the Scottish metropolis, on rhetoric and the belles lettres, the professorship for which had not then been founded. This Smith continued to do for two years, at the end of which he was sufficiently recognized as a man of talent and erudition to be elected to the Logic Chair in the University of Glasgow, where he discharged the duties with much ability. He departed widely from the course that had been pursued by his predecessors, and directed the minds of the students to subjects of a more useful and interesting nature than they had been accustomed to.

Smith was now, indeed, in a position which was favorable to the proper display of his extraordinary powers; and within twelve months of his election he had the good fortune to be nominated and chosen as Professor of Moral Philosophy. Such he continued for the next thirteen years, which, when they had long passed, he was in the habit of looking back on with a feeling somewhat resembling regret, as they had formed the happiest and most agreeable period of his existence. His public lectures, though delivered in a plain and unaffected manner, were always distinguished and rendered interesting by a luminous division of the subject, as well as by full, fresh and various illustration. They soon began to excite interest, and were attended no less for pleasure than instruction. The commercial community was agitated by a spirit of inquiry; the learned professor's name rapidly spread; and young men from all parts of the country were attracted to the College with a view of profiting by them. The science, from the novel method in which it was treated, became popular; and Adam was so much admired in his capacity of lecturer, that, as in the days of Hotspur,

> "The speaking thick which Nature made his blemish
> Became the accents of the valiant;"

so the students of moral philosophy admiringly exerted themselves to imitate their professor's peculiarities in pronunciation and manner of address.

At this period the men of letters in the Scottish capital projected and commenced the first "Edinburgh Review;" and Smith, besides contributing an article on Dr. Johnson's "Dictionary," addressed a letter to the editors, containing observations on the state of literature in the different countries of Europe. This effort at the establishment of a great Northern periodical proved premature, and it was reserved for another generation of "modern Athenians" to realize such a scheme. After two numbers the journal spread its wings no more, and the copies are now remarkably rare.

Fortune smiled more bountifully on the scientific Professor when he sallied forth into the literary field, single-handed, and under his own pennon. In 1759 he boldly challenged criticism with his "Theory of Moral Sentiments," which soon attracted public attention, and won no slight applause. His friends, David Hume and Wedderburn, afterward Lord Chancellor Loughborough, lent their aid to spread the reputation of the book in London; and the historian soon had the happiness of transmitting to the author flattering accounts of its reception. Among others who were captivated with the performance was Charles Townsend, then regarded as "the cleverest fellow in England," and subsequently immortalized in one of Burke's most marvelous parliamentary speeches "as the delight and ornament of the House, and the charm of every private society he honored with his presence." He had already become connected with Scotland by wedding a dowager of high rank, and vindicated his claims to respect as her consort in a very amusing way. On accompanying his titled bride to her residence in "the land of mountain and of flood," the relatives and dependants of the lady, in their eagerness to do her full honor, seemed rather inclined to forget that a welcome was due to the brilliant and ambitious husband. "For God's sake, gentlemen," exclaimed the prodigy, who could hit the House of Commons between wind and water, "remember that I am at least Prince George of Denmark!" He now declared that he would exercise the privilege of a step-father, and put the boy-Duke of Buccleuch under Smith's tuition. Hume wished to settle the matter at once by having the noble cub sent to Glasgow, but a different course was adopted. Townsend was somewhat uncertain in his resolutions, and four years were allowed to elapse before the necessary arrangements were made. Then Smith received a formal invitation to attend the young duke on his travels; and setting out, they arrived at Paris in the beginning of 1764.

Hume, whose ancient blood would naturally boil at the recollection of the indignities he had suffered while, for a brief period, enacting the part of keeper to an insane marquis, had been clearly of opinion that no terms offered by Townsend would induce Dr. Smith to renounce his professorship. He was mistaken. The latter considered that his new position afforded him an opportunity of observing the internal policy of Continental states, and thus completing the system of political economy which his brain was occupied in thinking out. On arriving in Paris, he immediately addressed to the Rector of the University a letter announcing his resignation. It was accepted by the professorial body with regret; a meeting was convened; a fitting tribute was paid to his genius, ability, and learning; and honorable testimony was borne to the high probity and amiable qualities which had secured their possessor lasting esteem among his colleagues. Meantime Smith and his pupil, having remained a fortnight in Paris, proceeded to Toulouse, and there fixed their residence for eighteen months, during which the Doctor formed intimacies with several men of distinction, and made himself acquainted with the internal policy of the kingdom. They then visited several places in the South of France, resided for a while at Geneva, and then retraced their steps to the borders of the Seine. There Smith counted among his associates many of the chief men of letters and science, among whom were several of the political philosophers known as Economists. The accredited founder of that sect was the celebrated Quesnai, though he had been preceded by the profound and acute Galiani. Harris and Hume had likewise done much to popularize the doctrines. But Smith, whose attention had already been occupied with the subject for the space of ten years, was the first to see the whole bearing of their principles, and to trace their consequences with care, and face them with confidence.

When Smith set foot on his native soil, in the autumn of 1766, he did not return to the scene of his former triumphs, but consigned himself to studious and laborious retirement under the roof of his worthy mother. Old friends urged him to come within their reach, and give them the benefit of his company; but his strong ambition to produce a great and influential work, "like Aaron's rod swallowed up the rest," and he was content to pursue his object in obscurity. He was in comfortable circumstances, as the Duke of Buccleuch had, in consideration of his tuition, settled on him an income of three hundred pounds a year, and in other respects he was not unprepared for the mighty task. His long residence in a commercial town, his foreign experience, and his intercourse with the French economists and statesmen, had trained his philosophic mind for the investigation of the subjects on which he aspired to throw a new and enduring light. When employed in preparing for the press, he generally walked up and down the room dictating to an amanuensis, and he is said to have composed with as much slowness and difficulty in his later years as in youth. The "Inquiry into the Nature and Causes of the Wealth of Nations" did not make its appearance in public till the spring of 1766. It was found to consist of five books. The two first contain the scientific portion. The third is a historical sketch of the progress of opulence. The fourth, the longest, treats of the legislative interference by which governments have attempted to make their subjects rich, and endeavors to show that all such schemes retard instead of promoting the object in view. The fifth, which points out the means by which the duties of sovereigns may be best performed, and how a public revenue may be most judiciously provided, is in reality a treatise on the art of government. This work, so important in its results, saw the light just six months before David Hume was laid in his lonesome grave, and he immediately wrote—"It has depth, and solidity, and acuteness, and is so much illustrated by curious facts that it must, at last, take the public attention.... If you were here, at my fireside, I should dispute some of your principles; but these, and a hundred other points, are fit only to be discussed in conversation." Gibbon, likewise, mentioned it with praise in his immortal History; and Fox lent his aid to increase its fame by saying in that House, where the author's name has since been familiar as a household word, and unquestionably too often used by others than parliamentary giants—"The way, as my learned friend Dr. Adam Smith states, for a nation, as well as an individual, to be rich, is for both to live within their income." It is admitted, however, that the doctrines enunciated made less impression on the minds of Fox and his allies, than on that of the young and disdainful minister who, toward the close of the century, had to stand the brunt of their impassioned eloquence. Johnson, whose love for Smith was not excessive, interposed his ponderous influence to shield him from Sir John Pringle's diverting allegation—that Smith, not being practically conversant with trade, could not be qualified to write on matters relating to it. "That is quite a mistake," said the sage, indignantly: "a man who has never been in trade may write well on trade; and there is nothing which requires more to be illustrated by philosophy than trade does. As to mere wealth, that is to say money, it is clear that one nation, or one individual, can not increase its store but by making another poorer; but trade procures what is more valuable, the reciprocation of the peculiar advantages of different countries. A merchant seldom thinks of any but his own trade. To write a good book upon it, a man must have extensive views. It is not necessary to have practiced, to write well upon, a subject."

During the two years following his greatest publication Dr. Smith resided in London, and spent much of his time in that "bright constellation of British stars," forming the club without a name, which Sir Joshua Reynolds had founded. But in 1778 he was appointed one of the Commissioners of Customs in Scotland, and removed to Edinburgh to attend to the duties attached to the office, which, though they required little exertion, were sufficient to divert his attention from literary undertakings. His mother, now an extremely aged woman, came to live with him; as did also Miss Douglas, an elderly cousin, who had formerly superintended his domestic arrangements at Glasgow. He had collected a valuable library, and being apparently of Horace's way of thinking, in regard to there being no splendor in money unless it shines in a temperate expenditure, he was generous in his gifts and hospitable in his manner of living. He soon began to feel some of the infirmities of age, but his health and strength did not give way till the death of his female relatives, when he was left in a position somewhat more solitary than he relished, and he became still more engrossed with his meditations.

Kay's series of portraits and caricature etchings enable the curious inquirer not only to have before him the style of dress and appearance of the author of the "Wealth of Nations" at this period, but even to form a tolerably accurate conception of what a day with him must have ordinarily been. One seems to see him, as he is prepared after breakfast to set out for the Custom House, standing before the table, with his cane in one hand, and the other on some page of his latest work, which lies open before him. He descends the stair, and issues slowly into the street, muttering to himself, and indulging in a laugh, which must be very favorable to the digestion of his morning meal. And what can it be that excites his risibility? Is he chuckling over the solution of some knotty problem in political science, or does the manly and dignified figure of his acquaintance, Lord Rockville, in the distance, recall to his memory the never-ending joke about the Grassmarket pavement, having one evening most suddenly risen up and struck that urbane and polished legal sage in the face? These two fishwomen, whom he meets, look as if they had some notion; but no, by St. Bride! the weather-beaten jades really mistake the philosopher for a lunatic, and express their surprise that he is not in custody. He neither sees nor hears them, however, but continues to laugh and soliloquize.

"Heigh, sirs! isn't that waesome?" ejaculates one, as she shakes her head and becomes mute from very pity.

"And he's so well put on, too!" observed the other, with a sigh, as she marked his careful attire, from the cocked hat and flowing wig to the ruffles at his wrists and the buckles on his shoes. Our venerable hero now approaches the Custom House, and as he reaches the door, the gigantic porter, who keeps guard, salutes him with ceremonious formality. But what is the Economist about now? Exercising his muscles, or teaching the big janitor sword exercise? Not at all. He is only, with the most complete unconsciousness of doing any thing of the kind, imitating with his gold-headed cane every flourish that the man has made, before entering the building where the Board is sitting for the transaction of business connected with the collection of the revenue. He exchanges courteous salutations with his colleagues, among whom are a tall, stately scion of the noble house of Cochrane, and Capt. Edgar, a gentleman of eccentric habits, but a thorough man of the world, and valued by the Doctor, because, being rather out of place at a Customs' Board, and luckily an excellent classical scholar, he is quite ready to devote the official hours to the task of amusing the philosopher. Accordingly, this personage, celebrated in verse as the *beau dîneur*, and Dr. Smith, renowned for having taught the world how nations are bound together by the reciprocal benefits of commerce, occupy their time with the recitation of passages from the Greek authors. Then a paper bearing the signature of one of the Commissioners is handed to the Economist, but instead of appending his own name, he copies that of the person who has already signed it. He now rises and sallies forth to indulge in a quiet walk about the Meadows, a fashionable place of resort; and after dining, he repairs to the "Poker Club," to spend the remainder of his waking hours in the company of Black, and Hutton, and John Home.

Now and then Dr. Smith paid a visit to London. On the last occasion of his being in the metropolis he had been engaged to dine with tall Harry Dundas, afterward Lord Melville, then the real "Cock of the North." He happened to arrive too late, and the guests, among whom were Pitt, Grenville, and Addington, had taken their places at table; but on his entrance, they, with one accord, rose to receive him. The Doctor offered an apology for being so late, and begged them to resume their seats; but they said, "No, we'll stand till you are seated, for we are all your scholars."

In the year 1787 the veteran philosopher was elected Rector of Glasgow University. He was touched by the compliment, and in acknowledging it, stated that no preferment could have given him so much real satisfaction, because the term of years, during which he had been a member of the Society, had formed by far the most useful, and therefore the happiest and most honorable, period of the life whose closing scene was now gradually drawing nigh. His last illness was painful and lingering, but in the summer of 1790 the angel of death gave no uncertain signals of approach. In accordance with an old Scottish custom, certainly more honored in the breach than the observance, Dr. Smith had been in the habit of inviting his intimate associates to supper on Sundays. This, it should be mentioned, was, at that date, practiced by men whose character for Christian piety was beyond all reproach or question; and the Economist's adherence to it can not, with any show of reason, be cited in support of the tendency to infidelity, which has been, rightly or wrongly, imputed to him. It was a July evening when they last assembled, and the gathering was, as usual, pretty numerous; but the host found himself incapable of taking that part which he had so often done; and feeling himself unable to entertain them, he requested their permission to withdraw. On taking his leave, he said, "Indeed, gentlemen, I believe we must adjourn this meeting to some other place." A few days brought release from his sufferings. He had just given orders for the destruction of all his manuscripts, with the exception of some detached essays, which, being left to the care of his executors, were afterward published; when he breathed his last in a state of complete mental resignation. He was most tenderly sympathized with in his pangs by a circle of sorrowing friends, who had learned fully to appreciate the powers of his intellect, the comprehensiveness of his views, the extent of his attainments, and the benignity of his disposition.